Unorthodox
Lawmaking

Unorthodox Lawmaking

New Legislative Processes in the U.S. Congress

Barbara Sinclair
University of California, Los Angeles

A Division of Congressional Quarterly Inc.
Washington, D.C.

To

Dick Fenno,
teacher, mentor, friend

Cover design: Paula Anderson

Library of Congress Cataloging-in-Publication Data

Sinclair, Barbara.
   Unorthodox lawmaking : new legislative processes in the
   U.S. Congress / by Barbara Sinclair.
      p.   cm.
   Includes bibliographical references and index.
   ISBN 1-56802-277-8 (cloth). — ISBN 1-56802-276-X (pbk.)
      1. Legislation—United States.   2. United States—Politics and
government—1993–   I. Title
KF4945.S58   1997
328.73'077—dc21   96-54276

Contents

---

c h a p t e r   s e v e n

National Service Legislation:
(Mildly) Unorthodox Lawmaking   101

c h a p t e r   e i g h t

Regulatory Overhaul: The Pitfalls of
Unorthodox Lawmaking   113

c h a p t e r   n i n e

The Omnibus Drug Bill: A "Designer"
Legislative Process   134

c h a p t e r   t e n

The Budget Process as an Instrument for Policy Change: Clinton's Economic Program   151

c h a p t e r   e l e v e n

The Republican Revolution and the Budget Process   175

c h a p t e r   t w e l v e

Tables

Preface

DURING THE TWENTY PLUS YEARS that I have been doing research on Congress and teaching courses about the institution, the gap between the legislative process that I observe on Capitol Hill and the legislative process described in U.S. government textbooks has become a chasm. Like most teachers, I tried to give my students a sense of the contemporary legislative process in all its variety while still presenting the "textbook" model as the standard. That, I believe, is no longer adequate or accurate.

This is a book about how the legislative process really works today. I show how the legislative process in the U.S. Congress has changed in recent years, explore the reasons for the change, and examine its consequences. Although based on original research, the book is written with the nonspecialist in mind. No extensive knowledge of Congress is presupposed. I believe that readers will be better prepared to pursue further studies of Congress if they so choose, but my primary aim is to enable them to make sense of congressional politics and to judge claims about congressional performance.

I refer to the contemporary legislative process as "unorthodox lawmaking" to distinguish frequently employed contemporary procedures and practices from what is still often presented in textbooks as the standard process. In fact, on major legislation the legislative process is now less likely to conform to the textbook model than to what I call "unorthodox lawmaking." I use that term to emphasize the extent of change. It also gives me a handy way of referring to a set of procedures and practices that are either new or much more frequently employed than they used to be.

The book begins with two short case studies that provide a vivid example of how much the legislative process has changed. Chapter 1 describes the passage of clean air legislation in 1970 and in 1990 and then, through a comparison of the process on the two bills, introduces unorthodox lawmaking and the questions it raises. Chapters 2 through 5 explain the procedures and practices that make up the new legislative process. Chapter 2 begins with the introduction of a bill and proceeds step-by-step through the process in the House, examining and illustrating with examples frequently used options at each stage. Chapter 3 traces a bill through the Senate. Before 1970 one could speak of a standard legislative process that most major legislation traversed, but as those chapters show there are now many routes from introduction to enactment. Once the House and Senate have passed legislation the two different versions must be reconciled, as I explain in Chapter 4. Chapter 5 addresses omnibus legislation, the budget process, and legislative-executive summits. In Chapter 6, the historical origins of the procedures and practices that characterize contemporary lawmaking are explored, and the change over time in their frequency is documented. Chapters 7 through 11 analyze unorthodox lawmaking through a series of case studies. Accounts of the process on the 1993 national service bill, regulatory reform legislation in 1995, and an omnibus drug bill in 1988 illustrate the range and variability of the contemporary legislative process. Case studies of the enactment of Clinton's economic program in 1993 and of the Republicans' attempt in 1995 to pass a balanced budget that included restructuring Medicare, Medicaid, welfare, and other major programs show how the budget process works and demonstrate its contemporary use as an instrument of comprehensive policy change. Chapter 12 examines the impact that the new procedures and practices have on legislative outcomes and on how Congress functions.

I chose to describe the contemporary legislative process in Chapters 2 through 5, followed by a chapter that analyzes the trajectory of change and the reasons for it. For those who prefer their history first, the order of those chapters could be reversed, with Chapter 6 read before Chapters 2 through 5. Chapters 7 through 9, the case studies of nonbudget legislation, could easily be read after Chapters 2 through 4 and before Chapter 5, which deals with the budget process.

In addition to the analysis of major legislation described in Chapter 1, this book is based on my observations and experiences in the office of the House majority leader in 1978–79 as an American Political Science Association Congressional Fellow; in the office of the Speaker in 1987–88 on an informal basis; and on interviews with members of Congress, their staffs, and informed observers over the course of more years than I am now willing to admit. I owe Jim Wright, Speaker of the House from 1987 to 1989, and his staff an enormous debt for giving me the opportunity to observe the legislative process from the inside. I am also grateful to all of those very busy people who made time to talk to me over the years and from whom I learned so much.

I would especially like to thank Peter Robinson, formerly of the House Parliamentarian's Office and of Speaker Wright's staff, and Stanley Bach, Richard Beth, and Walter Oleszek of the Congressional Research Service. All are incredibly knowledgeable and extremely generous in sharing their expertise. Stan Bach, Sandy Maisel, and Michael Kraft read the manuscript and gave me invaluable comments and advice. I want them to know how much I appreciate their detailed and thoughtful reviews; they significantly improved the manuscript. Bruce Oppenheimer, Steve Smith, and Robin Kolodny, who read the proposal and much of an early draft, provided perceptive and helpful advice. Much of the quantitative material has been presented in papers at professional meetings; I thank the many colleagues who commented on those papers. Of course, none of these people is responsible for any remaining errors. Finally, I would like to thank Brenda Carter of CQ Press, who has been a real pleasure to work with, and Barbara de Boinville, an excellent copy editor, for her willingness to work with a sometimes difficult author.

Clean Air: An Introduction to How the Legislative Process Has Changed

In 1970 Congress passed a path-breaking Clean Air Act, legislation *Congressional Quarterly* called "the most comprehensive air pollution control bill in U.S. history" (*Congressional Quarterly Almanac* 1970, 472).

Reported by the House Interstate and Foreign Commerce Committee, the bill was considered on the House floor under an open rule allowing all germane amendments. Of the nine amendments offered, eight were defeated, most on voice votes; only one technical amendment was accepted. The bill passed the House 375–1.

In the Senate the Public Works Committee reported a bill stronger than the House legislation or the administration's draft. After two days of floor debate during which ten amendments were accepted by voice vote and two rejected by roll calls, the Senate voted 73–0 to pass the strong bill. The conference committee, consisting of five members of the House committee and nine senators, came to an agreement on a bill much closer to the Senate's stringent version than the House's milder bill, and both chambers approved the conferees' version by voice vote.

Although far stronger than the legislation he had initially proposed, President Richard Nixon signed the bill, "one of the most far-reaching laws ever passed by Congress to regulate the domestic economy," in the words of a prominent journalist. The act set auto emission standards so stringent that it forced the development of new technology, and it directed the Environmental Protection Agency to establish national air quality standards (Cohen 1992, 13).

* * *

In 1989, when the 101st Congress began work on a major revision of the Clean Air Act, the political and institutional environment had changed, and the path the legislation traversed to enactment was very different from that of its 1970 predecessor. In the Senate the slightly renamed Public Works and Environment Committee again reported a strong bill. The bill was considered on the Senate floor for six days, but the majority leader, George Mitchell, D-Maine, could not muster the sixty votes needed to overcome a threatened filibuster. To construct a bill that could pass the chamber, the majority leader began negotiations with the administration and with a large and shifting group of senators. Members of the Environment Committee participated on a continuous basis, but many other senators with an interest in specific issues also took part. After a month of talks, an agreement was reached. To guard against the compromise unraveling on the floor, Mitchell and President George Bush pledged to oppose floor amendments, even those that reflected their policy preferences.

Mitchell offered the compromise worked out in the talks as a substitute amendment to the bill the Environment Committee had reported. He negotiated a complex unanimous consent agreement (UCA) for considering the bill on the floor. That UCA did not limit either debate or amendments; it simply required senators to put the amendments they wished to offer on a list. This provided a modicum of order to floor consideration of the bill. After ten days' debate over a month's time, the Senate passed the bill 89–11. Of about 250 amendments on the list, 25 were offered and pushed to a roll call vote; nine of these passed. None was a "deal breaker."

In the House the legislation was referred to three committees rather than just one as the 1970 bill had been. The Energy and Commerce Committee, successor to Interstate and Foreign Commerce, was the lead committee, and after protracted internal negotiations it reported legislation that represented a compromise among its factions. One key issue, however, had been decided by extremely close votes in both the subcommittee and the full committee, and Speaker Tom Foley, D-Wash., was concerned that the issue might well lead to a bitter party-splitting battle on the floor. He thus instructed the lead representatives of the two Democratic factions, Henry Waxman of California, chair of the subcommittee, and John Dingell of Michigan, chair of the full committee, to work out a compromise. In order to pressure them to act expeditiously, Foley set a deadline for floor action on the legislation. The Speaker and his aides then worked with Waxman and Dingell to help them come to an agreement. The other committees, also under Speaker-imposed deadlines, reported their legislative language.

Unlike its 1970 predecessor, the 1990 clean air legislation went to the floor under a rule that restricted amendments to nineteen listed in the Rules Committee report and carefully structured how they would be considered. The crucial Waxman-Dingell deal was offered as an amendment on the floor and approved 405–15. In all, six amendments were pushed to a roll call vote and five passed; none of these threatened the key compromises. The House then approved the bill 401–21.

Speaker Foley chose 130 conferees to represent the seven committees with some jurisdiction over the bill's subject matter; nine members from two committees represented the Senate. Protracted negotiations produced a bill that passed both chambers easily. A dramatic expansion of the Clean Air Act, the 1990 bill for the first time set up a program for controlling acid rain, established a stringent new program to control emissions of toxic air pollutants, and set new standards and timetables for improving urban air quality (*Congress and the Nation* 1993, 469, 473–474). Although considerably stronger than the draft he had proposed, President Bush signed the legislation.

* * *

These examples illustrate how greatly the legislative process has changed over the past two decades.[1] The legislative process on the 1970 Clean Air Act perfectly fits the bill-becomes-a-law diagram that is still a staple of American politics and legislative process textbooks (see Table 1.1). The 1970 bill was considered by a single committee in each chamber. It came to the House floor as drafted and approved by the committee, and it was considered there under an open rule allowing all germane amendments. The Senate also considered the bill as drafted by its committee; no senator mounted a filibuster or an amending marathon. After both chambers had passed the bill, a small group of senior members of the two committees got together in conference and worked out a compromise between the House and Senate versions.

The process on the 1990 bill, by contrast, was much more complex and not amenable to a nice, neat diagram. The legislation was considered by several committees in the House, and in both chambers the compromises arrived at through informal processes altered the bills after the

---

1. These accounts are based largely on primary documents, interviews (in the case of the 1990 act), and the following secondary sources: Congressional Quarterly's accounts, Cohen (1992), and Smith (1995, chap. 12).

TABLE 1.1   The 1970 Clean Air Act as an Example of the Textbook Legislative Process

Action	House	Senate
Committee	HR17255 referred to the Committee on Interstate and Foreign Commerce. Hearings held March 16–21 and April 14, 1970. Bill marked up. Bill reported June 3, 1970. Rules Committee grants open rule.	S4358 referred to the Senate Public Works Committee. Hearings held March 16–20, March 23–26, and April 17, 1970. Bill marked up. Bill reported September 17, 1970.
Floor	Considered in Committee of the Whole and passed by the House June 10, 1970.	Debated on the floor September 21–22 and passed September 22, 1970.
Conference	Conferees appointed. Conference meets. Conference agreement reached. Conferees file report December 17, 1970.	
Floor	House approves conference report December 18, 1970.	Senate approves conference report December 18, 1970.
Presidential	Sent to the president. President signs December 31, 1970.	

committees reported their legislation. Floor procedures were complex and tailored to the specific bill at issue. In the Senate the real possibility of a filibuster shaped the process, making it necessary for Majority Leader Mitchell to build through negotiations an oversized coalition. The final conference agreement was worked out by a much larger and more diverse group of members than in 1970.

In the contemporary Congress the textbook diagram describes the legislative process on fewer and fewer of the major bills. The seemingly unorthodox legislative process on the 1990 Clean Air Act is actually more characteristic of contemporary major legislation than the supposedly standard "textbook" process that the 1970 Clean Air Act traversed. To be sure, even during the "textbook" era not all legislation followed the relatively simple, straightforward process depicted by Table 1.1; there have always been alternative paths. Their use, however, was extraordinary, not ordinary; most major legislation followed the "textbook" process.[2]

Today the bill that, like the 1970 Clean Air Act, is reported by a single committee and considered on the floor under a simple open rule still exists but is not likely to be major legislation. Rather than being sent to one committee in each chamber, many measures are considered by several committees, especially in the House, while some measures bypass committee altogether. Not infrequently, after a bill has been reported but before it reaches the floor, major substantive changes are worked out via informal processes. Omnibus measures of great scope are a regular part of the legislative scene and formal executive-congressional summits to work out deals on legislation are no longer considered extraordinary. On the House floor most major measures are considered under complex and usually restrictive rules, often tailored to deal with problems specific to that bill. In the Senate bills are regularly subject to large numbers of not-necessarily-germane floor amendments; filibuster threats are an every-day fact of life, affecting all aspects of the legislative process and making cloture votes a routine part of the process. This book explores how and why the legislative process in the U.S. Congress has changed since the 1970s and examines the consequences of that change.

Although preceded by a long period of stability, the recent change in process is by no means unique. The Constitution does not specify how Congress is to carry out its core task of lawmaking; beyond a few basic requirements, it allows each house to determine its own rules and procedures. During its history of more than 200 years, the Congress has altered its legislative process a number of times.

In the very early years the legislative process in both the House and Senate emphasized the full membership's responsibility for lawmaking. The full membership debated a subject on the floor, decided whether legislation was warranted, and, if so, laid out substantive guidelines. Then a special or select committee was appointed to draft legislation according to those guidelines (Cooper and Young 1989; Risjord 1994).

Even in the early decades not all business could be given so much time and attention; minor business was sent first to small committees. The House then began to create standing—that is, permanent—committees to handle recurrent complex issues, and the Senate began to send to the same select committee all matters relating to the subject for which the committee had been initially created. During the second decade of the

---

2. Shortcut processes to handle noncontroversial legislation did and continue to exist.

1800s in the House and not much later in the Senate, standing committees became predominant. The committees did the initial work on legislation; only after they were finished did the rest of the membership have its
say.

Floor procedure, too, has changed over time. In the early years both
chambers' floor proceedings were relatively fluid and unstructured; even
the House placed little limit on members' debate time (Binder 1996).
Considering bills in the order they were introduced, the House was able
to dispose of all of its business. Soon, however, House floor procedures
became problematical. In 1811 the House adopted its first significant
restrictions on floor debate, and throughout the nineteenth century the
chamber struggled to develop a fair and efficient way of setting and ordering its floor agenda. Not until the 1880s and 1890s did the House develop
its premier device for scheduling major floor legislation: special rules
from the Rules Committee (Oppenheimer 1994). Special rules, which
required a simple majority of the House membership for approval,
allowed legislation to be taken up out of order; this innovation made it
possible for the majority party and its leaders, if they controlled the Rules
Committee in fact as well as in form, to control the House schedule.

Senate floor procedure changed in much less basic ways over the
course of its history (Bach 1994). The chamber's lack of limits on debate,
initially the result of no considered decision, became over time a revered
defining characteristic of the chamber (Binder forthcoming). In the
early years the Senate's small size made it unnecessary to limit the time
members could debate an issue. In time, however, senators' extended
debate prerogative became a problem. By then, the prerogative was well
entrenched; the formidable barrier the rules themselves erected against
change was fortified by the widely accepted myth that extended debate
reflected the framers' intent. Under extraordinary pressure from the
president and the public, the Senate in 1917 for the first time changed its
rules in such a way as to make cutting off debate possible. The cloture
procedure, however, was cumbersome and required a two-thirds vote for
success.

Why has the legislative process changed over time? The long evolu-
tion of the legislative process is far too complex to review here, and scholars do not agree about just why things happened as they did (Cooper
1981; Gamm and Shepsle 1989). Certainly workload increases, alterations
in the political and social environment, and the strategic behavior of parties and of members as individuals were important determinants. For
example, increases in the congressional workload and in the size of its
own membership put pressure on the House to modify procedures that
had adequately served a smaller, less busy legislature. Majorities, especially

partisan majorities, found their legislative goals stymied by chamber rules that facilitated minority obstructionism. These majorities were able to change such rules in the House but were largely blocked in the Senate. On a more abstract, theoretical level, changes in the legislative process can be seen as the responses of members to the problems and opportunities the institutional structure and the political environment present to them as they pursue, as individuals or collectively, their goals of reelection, influence in the chamber, and good public policy (Fenno 1973; Sinclair 1995).

The alterations in the legislative process since the 1970s are the latest installment in an ongoing story. They shed light not only on the contemporary legislative process (what is happening on Capitol Hill today) but also on the broader political process. The study of rules changes also provides insight into how democratic institutions like the Congress evolve and adapt.

Chapters 2 through 5 describe the procedures and practices that make up the new legislative process and document their frequency. Before 1970 one could speak of a standard legislative process that most major legislation followed. It is now more accurate to speak of legislative processes in the plural. Bills today follow many routes from introduction to enactment; the legislative process is characterized by variability, not uniformity. Multiple examples give the reader a broad sense of when the new procedures and practices are employed.

In Chapter 6 the historical origins of contemporary lawmaking are explored and the change in frequency of particular practices over time is documented. Chapters 7 through 11 use case studies to analyze unorthodox lawmaking. The 1993 national service bill, regulatory reform legislation in 1995, and an omnibus drug bill in 1988 illustrate the range and variability of the contemporary legislative process. The process on these three bills ranges from similar in many respects to the old standard process, though with some unorthodox elements, on national service to a radically unorthodox "designer" process on the drug bill. The enactment of Clinton's economic program in 1993 and the Republicans' attempt in 1995 to pass a balanced budget that included a restructuring of Medicare, Medicaid, welfare, and a number of other major programs show how the budget process works and illustrate its contemporary use as an instrument of comprehensive policy change.

Chapter 12 examines the impact that the new procedures and practices have on legislative outcomes and on how Congress functions. Congress is the least liked branch of the national government; only a fraction of the American people express confidence in the Congress. Never popular, Congress now evokes real hostility from many citizens. Americans are not happy with either the congressional process or the policy produced (Hibbing and Theiss-Morse, 1995). Is unorthodox lawmaking, in part, responsible, either directly or indirectly? Does it enhance or inhibit the likelihood of a bill becoming law? What other effects does the change in process have on how the Congress functions? Does it foster or discourage deliberation, the development and bringing to bear of expertise, the inclusion of a broad range of interests, and informed and timely decision making?

We expect a lot from Congress. Congress should represent the people; we expect members to bring into the legislative process the views, needs, and interests of the people they are elected to represent. We expect Congress to pass laws that reflect the will of the people; that is, Congress should be responsive to popular majorities. Congress should pass laws that deal promptly and effectively with pressing national problems. Has unorthodox lawmaking made the Congress more or less capable of carrying out the formidable tasks with which it is charged?

A Note on Data

I argue here that the legislative process on major legislation has changed. To show that is so, I need to define major legislation and then document change over time. Major measures are defined by the list of major legislation in the *Congressional Quarterly Weekly Report*, augmented by those measures on which key votes occurred (again according to Congressional Quarterly). This provides a list of about forty-five to fifty-five bills (and some other measures such as budget resolutions and constitutional amendments) for each Congress that close contemporary observers considered major. I then examined the course that major measures traversed in selected Congresses. I supplement my data by drawing where possible on the work of other scholars.

The Congresses selected are the 91st (1969–70), a prereform Congress; the 94th (1975–76), the first reformed Congress; the 97th (1981–82), the first Congress of the Reagan presidency and one in which the Republicans controlled the Senate; and the following recent Congresses—the 100th (1987–88), the 101st (1989–90), the 103rd (1993–94), and the 104th (1995–96). My 104th Congress data are perforce incomplete: the data set consists of the thirty-five measures that meet the above definition and had been considered on the floor of one of the chambers by the end of 1995. The measures include all of the Contract with America items but also the budget resolution, the rescission bill, the enormous reconciliation bill, and a number of other pieces of important legislation.

Multiple Paths:
The Legislative Process in the
House of Representatives

THE LEGISLATIVE PROCESS in the contemporary Congress is varied and complex. The old "textbook" process depicted in Table 1.1 was predictable and linear with one stage following another in an inevitable sequence. At many stages now there is no single, normal route but rather a number of different paths that legislation may follow. The best way to understand the contemporary legislative process is to begin with the introduction of a bill and proceed step-by-step through the process in each chamber, examining frequently used options at each stage. That is what this and the following three chapters do.

This is not a book on parliamentary procedure; procedures that are obscure and seldom employed are of no interest here. Rather, my aim is to make understandable the procedures and practices that occur on the major legislation considered during any contemporary Congress.[1]

For convenience, we begin the journey in the House of Representatives. Most legislation and other measures—budget resolutions and constitutional amendments—may begin in either chamber. The Constitution requires that tax legislation originate in the House, the people's chamber, and by custom the House also acts first on appropriations—

---

1. I have relied heavily on Tiefer (1989) and Gold et al. (1992) for the fine points of procedure. The interested reader should also consult Oleszek (1996). The people at the Congressional Research Service, especially Stanley Bach, Richard Beth, and Walter Oleszek, were invaluable sources of information. Peter Robinson was also extremely helpful.

that is, spending—bills. The Senate, however, is fully co-equal as a policy initiator. Even in the tax area, the Senate can initiate policy change by amending a minor House-passed tax bill. Yet because the House tends to act before the Senate (Strom and Rundquist 1977), we start with action in that chamber. Although action on the same *issue* may take place simultaneously in the two chambers, formal action on legislation is a sequential process: the House and the Senate cannot act on the same bill at the same time.

Bill Introduction

To introduce a bill, a member of the House simply drops it into the "hopper," a wooden box at the front of the chamber, when the House is in session.[2] Bill introduction has not changed in recent years. Only members of the House may introduce bills or resolutions in the House, and a member may introduce as many measures as he or she wishes. Thus even the president needs to find a member of the House to introduce his legislation, though doing so is seldom a problem.

In fact, the legislation members introduce has many different origins. Some bills are introduced at the behest of interest groups or even individual constituents; some come from federal government agencies and departments; some represent a member's own personal policy priorities. The legislative process in Congress is open and permeable. Although only members of Congress can perform official acts like introducing bills and voting, members' behavior is influenced by the president, interest groups, constituents, the media, and public opinion. That makes them significant actors in the legislative process.

---

2. The term "bill" is here used for bills, which are designated by the suffixes HR (for House of Representatives) and S (for Senate) and for joint resolutions, designated H.J. Res. and S.J. Res. There is no practical difference between the two in process and in effect; both become law. I try to use the term "measure" to indicate a broader class of legislative entities, including bills but also concurrent resolutions (H.Con. Res. or S.Con. Res.), which do not become law, and constitutional amendments. In process terms the difference between bills and joint resolutions, on the one hand, and concurrent resolutions and constitutional amendments, on the other, is that the latter do not require the president's signature. Resolutions, designated H. Res. or S. Res., deal with matters entirely within the purview of one body and do not require action by the other.

Bill Referral

Once introduced, the bill is referred to the committee or committees of jurisdiction. Because committees are the primary shapers of legislation and because they differ in membership and perspective, which committee receives the bill can make a difference to the legislative outcome. The parliamentarian, a professional, nonpartisan employee of the House, handles referrals under the supervision of the Speaker, whose prerogative it is to make this decision. Referrals are governed by the rules of the House, specifically Rule X that specifies what subject matters fall within the purview of each committee, and by precedents. Thus, referral decisions are usually fairly routine, but especially when new issues arise, there is some discretion (King 1994).

Multiple Referral

In 1975 the House changed its rules and permitted the referral of legislation to more than one committee. The prominent issues had changed, many had become more complex, and they no longer fit neatly into the jurisdiction of a single committee. Since the rules change, multiple referral has become increasingly common, especially on major legislation. By the Congresses of the late 1980s (1987–90), about 18 percent of all measures were referred to more than one committee (Young and Cooper 1993, 214). When only major legislation is considered, the likelihood of multiple referral is even higher. In recent Congresses about three out of ten major measures were multiply referred; in 1995, the first year of the 104th Congress, 40 percent were.[3]

Most routine multiply referred measures (about 80 percent) are sent to two committees (Davidson and Oleszek 1992, 132). Again, major legislation is different; in the Congresses of the late 1980s and early 1990s (100th, 101st, 103rd) more than half of multiply referred legislation went to three or more committees and, in some cases, to many more. President Bill Clinton's reinventing government legislation (the Government Reform and Savings Act of 1993), for example, went to seventeen House committees; his health care bill was referred to ten. The Republican bill to abolish the Department of Commerce was referred to eleven committees

---

3. Unless otherwise specified, data for recent Congresses are for the 100th (1987–88), the 101st (1989–90), and the 103rd (1993–94). The total number of major measures for these three Congresses is 158.

in 1995. The big trade bill passed by the 100th Congress (1987–88) was referred to six committees, and five other committees wrote trade-related legislation that was incorporated into the omnibus trade bill. In 1989 a bill to provide aid to Poland and Hungary was sent to seven committees.

It is easy to understand why many committees had jurisdiction over the bill to reinvent government; the bill concerned many federal agencies, each one under the purview of a different committee. But why was the trade bill referred to many committees? Even more curiously, why was legislation to aid two countries in eastern Europe multiply referred? The trade bill not only concerned unfair trade practices and authority to negotiate trade agreements. It also contained provisions on the retraining of workers displaced by plant closings and on grants to schools and colleges to improve the teaching of math, science, and foreign languages. The trade bill mandated negotiations with foreign governments to establish a competitive exchange rate for the dollar and to create an independent agency to buy loans owed by third world countries at a discount, required the identification of foreign owners of U.S. businesses and real estate, and prohibited government agencies from buying from companies in foreign countries whose governments restrict purchases from U.S. businesses (Cranford 1987, 813). On the Poland-Hungary bill, the Foreign Affairs Committee, which has jurisdiction over foreign aid, played the lead role, but Ways and Means was involved because of its jurisdiction over granting special trade benefits to foreign countries; programs for scholarships for Polish students, for technical training for Polish farmers and businesspeople, and for the promotion of U.S. exports to Poland and Hungary involved still other committees.

The original multiple referral rule instructed the Speaker to refer a bill to all committees with jurisdiction. Before 1995 the Speaker had three types of multiple referral to use (Davidson and Oleszek 1992). The most frequent type was a joint referral: a bill was sent to two or more committees simultaneously. Or a bill could be divided up and various sections and titles sent to different committees. Such split referrals have been relatively rare; dividing up complex legislation can be difficult. More common were sequential referrals: a measure is assigned to two or more committees in sequence. Typically, the first committee has the most jurisdiction and consequently the largest legislative role. The Speaker could combine types of referrals. Thus, legislation might be sent initially to the two or more committees with the most jurisdiction under a joint referral and then sequentially to other committees with lesser jurisdictional interests.

As amended in 1977, the multiple referral rule allowed the Speaker to set a reporting deadline for committees under any sort of referral. By custom, time limits were set on sequential but not on joint or split referrals. Since the Speaker could decide the type of referral to use, he exercised discretion as to time limits.

The 1995 rule, the aim of which was to streamline the process, abolishes the old form of joint referral and instructs the Speaker to designate a primary committee (Evans and Oleszek 1995). As interpreted, the rule actually allows several primary committees under a split referral. During the first 100 days of the 104th Congress, split referrals were frequently used. The welfare reform bill, for example, was split among the Ways and Means Committee, the Economic and Educational Opportunities Committee, and the Agriculture Committee. Joint referrals and, to an extent, sequential referrals have been replaced by the referral of legislation to a primary committee (based on "the weight of the bill") and additional initial referral to one or more other committees.

Committees that receive legislation on additional initial referral may consider it immediately; they need not wait for the primary committee to report before beginning their work. In that sense the new process is similar to the old joint referral procedure. However, when the primary committee reports, the other committees are, at the Speaker's discretion, subject to time limits, and if time limits are imposed, the committee must report within the specified time or be automatically discharged, that is, have the legislation taken away from it. The usual form of such a referral reads, "referred to the [primary] committee, and in addition to the [secondary] committees, for a period to be subsequently determined by the Speaker, in each case for consideration of such provisions as fall within the jurisdiction of the committee concerned." In the 104th Congress once the primary committee reported, the Speaker did impose time limits on the other committees if they had not yet reported, and those time limits were often short, in some cases one day. There were fewer turf fights than in previous years, but whether the new rule was responsible is unclear. With a new majority in control, committee chairs were under intense pressure from the party leadership and the membership to not allow turf fights to interfere with passing the Republican agenda.

What does multiple referral mean for how committees work and for how legislation is processed? Clearly, on much of the most important legislation of a Congress, committees must work together if they are to legislate successfully. Some committees—ones that frequently share jurisdiction—have developed standard operating procedures for working together. However, if the committees involved have substantially different and noncongruent perspectives, the relationship can be difficult and may make getting any legislation to the floor harder. In 1990, for example, the Ways and Means Committee and the Education and Labor Committee preferred distinctly different approaches to child care legislation; during months of negotiation, neither side was willing to budge. An agreement was finally reached only after the Speaker intervened and forced closure.

Some participants and knowledgeable observers contend that the multiple referral rule encourages committees to be even more turf conscious and to make even more, often tenuous, claims for jurisdiction than they otherwise would. Certainly in the House, members maintain their influence in the legislative process by aggressively asserting their committees' jurisdictional claims to legislation. Whether multiple referral has markedly exacerbated this tendency we cannot know; but without it there would still be turf fights and no method of handling them.

On the plus side, when legislation is referred to a number of committees, multiple perspectives are brought to bear on complex problems. More interests have a voice and a more diverse group of members a say at the committee stage where it counts most. Given the complexity of today's problems, this is certainly a benefit even if some delay is the cost.

For the Speaker, who is responsible for referral decisions, the high frequency with which major legislation is multiply referred presents both problems and opportunities. Until the 1995 rules change, a committee received a referral almost automatically; neither rules nor custom gave the Speaker discretion to withhold referrals. Yet when legislation is referred to several committees, the number of people who must come to agreement is multiplied, complicating and often slowing down the legislative process. Multiply referred legislation can present a variety of procedural problems on the floor. Frequently, multiple referral forces the role of jurisdictional and substantive mediator on the Speaker. That role, however, brings with it influence as well as headaches. And, of course, multiple referral also gives the Speaker the opportunity to set time limits for the reporting out of legislation. That power helped the Republican leadership speed things along during the first one hundred days of the 104th Congress. Under the new rule the Speaker has more discretion, particularly in terms of which additional committees receive referrals. Of course, he is still subject to pressure from members protecting their committee's clout (Evans and Oleszek 1995).

Bypassing Committee

Although legislation is now frequently considered by more than one committee, sometimes bills bypass committee consideration altogether. In the late 1980s almost one of five major measures was not considered by a committee in the House. In the Congresses of the 1990s, the frequency drops to about one in twenty in the 103rd Congress and one in ten in 1995. As we will see below, that low rate is somewhat deceiving.

The circumstances under which the committee of jurisdiction is bypassed in the House are varied. A majority of the House membership can bypass a nonresponsive committee by the discharge procedure: any member may file a discharge petition calling for a measure to be brought out of committee and to the floor; when half the House members—218—have signed the petition, the measure is taken away from the committee and considered on the floor. In the 97th Congress (1981–82), the 102nd (1991–92), and again in the 103rd (1993–94), a constitutional amendment to require a balanced federal budget was brought to the floor through the discharge procedure. In all three cases the committee of jurisdiction—the House Judiciary Committee—opposed the measure and had refused to consider or report it.

A House rules change in 1993 may have increased the chances of the discharge procedure succeeding—at least on high visibility issues. Previously, names on a discharge petition—and thus the names of those who had not signed—were kept confidential until 218 was reached. The rules change specified that the list of who had signed would be public from the first signature, making it easier to pressure members to sign on hot-button issues. Still, the discharge route is seldom successful (Beth 1994).

When a committee is successfully bypassed, the decision to do so is usually made by the majority party leadership.[4] The rationale for doing so varies widely. In early 1987, at the beginning of the 100th Congress, the Democratic Party leadership brought a clean water bill and a highway-mass transit bill directly to the floor because it wanted to score some quick victories. Both bills had gone through the full committee process and had passed by large margins in the preceding Congress. Thus, the committees could hardly claim they had been cut out of the process. In 1988 the Democratic Party leadership took the Senate's version of the Civil Rights Restoration Act directly to the floor because time for action was getting short, and it wanted to pass the bill without change to avoid a conference. The leadership feared delay in the Senate were further Senate action required. Most supporters were convinced that a bill more to their liking than the Senate version could never overcome a Senate filibuster nor a presidential veto.

In 1982 the House Democratic leadership and the chairman of the tax-writing Ways and Means Committee were unwilling to take the lead—and the blame—for a major tax increase made necessary by President

---

4. The most frequent means the leadership uses is extraction by the Rules Committee—that is, by the Rules Committee making the bill in order even though it has not been reported by committee (Tiefer 1989, 268–269).

Ronald Reagan's huge tax cut the year before. Thus, despite the constitutional requirement that the House initiate tax legislation, the Senate actually did so by attaching tax increase provisions as amendments to a minor House-passed revenue bill. The result was that the House Ways and Means Committee was effectively bypassed on the initial drafting of the legislation; members of that committee did have an impact on the legislation in the House-Senate conference committee that worked out the final version. Somewhat similarly, in 1985 the Senate attached the Gramm-Rudman budget-balancing requirements to a House-passed debt limit bill that had no similar provisions. No House committee had considered anything like the Gramm-Rudman requirements. The final form of that legislation was also worked out in conference.

Once in a while the majority party leadership believes an issue to be too politically delicate for the committee or committees of jurisdiction to handle. In 1988 the Speaker entrusted the drafting of the House Democrats' alternative to Reagan's plan for aiding the Nicaraguan contras to a task force headed by the deputy whip; no committee was involved. The political risks inherent in strongly opposing the president on a highly charged and highly visible foreign policy issue, as House Democrats were doing, were too great to leave the decision making to a committee.

Although most items in the Contract with America, the House Republicans' legislative agenda in the 104th Congress, went through the formal committee process, committee deliberation was largely pro forma. The unfunded mandates bill, for example, was referred to four committees on January 4, 1995, the first day of the session; the Government Reform and Oversight Committee ordered it reported on January 10, having spent only one meeting marking up the bill; Rules followed suit two days later; on January 19 floor consideration began. The Judiciary Committee ordered the balanced budget constitutional amendment reported on January 11, and floor consideration began within the month. The same two committees that reported the unfunded mandates legislation reported the enormously consequential line-item veto bill on January 26 and 30; it raced to the floor on February 2. In fact, these bills were actually drafted before the Congress began (the Contract was put together in the summer of 1994), and the Republican leadership was unwilling to brook changes of any magnitude (Owens 1996). During the campaign, the leaders had promised action on all the items in the first 100 days, an extremely ambitious schedule that allowed for little real deliberation in committee, and they feared being accused of not keeping their promises if significant changes were made.

The Republican leadership often used task forces to work out legislation in 1995 but in most cases did not formally bypass committee deliberation. For example, a "design team" led by Speaker Newt Gingrich, R-Ga., worked out the contours of the Medicare reform bill (see Chapter 8). Immigration policy also was crafted by a task force; according to a participant, about 80 percent of the task force's recommendations were incorporated in the bill reported by the Immigration Subcommittee of the Judiciary Committee. The membership of the task forces and of the key committees of jurisdiction often overlap. The task force device allows the leadership to involve other interested members in the process and puts pressure on committees to act expeditiously and with sensitivity to the sentiments of the party majority.

In early 1996 House Republicans decided to bypass committees altogether in a number of instances. They had failed to force President Clinton to accept their budget priorities, and for both policy and political reasons they needed to get the federal government running again. The party leaders and the chairman of the House Appropriations Committee, Robert L. Livingston, R-La., decided what programs to fund in a continuing resolution for the rest of the fiscal year; not even the usually influential subcommittee chairs (known in Hill parlance as the College of Cardinals) were in the room (Cohen 1996, 130). The continuing resolution was never considered by the committee but was taken directly to the floor.

Postcommittee Adjustments

After a bill has been reported from committee, supporters now often make substantive adjustments. The practice has become almost routine, with more than a third of major legislation subject to such postcommittee adjustments in most recent Congresses. Occasionally, legislation will be taken back to committee for formal revision. Much more frequently, changes will be negotiated and then incorporated into a substitute or an amendment. The substitute may supersede the committee bill and become the version (called the base bill) taken to the House floor, or it may be incorporated into the committee bill by the rule; alternatively, the substitute or the amendment may be offered by supporters on the floor.

Such postcommittee adjustments are made to enhance the legislation's chances of passage. Almost always both committee and party leaders are involved with the majority party leadership often taking the lead. Major legislation that involves difficult political, substantive, or procedural problems is most likely to require such alterations. The committee leaders have, in most cases, done in committee what they were willing and able to do to ensure passage; and the majority party leaders are ultimately held responsible for passing the legislation their party members and the House as an institution need and want.

Multiple referral has drawn the majority party leaders into the substantive side of the legislative process; when the committees to which major legislation has been jointly referred cannot come to an agreement among themselves, the party leadership may have to take over the job of negotiating enough of an agreement to avoid a bloody battle on the House floor. A 1987 bill to restructure the farm credit system provides a good example. The House Agriculture Committee reported legislation that included a provision setting up a secondary market in farm mortgages. Securities issues are in the jurisdiction of the Banking and Commerce committees, and the legislation was sequentially referred to both. The leaders of these two committees and of the Agriculture Committee were, however, far apart substantively; it took strong leadership intervention to get an agreement. The majority whip brokered the deal that was taken to the floor as an amendment. The amendment and the bill passed easily. Similarly, on the child care legislation mentioned earlier, the two committees with major jurisdiction took very different approaches to the problem and could not come to an agreement between themselves; the party leadership had to intervene to break the stalemate, and that intervention involved making substantive adjustments to the legislation. In 1995 the House Republican leadership produced the party's welfare reform bill by combining bills passed by three committees and, in the process, altered some controversial provisions (Katz 1995a, 815).

Controversy and saliency often prompt the need for postcommittee adjustments. Supporters may find that their bill as it emerged from committee does not command enough votes to pass. In 1988, for example, a welfare reform bill as reported from committee was viewed as too expensive by many in the House. Supporters believed it would be severely amended or fail if it went to the floor without change. The legislation could not be allowed to die. Democrats were committed to welfare reform. The committees had put a great deal of effort and time into drafting the bill, and the party leadership believed it would enhance the party's image. After extensive negotiations the leadership came up with a strategy: offer an amendment to cut the program enough to satisfy those Democrats who believed they needed to vote for cuts but not so much that the legislation's erstwhile supporters could no longer vote for it. The amendment was offered on the floor, and once it passed the bill did also.

A 1989 bill increasing the minimum wage provides another example of postcommittee adjustments. At the time the Democratic leadership believed there were probably enough votes to pass the bill that the liberal Education and Labor Committee had reported. The leaders, however, wanted the bill to pass by a big enough margin to discourage a presidential veto, and a number of Democrats were uncomfortable with the size of the committee's minimum wage increase. Both considerations argued for bringing more moderate legislation to the floor. Negotiations with committee supporters and southerners, who were most leery of voting for the bill, produced a substitute that was successfully offered on the floor.

Relatively minor postcommittee adjustments were sufficient to amass the necessary support in the House for Clinton's national service program and Goals 2000 education legislation at the beginning of his presidency. On the most important legislation of his second year, however, even major adjustments were not enough to save the legislation. Different versions of comprehensive health care legislation were reported by three committees (actually, one committee reported two different bills); the party leadership attempted to put together a single bill that could pass but was unsuccessful. The issue and the Clinton approach had become too controversial.

In the 104th Congress the Republican leadership often found it necessary to make postcommittee adjustments in legislation. To pass a big rescission bill (a bill cutting already appropriated spending) in 1995, the leadership had to agree to drop restrictive anti-abortion language and to accept a "lockbox" provision dictating that the savings go to deficit reduction and not to fund tax cuts. The first was necessary to get the votes of GOP moderates, the second to pick up some votes from conservative Democrats (Hager 1995a, 796–797). When the constitutional amendment imposing term limits on members of Congress emerged from the Judiciary Committee in a form that the majority of the Republican Party found unacceptable, the Rules Committee, at the direction of the leadership, dropped the committee draft and substituted another version (Salant 1995, 787). In early 1996 committee-approved provisions were deleted from the anti-terrorism bill and the immigration bill before they were taken to the floor. In the former case the leadership was eager to pick up the votes of the most conservative Republicans who opposed giving the federal government any new powers. The weakening of the anti-terrorism bill proved to be insufficient, and an amendment largely gutting the bill was adopted on the House floor. In the case of immigration legislation, business groups opposed a committee-approved provision requiring the verification of the legal immigration status of workers in five states. When the head of the Immigration Task Force complained about the change making the plan voluntary, the chair of the Immigration Subcommittee said, "The idea was to get the bill to the House floor with solid support" (Eilperin 1996, 1).

Legislation that involves many issues is likely to be both highly consequential and controversial and, as such, not infrequently requires postcommittee fine-tuning. The broad scope of such omnibus measures, which are discussed more in Chapter 5, means that most members have a keen interest in at least some provisions. Putting together a version that is satisfactory to most members of the majority party and to a majority of the House may be difficult for the reporting committee or committees. Budget resolutions that lay out a blueprint for federal spending in the following year—how much will be spent, for what, whether there will be a tax increase, and what the deficit will be—and reconciliation bills that bring law into accord with the budget blueprint (and thus may include changes in a multitude of programs as well as tax increases) are the sort of omnibus measures that frequently require postcommittee adjustments orchestrated by the majority party leadership. The case studies in Chapters 10 and 11 of the 1993 reconciliation bill, which in essence contained President Clinton's economic program, and of the even more ambitious 1995 reconciliation bill incorporating congressional Republicans' balanced budget plan provide several examples.

Special Rules

In the House the majority party leadership schedules legislation for floor debate. When a committee reports a bill, it is placed at the bottom of one of the House calendars, the Union Calendar if major legislation. Considering legislation in the order it is listed on the calendar would make little sense, since optimal floor scheduling dictates attention to a host of policy and political factors. The House has developed ways of getting legislation to the floor that provides the needed flexibility. The primary ways of bringing legislation to the floor are through suspension of the rules and through special rules from the Rules Committee, both procedures that the majority party leadership controls.

Noncontroversial legislation is usually considered under suspension of the rules. In 1991–92, for example, 52 percent of all bills that passed the House did so by way of the suspension procedure. Most legislation considered under suspension is narrow in impact or minor in importance. Examples include H.Con. Res. 146, a concurrent resolution authorizing the 1996 Special Olympics Torch Relay to be run through the Capitol Grounds, or S1341, a bill to provide for the transfer of certain lands to the Salt River Pima-Maricopa Indian community and the city of Scottsdale, Arizona. Legislation of more far-reaching significance also may be considered under suspension of the rules. This happens if the bill is so broadly supported that using much floor time is unwarranted. One example is HR2778, a 1995 bill affecting members of the armed forces performing services for the peacekeeping effort in the Republic of Bosnia and Herzegovina. The bill entitled them to certain tax benefits in the same manner as if their services were performed in a combat zone.

The motion to suspend the rules is in order on Mondays and Tuesdays. Legislation brought up under this procedure is debated for a maximum of forty minutes. No amendments are allowed, and a two-thirds vote is required for passage.

The Speaker has complete discretion over what legislation is considered under suspension. When a committee reports a bill that the committee chair considers appropriate for suspension, the chair writes the Speaker requesting that procedure. The Speaker is guided by party rules restricting the use of the procedure. The Democratic Caucus and the Republican Conference both have rules specifying that, to be considered under suspension of the rules, bills should be bipartisan, have strong committee support, and cost less than $100 million.

Most major legislation is brought to the House floor by a special rule that allows the measure to be taken up out of order. The Rules Committee reports such rules, which take the form of House resolutions, but a majority of the full membership must approve each one.

The rule sets the terms for a measure's floor consideration. A rule always specifies the amount of time allowed for general debate and who is to control that time. One or two hours of general debate are typical, though major measures are sometimes granted considerably more time. The time is always equally split between the chairman and the ranking minority member of the committee that reported the legislation; if several committees worked on the bill, each will control some of the general debate time.

A rule may restrict amendments, waive points of order (against what would otherwise be violations of House rules in the legislation or in how it is brought up), and include other special provisions to govern floor consideration. The extent to which a rule restricts amendments and the manner in which it does so also may vary. An *open rule* allows all germane amendments, while a *closed rule* prohibits all amendments other than those offered by the reporting committee. Between the two extremes are rules that allow some but not all germane amendments to be offered; the Rules Committee labels them a *modified open rule* or a *modified closed rule,* depending on just how restrictive the rule is. Some rules of this kind allow only specific amendments enumerated in the Rules Committee report to be offered. Others allow only amendments that have been submitted to the Rules Committee or printed in the *Congressional Record* by a specific time. Still other rules set a time limit on the amending process and allow all germane amendments that can be offered during that time period.

In the contemporary House most rules are somewhat restrictive; in the Congresses of the early 1990s, two-thirds or more of all rules were modified open or modified closed or, occasionally, closed. In recent Congresses three-fourths of all major bills were considered under a restrictive rule.

When major legislation is ready for floor consideration, a decision on what type of rule to use must be made. Given the variety in contemporary rules, the choices are many. The Rules Committee is officially charged with making the decision, and the leaders of the reporting committee make their preferences known, but since the majority party members of Rules are selected by the Speaker, the party leadership strongly influences what is decided. On major legislation the decision on the character of the rule is considered crucial to the bill's success; not surprisingly, the leadership decides.

Because there are many options in the design of a rule, special rules can increasingly be tailored to the problem at hand. Thus, when a bill is referred to several committees, setting the ground rules for floor consideration can present a host of complicated and delicate problems (Bach and Smith 1988, 18–23). Debate time must be divided. When two or more committees have reported different provisions on a given matter, a decision also must be made about which committee's language will constitute the base text and how the other committees' versions will be considered. The first rule for the consideration of the 1992 energy bill, which had been referred to nine committees, split five hours of general debate among the committees. The Energy and Commerce Committee received one hour; the other eight were allotted a half hour each. The committees worked out as many of the conflicts among themselves as they could. In the remaining cases, the Rules Committee decided which committee's version would go into the base bill that would serve as the original bill for the purpose of amendment on the floor. Other committees could offer their language as amendments on the floor. The rule limited the amendments to those listed in the Rules Committee's report, set debate time for each amendment—ranging from five to twenty minutes per side—and specified that those amendments "shall not be subject to amendment except as specified in the report" (*Congressional Record*, May 20, 1992, p. H3462). And this rule governed consideration of only the first seven titles of the bill. The remaining titles were considered under a second rule that again limited the amendments that could be offered and permitted the chairman of the Energy and Commerce Committee "to offer amendments en bloc consisting of the text of amendments printed in the report and germane modifications" (*Congressional Record*, May 21, 1992, p. H3705).

The Uses of Special Rules

Special rules can be used to focus attention and debate on the critical choices, to save time and prevent obstruction and delay, and sometimes to structure the choices members confront on the floor in a way that promotes a particular outcome. When the rule gives members a choice among comprehensive substitutes but bars votes on narrow amendments, it is focusing the debate on alternative approaches, on the big choices rather than the picky details. In recent years rules allowing a choice among comprehensive substitutes have been used to bring to the floor tax bills, budget resolutions, civil rights bills, and social welfare legislation on issues such as parental leave, minimum wage, and child care.

Rules that restrict amendments and waive points of order save time and prevent obstructionism. Before Republicans gained a House majority in the 1994 elections, they had promised, if they took control of the chamber, to use less restrictive rules than had the Democrats when in power. Yet House Republicans also promised to pass the Contract with America during the first 100 days of the 104th Congress. When they brought one of the early Contract items to the floor under an open rule, Democrats naturally enough offered multitudes of amendments. Thereafter, the Republican-controlled Rules Committee usually included in its otherwise unrestrictive rules a time limit on total amending activity.

Any restrictions on amendments, even simply the requirement that amendments be submitted to the Rules Committee several days before being offered on the floor, help the bill's proponents by reducing uncertainty. Proponents can focus their efforts and plan strategy more efficiently; opponents lose the element of surprise.

In addition to reducing uncertainty, carefully crafted rules can structure choices to advantage a particular outcome. The 1988 case of welfare reform legislation discussed earlier illustrates how. Most Democrats— enough to constitute a clear majority of the House—favored passing a welfare reform bill; they believed it constituted good public policy. Many, however, believed that, for reelection reasons, they had to go on record as favoring a reduction in the costs of the program. By allowing a vote on an amendment to cut the program moderately but barring one on an amendment that made Draconian cuts, the rule gave those members who needed it the opportunity to demonstrate fiscal responsibility and also ensured that legislation most Democrats favored would be enacted.

The rule for the reconciliation bill implementing Clinton's economic program in 1993 provides another example. That rule allowed only a vote on a comprehensive Republican substitute; amendments to delete various unpopular elements of the package—the BTU tax and the tax on high income recipients' social security payments—were not made in order. Passage of the bill was crucial for the new administration and for the Democratic Party, but the constraints imposed by the huge deficit and the need to reduce it made putting and holding together a package extremely difficult. The rule was intended to focus debate on the broad philosophical differences between the two parties' approaches to reducing the deficit and to protect Democrats from having to cast a series of excruciatingly tough votes. Many Democrats would have found it hard to explain to constituents back home why they voted against amendments striking unpopular taxing provisions. Allowing such amendments would have confronted Democrats with an unpalatable choice: cast a series of politically dangerous votes or contribute to the picking apart on the floor of the carefully constructed compromise, the passage of which, most believed, was crucial to the future of country and party. This rule also denied the minority a motion to recommit with instructions because, like amendments, that would have allowed Republicans to force a vote on the least popular provisions of the package.

In 1995 Republicans, now in the majority, used a cleverly constructed restrictive rule to protect their rescission bill. The rule specified that anyone wishing to restore spending that had been cut in the bill had to offset the cost by cutting something else in the same section of the bill. Thus, no money could be transferred to social programs from defense spending or from disaster relief for California, for example, since these programs were in different sections of the bill. The rule for the Republicans' omnibus tax-cut bill disallowed an amendment on one of its most controversial provisions. The bill gave families earning up to $200,000 a year a $500 per child tax credit; moderate Republicans wanted to reduce the eligibility to families making less than $100,000; conservative Republicans were adamantly opposed. Since Democrats agreed with moderate Republicans, had the amendment been made in order it would have passed and then conservative Republicans might have opposed the bill. The Republican leadership gambled that moderate Republicans would not desert their party and simply refused them a vote on their amendment.

New Parliamentary Devices

New parliamentary devices developed in recent years have made special rules even more flexible and potent tools for structuring choices. A "king-of-the-hill" provision in a rule specifies that a series of amendments or entire substitutes are to be voted on *ad seriatim* and the last one that receives a majority prevails. This device makes possible a direct vote on each of several alternatives; in ordinary parliamentary procedure, if an amendment or substitute receives a majority, no further alternative amendments to that part of the bill already amended can be offered. Clearly, when this procedure is employed, the amendment or substitute voted on last is advantaged. The procedure also makes it possible for members to vote for more than one version, which is sometimes politically advantageous. When Democrats were in the majority, budget resolutions were often considered under "king-of-the-hill" rules. Members were thus guaranteed a vote on each of the substitute versions of the resolution made in order by the rule. The House Budget Committee version was always placed in the advantageous last position.[5]

The rule for the 1991 civil rights bill illustrates how the procedure can be used strategically. The rule stipulated that the three substitutes made in order were to be offered in a specific order under the king-of-the-hill procedure. The rule gave liberals a vote on their much stronger version but put that substitute first in line. Having cast a vote in favor of the tough bill favored by civil rights activists, these members then could support the leadership's more moderate compromise. The rule next gave House Republicans and the Bush administration a vote on their preferred version. It put the Democratic compromise last—that is, in the advantaged position.

In the 104th Congress Republicans began using a "queen-of-the-hill" variant, which allows a vote on all the versions but specifies that whichever version gets the most votes, so long as it receives a majority, wins. The rules for the welfare reform bill and the term-limits constitutional amendment took this form; in the former case, a liberal Democratic substitute, a more conservative Democratic substitute, and the Republican version were considered under the queen-of-the-hill procedure. On term limits, votes on four versions were made in order. In both cases the option the Republican leadership supported was placed last, which is still the preferred position. Supporters of the last option, unlike those of earlier ones, know how many votes they need in order to win.

Another new device—a self-executing rule—provides that when a rule is adopted by the House, the accompanying bill is automatically amended to incorporate the text of an amendment either set forth or referenced in the rule. The procedure provides a simple way of inserting last-minute corrections or compromises into a bill and prevents a direct and

---

5. When the leadership was confident that it could defeat all the alternatives and no postcommittee adjustments in the budget resolution were needed, the Budget Committee version was not offered as an amendment at all but constituted the base bill.

separate vote on the language in question. Thus, in 1993 after the reconciliation bill implementing President Clinton's economic program was
reported from committee, the leadership, in order to amass the votes
needed to pass the bill, worked out a compromise on entitlements with
conservative Democrats. The language was incorporated into the legislation by a self-executing provision in the rule. The Republican leadership
used the device frequently in 1995, as the case study in Chapter 11 shows.

On the Floor

Floor consideration of a bill begins with debate on the rule. One
hour is allotted, half controlled by a majority member of Rules and half by
a minority member. The majority member explains and justifies the rule,
the minority member gives his party's position, and then both yield time
to other members who wish to speak. If neither the rule nor the legislation is controversial, much less than the full hour may be used. If the legislation is controversial but the rule is not, members frequently will use the
time to discuss the legislation substantively. Since rules today are often
restrictive and complex, they are often highly controversial, and debate
may well revolve around the character of the rule itself and consume the
entire hour. During this period, no amendments to the rule are in order.

The House must approve the rule before consideration of the legislation can begin. The Rules Committee member managing the debate on
the rule for the majority party will *move the previous question.* If successful,
the motion cuts off debate, and the House then proceeds to vote on the
rule itself. The only way to amend the rule is to defeat the previous question motion. If opponents defeat the previous question motion, they control the floor and may propose the special rule they would like to see. Losing on the motion to order the previous question is devastating for the
majority party and seldom happens; a member who votes against his or
her party on this crucial procedural motion is not quickly forgiven.

One memorable vote on the previous question occurred in 1981 on
the reconciliation bill that implemented President Reagan's economic
program. The key battle on that legislation was over the rule. Reagan and
House Republicans wanted a single vote on Reagan's package of spending
cuts; they could then make the vote a test of whether members supported
or opposed the popular president's program to rescue the economy.
Democrats, who controlled the House, proposed a rule that forced a
series of votes on cutting specific popular programs. Knowing they were
likely to lose at least some of those votes and thereby major chunks of Reagan's economic plan, Republicans decided to try to defeat the previous

question on the rule. With the help of some conservative Democrats, they were successful and so were able to substitute their own rule that called for a single vote on the package as a whole.

Votes on the previous question are usually far less visible, and disgruntled majority party members can be persuaded by their leadership to vote "yes" on that motion and show their displeasure, if they must, by voting against the rule. Fearing they lacked the votes to pass their rule for the consideration of the Department of Interior appropriations bill in the summer of 1995, Republicans nevertheless made an attempt to do so—but only after forcefully explaining to their freshmen members that they had better not join the minority in voting against the previous question (Burger 1995, 22). The rule was, in fact, defeated. The leadership then worked out a compromise among House Republicans, got the Rules Committee to incorporate it in a new rule, brought that to the floor, and passed it. When the majority party lost the rule, it did not lose control of the floor as it would have had it lost the previous question vote.

Once the previous question has been approved, the House votes on the rule itself. When the rule is not controversial, these votes may be by voice; on controversial rules the votes will be recorded. They are called roll call votes, although the House seldom calls the roll as it once did in the days before electronic voting. Because rules are frequently contentious, recorded votes are likely. In the 100th and 101st Congresses (1987–90), seventy-one major measures were brought to the floor under special rules, and fifty-two (73 percent) of the rule votes were decided by roll call; in 1995, 58 percent of all the rules provoked roll calls.

The majority party sometimes loses votes on rules but not often. The vote on the Interior appropriations rule was the first that Republicans lost during 1995; from 1981 to 1992, Democrats lost on average just over one rule per year. During the highly charged 103rd Congress (1993–94), Democrats lost five rules. Increasingly, majority party members are expected to support their party on such procedural votes. Over the period 1987 to 1991, the mean Democratic vote in favor on passage or on ordering the previous question (whichever was closer) was 93 percent. Votes on rules as well as votes on ordering the previous question tend to fall along party lines, especially when the rule is restrictive. Of rules for major legislation in the 100th and 101st Congresses, 48 percent saw a majority of Democrats supporting the rule and a majority of Republicans opposing it; 72 percent of modified closed rules were decided by such party votes.

If the House approves the rule, it thereby resolves itself into the Committee of the Whole, where the debate and amending of the legislation takes place. A sort of parliamentary fiction, the Committee of the Whole has the same membership as the House but somewhat more streamlined rules. The quorum for doing business in the Committee of the Whole is 100 members rather than 218 members (half the full membership, which constitutes a quorum in the House). In the Committee of the Whole when a member is recognized to offer or speak on an amendment, it is for only five minutes. The Speaker does not preside over the Committee of the Whole, but since he chooses the presiding officer and always picks a majority party member, the majority party remains in control of the chair.

General debate begins the consideration of the bill in the Committee of the Whole. The rule has specified who controls the time. The chair of the committee or of the subcommittee that reported the bill serves as floor manager for the majority and actually controls the time allotted to the committee majority; his or her minority counterpart controls the minority's time. The majority floor manager begins with a prepared statement explaining what the legislation does and why it deserves to pass.

The minority floor manager then makes a statement, which may range from wholehearted agreement with his or her opposite number to an all-out attack on the bill. When the committee has come to a broad bipartisan agreement, general debate may be a lovefest, with committee members congratulating each other on the wonderful job they did and on the admirably cooperative way in which they did it. When the committee reporting the legislation is split, especially if it is split along party lines, the tone of floor debate will be contentious and sometimes bitter. If the legislation is the product of several committees, each will have floor managers, who will each make an opening statement.

After opening statements the floor managers yield time—usually in small amounts—to other members who wish to speak. By and large, the majority floor manager yields time to supporters of the legislation and to majority party members, while the minority floor manager yields time to minority party members and, assuming the bill is controversial, to bill opponents. Often not all majority party members support the bill and not all minority party members oppose it. Therefore, both managers may yield time to opponents of their position. An opponent today, especially if a fellow party member, may be a supporter tomorrow and should not be alienated.

When general debate time has expired, the amending process begins. What happens now depends on the rule. If all germane amendments are allowed, members are recognized to offer amendments. House rules give the chair of the Committee of the Whole discretion to determine the order of recognition, but by custom members of the reporting committee are given preference in gaining recognition, and they are recognized in order of seniority (Tiefer 1989, 231). Once a member is recognized to offer his or her amendment, the member has five minutes to explain it. The floor manager has five minutes to reply, then other members may speak. They gain time by offering pro forma amendments "to strike the last word" or "to strike the requisite number of words." The member who offers a pro forma amendment does not actually want it to pass, but by offering it he or she gets five minutes to speak on the amendment that is really at issue.

A House member may offer an amendment to the amendment being considered. Such a second degree amendment may be intended sincerely to improve the amendment to which it is offered. Alternatively, the purpose behind a second degree amendment may be to lessen the impact or even negate altogether the effect of the original amendment. If a bill's supporters believe they cannot defeat a popular but, in their view, harmful amendment, they may try to come up with a second degree amendment to at least weaken its effect.

Debate on an amendment under the five-minute rule may go on for a considerable period of time, but eventually when everyone who wants to has spoken, a vote on the amendment occurs.

Sometimes a floor manager has no objections to an amendment or actually supports it and will simply "accept" the amendment without asking for a recorded vote. In that case the amendment is usually approved by voice vote. If the floor manager—or another member—opposes the amendment, a vote will be demanded. The first vote may be by voice, but if the amendment is at all controversial, the losing side in a voice vote will demand a recorded vote. Only twenty-five members are needed to force a recorded vote.

The House's electronic voting system works in this way. Members have individualized cards that look rather like a credit card; they insert their card into one of the ten voting stations attached to the backs of seats on the House floor and punch the "yea," "nay," or "present" button. The vote is recorded by a computer, and it also shows up as a green, red, or amber light next to the member's name on a huge lighted display behind the Speaker's dais.

After the amendment has been disposed of, another member is recognized to offer another amendment. Under an open rule the amending process continues as long as there are members wishing to offer amendments and on the floor prepared to do so. The House can by majority vote cut off debate, though amendments that have been "preprinted" in the *Congressional Record* at least one day before floor consideration are guaranteed ten minutes of debate (Tiefer 1989, 401–403). Unlike senators, House members have limited patience for protracted floor debate. In January 1995 Republicans brought the unfunded mandates bill to the floor under an open rule; after six days of debate and with 170 amendments still pending, they voted to cut off debate.

A more frequently used way of controlling the length of the amending process is through the rule. Under many rules the amending process proceeds pretty much as described above except that the amendments allowed are limited, perhaps to those preprinted in the *Congressional Record*. In other cases the rule specifies the amendments that are in order and the member who may offer them. In these cases the rule frequently specifies a time limit on debate on a specific amendment—perhaps twenty minutes or one hour if a major amendment. The rule also is likely to prohibit amendments to the amendments made in order.

What happens in the Committee of the Whole thus varies depending on the number of committees involved and the character of the rule. Clearly, a structured rule makes floor proceedings more orderly and predictable.

After general debate and whatever amending is allowed have been completed, the Committee of the Whole rises and reports back to the House. The Speaker again presides and the rules of the House again are in effect. Amendments adopted in the Committee of the Whole must be approved by the House, which gives opponents of an amendment a second chance to defeat it. Usually, however, the House votes on all the amendments adopted as a package and approval is certain. Occasionally, if a vote was very close and the amendment makes major and unacceptable changes in the legislation, an effort to change the outcome will be made. In 1995 Democrats, with some help from moderate Republicans, successfully passed in the Committee of the Whole an amendment to an appropriations bill deleting controversial language barring the Environmental Protection Agency from enforcing various environmental laws. The amendment won on a close 211–206 vote and the provision was important to many staunchly anti-regulatory Republicans, so the leadership called for a second vote in the House and defeated the amendment on an even closer 210–210 vote. (Motions die on a tie vote.) In that case the leadership got lucky; although no Republicans switched their votes, several Democrats who had supported the amendment the first time were absent for the second vote. Usually, however, amendments that win in the Committee of the Whole win again in the House. After all, the membership of the two bodies is identical.

The minority may now offer a motion to recommit the legislation to committee with or without instructions. A motion to recommit without instructions is essentially a motion to kill the bill and seldom prevails. By this point too many members have a stake in the legislation's enactment; if it lacked majority support, it would probably not have gotten so far. A motion to recommit with instructions—that is, instructions to report the bill back with specified changes—is, in effect, a motion to amend the bill. It is the minority's last chance to change the legislation. The motion may propose substituting the minority's version of the bill for the majority's, or it may propose much more modest changes. Again, because it is the minority's motion, it seldom wins—though more frequently than the motion to recommit without instructions. Assuming the legislation survives, a vote on final passage is taken, usually by recorded vote. At this point the legislation will almost certainly pass. Constitutional amendments requiring a two-thirds vote have been defeated on a floor vote in the House, but they are an exception from the norm; in the 100th, 101st, and 103rd Congresses, the only major measures to be defeated at this stage were two competing proposals to aid the Nicaraguan contras, one President Reagan's and the other sponsored by the Democratic leadership in 1988, and the first 1990 budget summit agreement (though that technically was the defeat of a conference report).

If the legislation does pass, a motion to reconsider is made and laid upon the table. This ensures the issue cannot be reopened. The legislation is then sent to the Senate.

Unorthodox Lawmaking in the House

If the textbook legislative process can be likened to climbing a ladder, the contemporary process is more like climbing a big old tree with many branches. The route to enactment used to be linear and predictable; now it is flexible and varied. To be sure, the textbook model was never a complete description of how bills became laws. There have always been alternative routes. In the past, however, the alternatives were infrequently used on major legislation. Now variation is the norm. As the case studies in Chapters 7 through 11 show, no two major bills are likely to follow exactly the same process.

Although the new practices and procedures arose in response to different problems and opportunities (see Chapter 6), their consequences are similar. The new practices and procedures in the House facilitate lawmaking. Most make it easier for the majority party leadership to advance its members' legislative goals. The leadership now has more flexibility to shape the legislative process to suit the particular legislation at issue. When climbing a ladder there isn't much one can do if a rung is broken; when climbing a tree with many branches, if one route is blocked there is always another one can try.

Routes and Obstacles:
The Legislative Process
in the Senate

IN THE SENATE LEGISLATION MUST TRAVERSE the same basic path as in the House, and the alternatives at the various stages are, in many cases, similar—at least on the surface. Yet the Senate is a quite different body than the House (Matthews 1960; Sinclair 1989; Smith 1989). Smaller in membership, the Senate is less hierarchical and less formal. Senate rules give senators as individuals great power: a senator may hold the floor indefinitely unless the Senate invokes *cloture,* which requires an extraordinary majority, and any senator may offer an unlimited number of amendments to almost any piece of legislation, and those amendments need not even be germane. Current norms allow senators to use extended debate and their floor amending rights expansively (Sinclair 1989).

The differences in the two bodies are reflected in their legislative processes. The Senate does much of its business by unanimous consent—both an acknowledgment and an augmentation of the power of senators as individuals. Any one senator can block a unanimous consent request. The Senate is not a majority-rule chamber like the House. In the House the majority can always prevail; in the Senate minorities can often block majorities.

Bill Introduction

In the Senate, as in the House, only members—that is, senators—may introduce legislation, and each may introduce as many measures as he or she pleases. Senators may introduce their bills from the floor or just submit them to the clerks while the chamber is in session. The sources of legislation—the executive branch, interest groups, constituents, the legislator's pet projects—are similar in the two chambers. Because senators represent whole states and serve on more committees than the typical House member, they tend to offer legislation concerning a broader range of issues.

Bill Referral

When a bill is introduced or arrives from the House of Representatives, it is normally referred by the presiding officer, on the advice of the parliamentarian, to the committee of *predominant* jurisdiction. Senate rules do not encourage multiple referral as House rules do.

Multiple Referral

Sometimes bills are sent to more than one committee in the Senate. A 1977 rule provides that the joint party leadership (that is, the majority and the minority leaders acting together) can by motion propose that legislation be multiply referred, but this route is never used (Davidson 1989, 379–380). When legislation is multiply referred, it is done by unanimous consent; the consent request may specify time limits for each committee's consideration of the legislation as the 1977 rule had allowed. Agreements are usually negotiated by the affected committee leaders; in the Senate party leaders seldom take an active role (Davidson 1989, 388). "One just can't imagine the Senate giving its leaders the kind of power the Speaker has with respect to referral—determining what committees can do what to legislation, sometimes even to specifying what language they can work on, specifying committee reporting deadlines, and the like," a knowledgeable observer explained.

In the Senate several different committees sometimes consider bills that, while not identical, deal with the same topic. For example, in 1995 three committees—Judiciary, Governmental Affairs, and Energy and Natural Resources—reported out regulatory reform legislation (see Chapter 7). Even when not technically multiply referred, such legislation entails many of the same complications.

Multiple referral is less frequent in the Senate than in the House; only a little more than one in ten major measures were sent to more than one committee in recent Congresses. Much of the legislation sent to multiple committees in the House is referred to only one committee in the Senate; about two-thirds in recent Congresses. The reverse is seldom the case; in recent Congresses only about 10 percent of all major measures multiply referred in either or both chambers was multiply referred in the Senate but not in the House.

Legislation that is multiply referred in the Senate is also less likely than in the House to be sent to a large number of committees. The big trade bill in the 100th Congress was referred to nine committees in the Senate and the bills implementing the North American Free Trade Agreement (NAFTA) and the recent General Agreement on Tariffs and Trade (GATT) were each sent to six. More typical, however, is referral to two committees.

Part of the difference in the frequency of multiple referral in the Senate and the House is a result of differences in how jurisdictional boundaries are drawn in the two chambers; the Senate made significant changes in 1977, and its committee jurisdictions are somewhat more consonant with contemporary issues. But the difference also reflects more basic differences between the chambers; in the Senate when legislation impinges on the jurisdiction of more than one committee, the committee chairs often informally work out any problems among themselves.

Bypassing Committee

In the Senate, as in the House, committees are sometimes bypassed altogether. In recent Congresses about one in seven major measures went to the Senate floor without going through committee; in 1995, however, more than one in four did so. In the Senate bypassing a committee is technically simple; if any senator objects to committee referral (more precisely, objects on the floor to further proceedings on the measure after the second reading, which occurs right before the bill would be referred to committee), the bill goes directly to the calendar (Tiefer 1989, 594). When legislation reported by a Senate committee awaits floor action and a companion House-passed bill arrives in the Senate, this procedure is frequently used to put the bill directly on the calendar rather than sending it to a committee that has already dealt with the issue. In a similar vein when a Senate committee is still working on a bill and the House sends over its version, the House-passed bill is commonly held at the desk by unanimous consent. The use of these procedures does not, of course, constitute bypassing the committee in any real sense.

Any senator's power to put legislation directly on the calendar simply by objecting to the bill's being referred to committee would seem to make bypassing committee easy. However, the majority leader, through his scheduling powers, effectively has a veto over senators bringing bills to the floor directly by this route. Although procedurally simple, it really requires the majority leader's assent to work.

Senate committee chairs, with the majority leader's agreement, sometimes use this rule to speed up the legislative process, particularly on relatively uncontroversial legislation. In early 1987, for example, a clean water bill that had overwhelmingly passed late in the previous Congress but had been vetoed by Reagan was brought directly to the floor. In 1988 legislation protecting whistleblowers had passed, but again late in the year, and Reagan killed it by pocket veto. When the next year the sponsors and the Bush administration worked out a compromise, the bill was no longer at all controversial, so supporters took it directly to the floor. On fair housing legislation in 1988, extensive negotiations among Senate committee leaders, administration officials, and interest group representatives produced a broadly supported compromise, which was taken directly to the floor. Doing so enabled the bill to pass before the August recess and avoid the end-of-the-session rush. Republicans, newly in the majority in 1995, were determined to pass quickly legislation requiring that Congress abide by various regulatory laws; the House had passed its bill on the first day of the session. A similar bill had passed before and had bipartisan support, so the Senate by unanimous consent placed it directly on the calendar. Despite this maneuver, the Senate still took a week to pass the legislation.

Political considerations may dictate bypassing committee. In the wake of the Oklahoma City bombing, President Bill Clinton proposed anti-terrorism legislation. To demonstrate his and the Republican Party's concern about the issue as well as his ability to get things done, then majority leader Bob Dole of Kansas wanted swift action. He and Judiciary chairman Orrin G. Hatch, R-Utah, drafted legislation and took it to the floor, bypassing committee consideration. Dole attempted a similar move on the so-called partial birth abortion ban; when the House passed the bill and sent it to the Senate, Dole took it directly to the floor. However, he found himself unable to marshal the votes for passage and so supported a motion by Sen. Arlen Specter, R-Pa., to commit the bill to the Judiciary Committee with instructions that the committee hold hearings and report the bill back to the Senate within ten days. Hearings were held, but the committee chair, hoping to pass the bill without change, opposed marking up the bill and let it be sent back to the Senate automatically. There it passed but only after Dole offered a weakening amendment. In both these cases the chair of the affected committee actively supported the majority leader's strategy of bypassing the committee.

Occasionally, the Senate bypasses committees to, in effect, avoid multiple referral. An omnibus drug bill in 1988 involved the jurisdiction of more than half the committees; rather than referring the legislation to all the various committees with jurisdiction, Senate leaders bypassed committee consideration. Instead, the bill was based on the recommendations of party task forces and drafted through months-long, bipartisan negotiations among key senators. Although the senators who were involved were largely the same ones that would have taken the lead had the legislation gone to the committees, the informal process allowed for more flexibility (see Chapter 9).

Senators have available another and, in some ways, even easier way to bypass committee; they can offer their legislation as an amendment to another bill on the floor. In most cases the "amendment" need not even be germane. The original Gramm-Rudman budget-balancing legislation was never considered by committee; Texas Republican Phil Gramm, its lead sponsor, simply offered it on the floor as an amendment to legislation raising the debt ceiling. Similarly, the Gramm-Rudman "fix" revising the law after parts of it were declared unconstitutional was also offered as a floor amendment to a debt ceiling bill. In 1984 Democrats, then in the minority in the Senate, brought civil rights legislation that Republicans opposed to the floor as an amendment to a continuing appropriations resolution, a must-pass bill.

Senate handling of the ethics–pay raise issue in 1989 represented a combination of these procedures. When the bill came over from the House (without any Senate provisions, since each chamber handles its own internal matters), the Senate leaders placed it directly on the calendar, thus bypassing committee. Time was short, and the issue was too delicate for a committee to handle. Then the majority and minority leaders jointly offered a leadership amendment to apply House pay-raise and honoraria-ban provisions to the Senate (*Congressional Quarterly Almanac 1989*, 57). Insufficient votes to pass their amendment later forced them to scale back the pay raise, again through a floor amendment.

As these examples suggest, the legislative process is often less formal in the Senate than in the House. Individual members are more important and committees less important than in the House. Given the power that senators as individuals wield and each senator's enormous workload, informal negotiations and agreements sometimes supplant more formal procedures.

Postcommittee Adjustments

To enhance its chances of passage, legislation in the Senate, as in the House, may be altered after it has been reported from committee. In recent Congresses about a third of major measures were subject to such postcommittee adjustment; in 1995 the proportion shot up to almost two-thirds.

The effort to craft a postcommittee compromise may be led by the party leadership. Majority Leader George Mitchell, D-Maine, played the lead role on the clean air bill in 1990. He orchestrated the complex negotiations that finally produced a bill that could pass the Senate (Cohen 1992, 81–98). He was similarly active on child care legislation in 1989, putting together a substitute based on elements of the Finance and Labor committees' versions when it became clear the liberal Labor Committee's bill could not pass on its own. In 1995, when Republican supporters of two line-item veto bills could not work out their differences, Majority Leader Dole helped craft a draft quite different from either one (Taylor 1995, 855).

More frequently than in the House, committee leaders or even individual senators take the lead. In 1993, for example, Senate Banking Committee leaders faced the daunting task of passing highly unpopular legislation to provide funds to finish the savings-and-loan bailout. In a time of big deficits and not enough money for popular programs, no senator relished voting for what appeared to be a bailout of the greedy savings and loan industry, even though, in effect, the bailout was of depositors that the federal government had guaranteed. After the Senate Banking Committee had reported the legislation, it became clear it would not pass, so the chair and the ranking minority member, after negotiations with the Clinton administration, offered a less generous substitute on the floor and thereby engineered passage. Similarly, when Clinton's national service program ran into some trouble on the Senate floor, Massachusetts Democrat Edward M. Kennedy, chair of the Senate Labor Committee, made changes via an amendment that picked up the needed votes. In 1989 two southern Democrats offered on the floor an amendment scaling back a minimum wage bill; they did so with the blessing of the Democratic committee leaders, who hoped thereby to garner enough support for the bill to discourage a presidential veto.

Of course, the strategy of altering the bill substantively to increase support is not always successful; it may not be possible to make sufficient changes to pick up needed new votes without altering the measure in a way that alienates its supporters. In 1995 Senate supporters of a balanced budget constitutional amendment engaged in a succession of very public negotiations as they scurried to get the necessary votes. Majority Leader Dole and the chair of the Judiciary Committee, as well as other core supporters, crafted an amendment restricting the judiciary's power over the constitutional amendment's enforcement and thereby won the support of Sen. Sam Nunn, D-Ga. Despite lengthy attempts, they were never able to satisfy senators concerned about the impact of the balanced budget amendment on the social security system, and the amendment failed.

Passage of a constitutional amendment requires a two-thirds vote, an intentionally high barrier to success. Ordinary legislation, if it is controversial, may well need an extraordinary majority as well. Senators now use their right of extended debate—their right to talk and thus block action indefinitely—much more frequently than in the past. Since cutting off debate requires sixty votes, supporters of legislation must build a coalition that is bigger than a simple majority. Doing so will likely require extensive compromise and may require the sort of postcommittee adjustments discussed here. On the national service legislation sponsors never had a problem getting a majority; they had to make more concessions in order to amass the sixty votes that overcoming a threatened filibuster takes (see Chapter 7).

Scheduling Legislation for the Floor

The Senate does not use special rules to bring legislation to the floor. The majority leader, by motion or unanimous consent, just takes the bill to be considered off the calendar. Senate precedent provides the majority leader with the right of first recognition; when several senators seek recognition, the majority leader is recognized first and the minority leader second. Otherwise, Senate rules require the presiding officer to recognize the first senator to seek recognition, giving the presiding officer much less discretion than his House counterpart has. (When the Senate is debating legislation, the bill managers have the right to be recognized after the leaders but before other senators.)

Although the procedure seems simpler than that used by the House, the Senate majority party leadership actually has much less control over the scheduling of legislation and over the terms for its consideration. On any debatable motion any senator can hold the floor indefinitely unless or until sixty senators vote to shut off debate. The motion to proceed to consideration of a bill is debatable, so senators can filibuster against bringing legislation they oppose to the floor.

This fact shapes the process by which legislation is actually scheduled for floor debate in the Senate. The majority leader usually moves bills off the calendar for floor consideration by unanimous consent; a study of 247 matters considered by the Senate in the 98th Congress (1983–84) found that 98 percent came up by unanimous consent (Tiefer 1989, 563).

The Consultation Process

Since any senator can block a unanimous consent request, the majority leader, if he wishes floor business to proceed smoothly, must check with all interested senators before bringing legislation to the floor. He always consults with leaders of the reporting committee and with the minority leader; in the Senate effective scheduling requires bipartisan cooperation and that requires intensive consultation between the majority and minority leaders.

Since any senator could object to considering the legislation and since time constraints make it impossible for the leaders to check with every senator on every piece of legislation, senators without an obvious interest in the bill are expected to inform their party leadership if they do have an interest. For every bill the staffs of the majority and minority leaders keep a record of senators who have asked to be informed before it is brought to the floor, and these senators must also be consulted. Senate party leaders contend that their only responsibility is to inform those senators when they are ready to bring a bill to the floor, and that may well be all a particular senator expects. She may simply want to be sure the legislation comes up when she is in town.

In other cases, however, a senator may object to the legislation's floor consideration at any time or until the bill's supporters have altered it to her liking. Such a notification by a senator to her party leader is called a *hold*; what gives holds their bite is the implicit or explicit threat to filibuster the motion to proceed. The majority leader sometimes will go ahead with the legislation despite a hold, but he then may face a filibuster on the motion to proceed and, if that is overcome, a filibuster on the bill itself. Even if both filibusters can be overcome, the time consumed is substantial. Especially when floor time is short—before a recess or near the end of the session—only the most essential legislation is likely to be considered as worthy of so much time. After all, if scarce time is used trying to end a filibuster, other legislation will be sacrificed. Supporters of legislation are under increasing pressure to make concessions that will remove the threat of a filibuster. As time becomes scarcer, a hold increasingly becomes a veto.

The majority leader thus schedules legislation under severe constraints. When he rises to make a unanimous consent request that the Senate proceed to consider a particular bill, he has almost always cleared it with those of his party colleagues who asked to be consulted and received agreement from his minority counterpart, who has cleared it with his party members.

Unanimous Consent Agreements

The Senate often considers legislation under a formal unanimous consent agreement (UCA). The majority leader, his staff, or committee leaders under his general supervision negotiate an agreement setting terms for the consideration of the legislation. A UCA may specify time for general debate and time limits for the debate of specific amendments; it may bar nongermane amendments or nongermane amendments that are not explicitly listed; and it may specify the time for votes on specific amendments and on final passage (Tiefer 1989, 573–584; Smith and Flathman 1989). Here is an example of a fairly typical unanimous consent agreement. It was offered by George Mitchell on February 4, 1994:

> Madam President [the member presiding over the Senate who in this case was a woman], I now ask unanimous consent that the Senate proceed to the consideration of S1361, the school-to-work bill, no later than 10 a.m. on Monday, February 7, and that it be considered under the following limitation:
>
> • That there be 1 hour for debate on the bill equally divided in the usual form, with an additional 20 minutes for debate under Senator Gregg's control; that the only first-degree floor amendments in order be the following, and that they be subject to second-degree amendments if they are relevant to the first-degree amendment, and limited to the following time limitations if applicable:
>
> An amendment by Senator Kassebaum that is relevant;[1] an amendment by Senator Kassebaum that is relevant [duplication means two amendments]; an amendment by Senator Simpson regarding vocational education; an amendment by Senator Coverdell that no new programs be funded until the earthquake supplemental is paid for; an amendment by Senator Nickles regarding funding, 2 hours equally divided in the usual form; an amendment by Senator Gorton regarding privatization, 2 hours equally divided in the usual form; an amendment by Senator Dole that is relevant; an amendment by Senator Thurmond that is relevant; an amendment by Senator Pressler that is relevant; an amendment by Senator Thurmond that is relevant; an amendment by Senator Chafee that is relevant; an amendment by Senator Kerry of Massachusetts that is relevant; an amendment by Senator Lautenberg that is relevant; an amendment by Senator Kennedy that is relevant; an amendment by Senator Kennedy that is relevant;
>
> • That all first-degree amendments must be offered by 6 p.m. on Monday, February 7; that all time is to be equally divided in the usual form; that upon the disposition of the above amendments and the committee substitute, the bill be read a third time; . . . and the Senate proceed to vote on passage . . . (*Congressional Record*, February 4, 1994, S846).

In recent years unanimous consent agreements have become increasingly individualized as Senate leaders seek to accommodate individual

---

1. Relevance is, in most cases, a less strict standard than is germaneness.

senators' demands (Smith and Flathman 1989, 361). Thus each senator may bargain for particular amounts of debate time on his or her amendments and also expect to have the date and time when those amendments will come up specified. For example, on September 21, 1993, Majority Leader Mitchell made the following unanimous consent request:

> Madam President, I ask unanimous consent that when the Senate resumes consideration of HR2419, the VA-HUD appropriations bill, at 9:15 a.m., on Wednesday, September 22, that Senator Bryan be recognized to offer an amendment on the SETI Program; that there be a time limitation of 1 hour for debate on the amendment with no second-degree amendment in order thereto, with the time actually divided and controlled in the usual form; that when the time is used or yielded back, the Bryan amendment be temporarily laid aside and that the Senate then resume consideration of the Bumpers amendment No. 910; that there be 20 minutes remaining for debate on the Bumpers amendment No. 910, with the time equally divided and controlled in the usual form; that at noon tomorrow the Senate, without intervening action or debate, vote on or in relation to the Bumpers amendment No. 910; and that upon disposition of the Bumpers amendment, without intervening action or debate, the Senate proceed to vote on or in relation to the Bryan amendment (*Congressional Record*, September 21, 1993, S12117).

Comprehensive unanimous consent agreements that are worked out before the bill comes to the floor and that govern the entire process of consideration are relatively rare (Smith and Flathman 1989, 366). More often, the leader will be able to work out only a partial agreement before debate begins. As consideration progresses, senators are likely to become clearer about what amendments they want to offer and how much time they will need, and further agreements may become possible. Recently reaching a preconsideration agreement, even a limited one, has proven difficult on major legislation and such bills have often had to be called up without any UCA in place. After an often substantial period of floor consideration, the leader may be able to work out one or more agreements. Thus, several partial UCAs may govern a bill's consideration.

A unanimous consent agreement provides some of the same predictability that a special rule provides in the House. The difference between them is that, while a simple majority can approve a special rule, a UCA requires unanimous consent; one senator can veto it. This difference, of course, has an enormous impact on the legislative process in the two chambers.

Why do senators agree to unanimous consent agreements? Clearly, they make the majority leader's job easier; once a UCA is in effect, he has a much better idea of how long the legislation will take on the floor. The bill's supporters value the reduction in uncertainty that a UCA accomplishes. For other senators, with their extremely busy schedules and their own legislative priorities, the more predictable schedule and the more efficient use of time that UCAs make possible are important benefits and may dictate acquiescing in a UCA even for a bill the senator does not support. But, if the senator strongly opposes the legislation, he can always object.

The Senate Floor

Assume the Senate has agreed to consider the legislation. Floor debate begins in the same way it does in the House: with opening statements by the majority and minority floor managers. As in the House, the chairman and ranking minority member of the committee or subcommittee usually manage the legislation on the floor, but in the Senate a bill sponsor who holds no such official role may act as floor manager. Other senators may also speak.

Debate is unlimited unless constrained by a unanimous consent agreement, and even then it will not be as tightly restricted as in the House. Senators' statements are likely to be considerably longer than those in the House. When the Senate is engaged in a great debate, such as on the resolution in 1991 to authorize the Persian Gulf War, the lack of tight time limits makes for better and certainly more dramatic debate. On less momentous occasions Senate debate can drag on interminably, and the lack of time limits provides no incentive for senators to prepare their remarks carefully.

Especially if the Senate is operating without a UCA, debate on amendments is quite unstructured. The floor manager will usually know when a senator intends to offer an amendment, and if that senator is not on the floor at the appropriate time, the floor manager is likely to wait! The House, in contrast, waits for no member and certainly not for a rank-and-file member who wants to offer an amendment.

Quorum calls are used to kill time. A senator can make a point of order that a quorum is not present, and the presiding officer will ask the clerk to call the roll.[2] The Senate does not use electronic voting. The clerk will very slowly call the names of the senators, while everyone waits for the senator who is supposed to be offering his amendment to show up. When he does, the quorum call is vacated (that is, called off) usually without a

---

2. In fact, a quorum is seldom present since senators are in their offices or in committee working. Even if a quorum is present, the presiding officer must have the roll called; only under cloture may the presiding officer determine the presence of a quorum by counting.

quorum ever having shown up. Similarly, when senators need some time in the midst of floor consideration to negotiate in private, quorum calls make possible a kind of "time out." For example, the floor manager and a senator offering an amendment may want to see if they can work out a compromise version of the amendment that both find satisfactory.

Amendment Rules and Their Consequences

Senate rules, under most circumstances, allow any senator to offer as many amendments as he or she wishes to legislation on the floor. For most bills the amendments need not even be germane to the legislation; that is, if a senator wants to offer a civil rights provision to an agriculture bill, Senate rules do not prohibit it. Amendments to general appropriations bills (that is, spending bills) must be germane according to Senate rules, but senators often prefer not to enforce the rule. Many unanimous consent agreements do bar nongermane amendments unless they are explicitly listed, and after cloture is invoked amendments must be germane. The Congressional Budget and Impoundment Control Act of 1974 (hereafter the Budget Act) requires that amendments to budget resolutions and reconciliation bills be germane.

In fact, senators frequently offer nongermane amendments. Throughout his Senate career Jesse Helms, R-N.C., has used nongermane amendments on hot-button topics such as busing, homosexuality, pornography, and abortion to get his issues to the floor and force senators to vote on them. In the late 1980s he successfully attached to an education bill an amendment outlawing dial-a-porn services (900-number telephone services that provide explicit sexual messages for a fee). But Helms is by no means alone; most senators use the tactic at least occasionally. In early 1993 Senate Minority Leader Bob Dole attempted unsuccessfully to attach an amendment on homosexuals in the military to family and medical leave legislation. His purpose was to embarrass President Clinton and, if possible, to impede passage of the bill. In this case Majority Leader Mitchell successfully countered Dole's strategy by offering an amendment to Dole's amendment that, in effect, removed its sting. In 1994 senators offered to the bill reauthorizing the Elementary and Secondary Education Act amendments limiting the application of the Davis-Bacon labor law, inserting provisions of the omnibus crime bill that had been dropped by crime bill conferees, and prohibiting the secretary of education from issuing new regulations to carry out the Vocational Education Act.

Senators' ability and willingness to offer nongermane amendments have major implications for the majority leadership's control of the schedule and of the agenda more broadly. The leadership cannot keep issues off the floor by refusing to schedule legislation. A senator can simply offer the legislation as a nongermane amendment. In the 104th Congress Majority Leader Bob Dole and most Republicans would have dearly loved to keep off the floor the issue of open hearings on the ethics case involving Sen. Bob Packwood, R-Ore. But Sen. Barbara Boxer, D-Calif., offered it as a floor amendment to the defense authorization bill and forced a recorded vote. Sen. Carl Levin, D-Mich., and other supporters of lobbying reform and gift ban legislation forced Dole to schedule that legislation although he would have preferred not to. They threatened to add the provisions as an amendment to the telecommunications bill, one of Dole's highest priorities. The agreement that Dole announced on June 9, 1995, committed the Senate to considering lobbying reform and the gift ban no later than July 28 and explicitly barred consideration of such measures before then. Dole finished his exposition of the unanimous consent agreement by saying, "Finally, I ask unanimous consent that no bill, resolution or amendment regarding the congressional gift ban rule or lobbying reform bill be in order prior to the execution of this agreement" (*Congressional Record*, June 9, 1995, S8086).

In 1996 Senate Majority Leader Dole and most Senate Republicans did not want to vote on a minimum wage increase that most opposed but that was popular with the public. Senate Democrats were prepared to offer the minimum wage increase as an amendment to every important piece of legislation brought to the floor and, to avoid a vote, Dole was forced to put off votes, bringing the legislative process in the Senate to a standstill. Eventually, Dole's successor as majority leader, Sen. Trent Lott of Mississippi, capitulated, the bill came to a vote, and it passed handily. Amending rules make it much more difficult for the majority party and the leadership to control the agenda in the Senate than in the House.

Senators today exercise their right to offer as many amendments as they wish on the floor, though the majority are relevant to the legislation at issue. On major legislation the number of amendments offered and pushed to a recorded vote is often high, and amending marathons (when ten or more amendments are offered and pushed to a recorded vote) are far from rare. In recent Congresses 27 percent of major measures were subject to ten or more amendments decided by recorded vote.

What sort of legislation is likely to provoke a high rate of amending activity, and does such activity usually represent an attempt to legislate or to stop legislation? Legislation that must pass, as well as legislation that seems highly likely to pass, more often than other legislation evokes high amending activity, suggesting that senators are using such bills as vehicles for legislating. Appropriations bills, which must be enacted to keep the government functioning, make up a regular part of legislation on which amending marathons take place. Legislation that is very broad in scope often provokes extensive amending activity; the big trade bill in the 100th Congress, budget resolutions, and major tax bills are examples. More than forty amendments were offered and pushed to a recorded vote on the trade bill and on the 1993 budget resolution; almost fifty, on the enormous tax bill of 1981. And, of course, controversial legislation stimulates amending activity as opponents attempt to alter or even kill it, and barring that to place supporters on the record on controversial provisions. In the 103rd Congress amending marathons accompanied much of Clinton's controversial agenda; campaign finance legislation, family leave, the stimulus program, national service, the Goals 2000 education program, and the omnibus crime bill, among others, had ten or more amendments offered to them on the floor.

The 1993 reconciliation bill that implemented Clinton's economic program had all three characteristics: it was must-pass legislation in the view of the majority party, it was extremely broad in scope, and it was very controversial. Twenty-five amendments were offered and pushed to a recorded vote. Some were sincere attempts to alter the legislation. Amendments in this category included one that knocked out a provision requiring small businesses to report all transactions over $600 to the Internal Revenue Service and another amendment, offered by the majority leader, that was crafted to pick up the votes to pass the bill. Other amendments were intended to gut the legislation or, if they did not pass, at least force supporters to go on the record on some very unpopular provisions. For example, Republicans offered amendments to eliminate the gas tax, to strike the provision raising the proportion of social security benefits that are taxable for high-income retirees, and to exempt small business from the increased taxes in certain circumstances. All were defeated, but Democrats were forced to take some tough votes.

Early in the 104th Congress Democrats, then in the minority, reciprocated. On the unfunded mandates bill, which Republicans had hoped to pass quickly, they forced fifty-nine hours of debate and roll call votes on more than forty amendments. Republicans were put in the uncomfortable position of voting against amendments that exempted federal mandates regulating radioactive substances, those designed to mitigate child pornography, child abuse, and illegal child labor, and those that regulated known human carcinogens (Hosansky 1995a, 276, 307–309).

Senate party leaders cannot protect their members from tough votes the way that House leaders sometimes can. To be sure, bill proponents often move to table an amendment. This is a nondebatable motion, and if an amendment is successfully tabled—which requires a majority vote— debate on it is cut off and it is killed without a vote ever being taken on the amendment itself; but this provides a pretty ineffective fig leaf for senators who opposed the amendment but fear the political consequences of voting against it.

The consideration of reconciliation bills is governed by Budget Act rules that are highly complex and require sixty votes to waive. Many of the amendments offered to reconciliation bills can be killed by making a point of order against them for violating the Budget Act, and this was done in 1993. The amendment's sponsor can, however, demand a recorded vote on waiving the act. While the requirement of sixty votes to waive makes it relatively easy to defeat the motion, senators are forced to go on the record. The parliamentary language does not provide much of a screen hiding the opposition of senators to the substance of the amendment. (In fact, a senator who believes that waiving budget rules is a mistake, and thus votes against such motions on principle regardless of the substance of the amendment at issue, may have a hard time convincing his constituents of that.)

Each senator's prerogative under the rules to offer as many amendments as she or he desires on almost any piece of legislation has many uses and, in fact, is employed to a variety of ends. Committee and party leaders know that the Senate's permissive amending rules give disgruntled senators a potent weapon. Therefore, leaders have a considerable incentive to bargain and compromise before the bill reaches the floor with any senator who expresses dissatisfaction. Senators not on the committee of jurisdiction can influence the shape of legislation at the prefloor stage in a way not possible for similarly situated House members. If a senator alerts a bill's sponsor, informally or through a hold, that she "has trouble" with certain of a bill's provisions, the sponsor must seriously consider trying to placate her. A single dissatisfied senator, even if she is junior and a minority party member, can cause a great deal of trouble.

Extended Debate and Cloture

A bill's supporters must concern themselves not just with the barrage of amendments opponents may offer on the floor but also with the possibility that opponents will use extended debate to block action altogether. In the Senate debate ends on a matter when every senator has said all he or she wants to say or when cloture is invoked. The cloture process is the only way in which debate can be shut off in the Senate over any senator's objection.

Any senator may circulate a cloture petition. When the senator has gathered sixteen signatures the petition is filed; after a one-day layover, the Senate votes. On most matters three-fifths of the entire Senate membership (usually sixty) must vote for cloture for the motion to pass. If the measure at issue changes Senate rules, two-thirds of those present and voting are required to shut off debate.

Even after a successful cloture vote, debate does not necessarily end immediately. Senate rule 22, the cloture rule, places a cap of thirty hours on consideration after the cloture vote. The thirty hours does include time spent on quorum calls and voting as well as on debate. The rule also requires that amendments considered after cloture must be germane.

If cloture fails, the bill's supporters may try again. There is no limit on the number of cloture petitions that may be filed on one measure, and sometimes supporters file a new petition even before a vote has been taken on a previous one so as to minimize the delay caused by the requirement that there be a day in session between the filing of the petition and the vote. In 1987 and 1988 Majority Leader Robert C. Byrd, D-W.Va., made eight attempts to impose cloture on campaign finance reform legislation before he gave up.

The cloture process is time consuming and cumbersome. Furthermore, if the opponents are determined, supporters may need to impose cloture at more than one stage in the measure's progress through the chamber. Thus, extended debate can occur on the motion to proceed to consider the measure, on specific amendments, on the measure itself, on various motions related to going to conference, and on the conference report. No single measure has ever been subject to filibusters at all these stages, but it is not uncommon for cloture to be sought at several stages. On the motor voter bill in 1993, for example, cloture votes took place on the motion to proceed, on the measure itself, and on the conference report.

The purpose of the cloture rule is to give the Senate some way to end a filibuster—the use of extended debate to block or delay legislation. Yet filibusters are not as easy to identify as one might think, especially since modern filibusters seldom resemble the famous ones of the past (Beth 1995). The word "filibuster" conjures up images of Sen. Huey Long, D-La., in the 1930s reading from the Constitution, quoting the Bible, and offering recipes; of Sen. Strom Thurmond, R-S.C., in the 1950s holding the floor for twenty-four hours at a stretch; or of round-the-clock sessions with senators sleeping on cots in the Capitol as occurred during the great civil rights battle of 1964. Modern filibusters are seldom so dramatic and threats of filibuster now frequently take the place of actual filibusters. A "hold" may keep legislation off the floor altogether. Sometimes after a bill is brought to the floor, nothing happens: no senators step forward to offer their amendments, but proponents make no move to call a vote on passage. This happened with the 1990 clean air bill reported by the Environment Committee. In such cases supporters of the legislation know they lack the votes to invoke cloture and so refrain from forcing a showdown; opponents are consequently saved the trouble of staging an overt filibuster. Eventually, supporters must take their chances, or give up on the bill, or negotiate with opponents, as happened on the clean air bill.

Because filibuster threats are frequent and may also be nebulous, a bill's supporters may file for cloture before opponents have clearly indicated they intend to engage in extended debate and undoubtedly sometimes when opponents actually had no such intention. All amendments must be germane after cloture is invoked, and this may sometimes encourage supporters to try for cloture. Finally, when senators spend a long time debating and amending a measure, they may simply be performing their deliberative function rather than trying to kill the measure. Many filibusters have as their purpose forcing a compromise on the legislation rather than killing it outright. Therefore, distinguishing between deliberation and filibustering becomes even harder.

Filibusters, defined as those instances where an attempt to invoke cloture was made, are now very frequent in the Senate. Recent Congresses have averaged almost thirty each (Beth 1995 and DSG 1994). The number of cloture votes averaged about forty per Congress, indicating that on many measures more than one cloture vote was taken.

Filibusters occur on a broad variety of matters. Not just legislation but presidential nominations may be subject to extended debate. In 1995 Republicans killed the nomination of Henry Foster to be surgeon general of the United States by a filibuster. A majority of senators was ready to confirm Foster, but since only fifty-seven voted to cut off debate, no vote on confirmation ever took place. Extended debate is not confined to the great issues of the day; senators sometimes hold up minor and parochial legislation or more major bills for parochial reasons. During the 1980s, a bill adjusting Hoover dam rates was filibustered, senators concerned that Cuba would interfere with radio broadcasting in their states filibustered a bill setting up Radio Marti to broadcast to Cuba, and a Maryland senator filibustered the Metropolitan Washington Airports Transfer Act. As the 102nd Congress was rushing to adjourn in October 1992, Sen. Alfonse D'Amato, R-N.Y., held the floor for fifteen hours and fifteen minutes to protest the removal from an urban-aid tax bill of a provision he said could have restored jobs at a New York typewriter plant (Kuntz 1992, 3128).

Major legislation is especially likely to encounter an extended-debate-related problem—a hold, a filibuster threat, or a filibuster. In the late 1980s and early 1990s just under 30 percent ran into some extended debate–related problem that was identifiable from the public record; in the first Congress of the Clinton presidency, almost half of major measures did. A Republican filibuster killed Clinton's stimulus package; Republicans used the filibuster or a threat thereof to extract concessions on voter registration legislation ("motor voter") and the national service program, for example. Republican attempts to kill or water down legislation via a filibuster were not always successful, of course. For example, the Republican filibuster of the Brady bill imposing a seven-day waiting period for buying a gun collapsed when a number of Republican senators began to fear the political price of their participation.

Time pressure makes extended debate an especially effective weapon of obstruction at the end of a Congress, and the greater the backlog of significant legislation, the more potent any threat of delay is. At the end of the 103rd Congress, Republican filibusters killed campaign finance and lobbying reform bills. Although unsuccessful in the end, Republicans filibustered and tried to prevent passage of a massive crime bill, the California Desert Protection Act, and a comprehensive education bill. In some cases filibusters were waged to prevent legislation from being sent to conference or, more frequently, to prevent approval of the conference report. Republican threats of obstructionist floor tactics contributed to the death of important bills revamping the superfund program, revising clean drinking water regulations, overhauling outdated telecommunications law, and applying federal labor laws to Congress.

In the 103rd Congress the filibuster was used as a partisan tool to an extent unprecedented in this century. In the first year of the 104th, Democrats, then in the minority, returned the favor. In 1995, 44 percent of major legislation encountered extended debate–related problems; Democrats killed regulatory overhaul and property rights legislation and forced majority Republicans to compromise on a number of major bills. For example, under threat of a filibuster, the regulatory moratorium legislation that sailed through the House was radically weakened.

The filibuster, however, is not a tool of the minority party alone. In 1994, for example, product liability reform was killed when liberals filibustered. Even more than the Senate's permissive amending rules, the right of extended debate provides the individual senator with a powerful weapon few can refrain from using. As a consequence, controversial measures increasingly need sixty votes to pass the Senate, and amassing the necessary support often requires significant concessions.

If legislation reaches the point of a passage vote, it almost certainly will pass. In recent Congresses the only major measures that lost on passage votes in the Senate were constitutional amendments, which require a two-thirds vote.

Unorthodox Lawmaking in the Senate

Because the Senate's legislative process has always been less formal than the House's and thus more flexible, the distinction between the orthodox and the unorthodox is less clear in the Senate than in the House. Senators have always had the right under the rules to talk as long as they wished, offer multitudes of amendments, and propose nongermane amendments. They have always used those prerogatives. Yet all the evidence we have indicates that the frequency of such behavior has increased enormously in recent decades. The contemporary legislative process in the Senate is of necessity predicated on the assumption that senators will regularly and fully exploit their prerogatives. The extensive consultation that is a standard part of legislative scheduling, the "individualized" unanimous consent agreements, and the deference to senators as individuals are all responses to senators' hyper-exploitation of their prerogatives under the rules.

Unlike unorthodox lawmaking in the House of Representatives, the changes in the legislative process in the Senate, on balance, make legislating more difficult. Given senators' willingness to exploit their prerogatives and the lack of any cost to them within the chamber of doing so repeatedly, successful lawmaking requires accommodating individual senators and most controversial legislation requires sixty votes for Senate passage. To be sure, other changes in the legislative process (the increased frequency of postcommittee adjustments, for example, and sometimes the bypassing of committees) seem to facilitate lawmaking. Such changes are a response to the problems created by senators' exploitation of their debate and amending prerogatives and may ameliorate but certainly do not solve those problems.

Getting One Bill:
Reconciling House-Senate
Differences

SINCE THE HOUSE AND SENATE DIFFER in membership and rules, major legislation is unlikely to emerge in identical form from the two chambers. Even if exactly the same bill was introduced in the House and the Senate, the changes necessary to pass it are likely to result in differences by the time it has worked its way through the two chambers' quite different legislative processes. Yet, before the bill can become law, both chambers must approve the identical wording; after all, a law cannot exist in several different versions. How would people know which they were expected to obey?

A number of alternative ways of reconciling House-Senate differences are used. One chamber can simply accept the other chamber's version of the legislation. A procedure based on amendments between the chambers entails a kind of public bargaining back and forth. A conference committee of members from both chambers can be appointed and charged with coming up with a compromise, which is then taken back to both chambers for approval.

Nonconference Reconciliation Procedures

On minor legislation or when the differences between the chambers are small, one chamber may be willing to accept the other's bill. Early in 1995 the House accepted the Senate's version of legislation applying labor and other regulatory laws to Congress. The two chambers' bills were very similar, and House and Senate Republicans were eager to complete an early legislative victory. This means of settling interchamber differences is, however, especially likely to be used late in a Congress when time is tight and the alternative is the probable death of the bill. Such circumstances may prompt one chamber to accept the other's version even of major legislation; if the choice is to let the legislation die and start over in the next Congress or to take a less preferred version, supporters may well opt for the latter. In 1980 the House in a lame-duck (that is, after the election) session accepted the weaker Senate version of the massive bill on Alaska lands. Since Republicans had won control of the Senate in the elections, House supporters of a strongly pro-environment bill knew they would fare worse if they waited until the next year. They also knew that, if they did anything other than simply accept the Senate bill, Senate opponents of a strong bill could easily use extended debate to kill the legislation in the few remaining days of the session. The power of extended debate as an obstructionist tool, especially late in the session, can put the House at a disadvantage, confronting the chamber with the choice of accepting Senate legislation as is or taking a chance that opponents in the Senate will kill it if more action is required.

House-Senate differences on most minor and some major legislation are reconciled through a process known as amendments between the chambers. Assume the House passed legislation and sent it to the Senate. The Senate then amends the bill, perhaps by substituting its own version for the House's, and sends it back to the House. At this point the House floor manager of the bill may ask that the House by unanimous consent (or under suspension of the rules or by a special rule) "agree to the Senate amendment with an amendment." The Senate amendment referred to is actually the Senate version of the bill, and the amendment the House is adding is the House's initial offer of a settlement of interchamber differences. Generally, the House will stick to its own position or move least on those issues its members care about most; it will move toward the Senate position on issues considered less important by House members. If the House agrees to the motion, the bill as amended goes back to the Senate, and the Senate can either accept the House offer or respond with an offer of its own. Although the parliamentary language soon becomes mind-bogglingly complex, what is actually going on is fairly straightforward bargaining, with each chamber making offers in succession. The legislation may go back and forth between the chambers several times (Tiefer 1989, 778). Often the differences are resolved through informal, behind-the-scenes negotiations between House and Senate committee leaders and then incorporated in the amendment one house sends the other. For example, in late 1988 a marathon series of informal negotiations settled the differences between the chambers on the omnibus drug bill. The highly complex deal was then incorporated into an amendment that the House adopted and sent to the Senate in the last hours of the session, and the Senate then accepted (Lawrence 1988c, 3145, 3170).

Conference Committees

The most common way of resolving interchamber differences on major legislation is by conference committee (Longley and Oleszek 1989). In recent Congresses 75 percent of major measures that both chambers passed were sent to conference; in some of these cases, amendments between the chambers were also used. By and large, conferences are restricted to settling differences on major legislation. This can be seen by examining all measures. When Steven Smith did so for 1985–86, he found that only about 12 percent of all measures went to conference (Smith 1995, 406).

Both chambers must approve sending legislation to conference; the first house requests a conference and the second agrees. Usually this is done by unanimous consent, but it can be done by motion and a majority vote, though in the Senate the motion can be filibustered.

The Appointment of Conferees

In both chambers the presiding officer appoints conferees; House rules give the Speaker sole power to do so; the Senate's presiding officer must receive unanimous consent. In the Senate, with its weak presiding officer, committee leaders almost always actually make the choice. The chair of the committee of origin, after "consultation" with the ranking minority member, "recommends" a list of conferees to the presiding officer, who accepts it without change. By tradition, conference committees are bipartisan; the ratio of majority to minority members roughly reflects the ratio in the chamber; and the majority allows the minority to choose its own members. The process is similar in the House, except the Speaker has more discretion. House rules explicitly require the Speaker to appoint "no less than a majority of members who supported the House position as determined by the Speaker." The rule continues:

> The Speaker shall name Members who are primarily responsible for the legislation and shall, to the fullest extent feasible, include the principal proponents of the major provisions of the bill as it passed the House. (Gold et al. 1992, 339)

Since the decision about which members meet these criteria is solely the Speaker's, the rule actually gives him more leeway to choose, if he so desires, junior members or members not on the committee of origin. During the 104th Congress, Rep. Newt Gingrich, R-Ga., was unusually assertive in exercising the Speaker's discretion; he appointed freshmen and even on occasion Democratic supporters of the legislation that the minority had kept off its conference delegation. Nevertheless, in both chambers most of the conferees will be members of the committee that reported the bill and, by and large, fairly senior ones. Today both chambers usually include leaders of the subcommittee responsible for the bill. Therefore, the conference delegation will not simply consist of the most senior members of the committee, as was often the case before the mid-1970s.

The multiple referral of legislation, as well as the frequency of bills of very broad scope, complicate the conference process. When several committees have considered the legislation, all expect representation on the conference committee. The consequence is very large conference delegations, especially from the House where multiple referral is more prevalent. On the conference committee for the 1988 trade bill were forty-four senators from nine Senate committees and 155 House members from fourteen House committees (Tiefer 1989, 798–799). Although this is an extreme example, multicommittee conference delegations are common. Of the fifty-one nonappropriations bills that completed conference in 1981–82, twenty—almost 40 percent—had conference delegations from more than one committee (Tiefer 1989, 799). Of these twenty, ten had multicommittee representation from both chambers, nine from the House only and one from the Senate only.

When the Senate has added nongermane amendments to a bill, House conferees are often appointed from the appropriate House committees even if the original bill was reported from only a single House committee. For example, when the Senate added to an education bill an amendment outlawing dial-a-porn operations, the Speaker appointed as conferees not just members of the Education and Labor Committee, the single House committee to consider the bill, but also members of the Commerce Committee, which has jurisdiction on communications issues. A 1991 State Department authorization bill had been reported solely by the House Foreign Affairs Committee, but when the much-amended bill came back from the Senate, the Speaker appointed as conferees members from the Banking, Judiciary, Post Office and Civil Service, and Ways and Means committees as well (Gold et al. 1992, 70).

The Speaker's discretion in the choice of conferees and in the charge he gives them is increased significantly when multiple committees are involved. Although he is effectively bound—by custom and expectations, not by rules—to appoint conferees from all the committees that reported the legislation, he decides the number of conferees from each and the breadth or narrowness of each conferee's authority (that is, over all of the bill or only specific parts). Conference appointments for large, complex bills often specify in great detail the precise titles or sections that particular conferees can negotiate as well as those conferees who have authority to negotiate on the entire bill (see, for examples, Gold et al. 1992, 340–341; Smith 1995, 413). In addition, when many committees receive conference representation, the Speaker can more easily add conferees who are not members of any of the committees that reported the bill—perhaps a leadership representative or the sponsor of a major amendment.

Reaching Agreement

The conferees are charged with coming up with a compromise between the House and Senate positions that can win the assent of a majority in both chambers. Sunshine rules instituted in the mid-1970s require that conference committee meetings be open to the public. However, because a public forum inhibits the hard bargaining that is often necessary, much negotiation takes place informally behind the scenes. To reach a compromise, members may need to retreat from positions they have advocated, often ones they have argued for strongly and ones with ardent interest group and constituency support; that is easier done behind closed doors. Sometimes formal, open conference meetings simply ratify deals worked out elsewhere.

The difficulty of reaching agreement depends, of course, on how far apart the two chambers' bills are, as well as on how strongly the participants feel about their positions. Certain kinds of differences lend themselves to compromise more easily than others. When an appropriations bill goes to conference, it typically includes hundreds of items in disagreement, but the differences in dollar figures are usually resolved easily by splitting the difference or trading off among items. The tough fights are more likely to be over substantive provisions (for example, the Hyde amendment barring federal funding for abortions).

When the two chambers take completely different approaches to a problem, the conference faces the most difficult task; splitting the difference is meaningless in that context. In 1995 the House passed a line-item veto bill that would allow the president to make a proposal to rescind spending for specific items previously approved by Congress. Unless both chambers of Congress voted to overturn his proposal, it would become law. The Senate's line-item veto bill was very different. The Senate proposed that, after passage, appropriations bills be broken down and sent to the president as hundreds of separate bills, thus enabling him to veto individual items. Clearly, there was no way of splitting the difference between the two approaches; the conferees had to choose one or the other or come up with a different approach altogether.

Conferences with many conferees from a number of different committees are much more unwieldy than the traditional small, one-committee conferences. Often with the really large delegations, many conferees have authority over only a limited part of the bill, and the conference splits up into subconferences. The trade bill conference in 1988, for example, operated through seventeen subgroups. Even then, someone must coordinate the work, making sure progress is made and that the parts are reassembled into a coherent whole at the end. The committee chairs have the primary responsibility, but the party leadership and the leaders' senior staff often are actively involved as well.

As the legislative process has changed, drawing party leaders more deeply into the process, members have come to expect that their leaders will take a hand at the conference stage when legislation is in trouble. Stalemate between the two chambers often requires leadership intervention. When conferences on four appropriations bills bogged down in late 1995 over the abortion issue, House Majority Leader Dick Armey of Texas and Senate Republican Whip Trent Lott of Mississippi stepped in to broker agreements that both adamantly anti-abortion House Republicans and more moderate Senate Republicans could accept (Koszczuk 1995b, 3376). In March 1996 Senate Majority Leader Bob Dole almost single-handedly broke the stalemate on the line-item veto bill. Having established himself as the almost certain presidential nominee of the Republican Party, Dole made getting a bill out of conference and to the president a top priority and so a test of his ability to get things done. Under these special political circumstances Republican senators, even those with severe substantive doubts about the bill, were unwilling to hold out against Dole's position of basically agreeing to the House version of the bill. Doing otherwise would have crippled their nominee. The line-item veto bill was approved by the conferees and signed by the president, who in negotiations with Majority Leader Dole and Speaker Gingrich had decided what the effective date of the legislation would be.

Party leaders now regularly take a hand in resolving differences on the big budget bills that make up an increasingly important part of the Congress's agenda. On the really high visibility bills of a Congress, members now expect leadership involvement in settling interchamber differences. When the choices facing conferees are highly salient and highly consequential ones that affect the political fate of members and of their party, party leaders are likely to make the final decisions.

In conference decisions require the assent of both the House and Senate, the position of a chamber being determined by the majority of its conferees. (Because of this voting rule, the fact that the House usually has more conferees than the Senate does not give it an advantage.) The final agreement must also be approved by a majority of the conferees of each chamber. Conferees formally indicate their approval by signing the conference report, which consists of the compromise legislative language agreed upon by the conferees.

Rarely, conferees are unable to reach an agreement, and the legislation dies in conference. In the late 1980s, for example, the Senate added to an airline consumer protection bill an amendment requiring drug testing of airline employees; House conferees were adamantly unwilling to accept the provision, the conferees were unable to come to an agreement, and the bill died in conference. In 1994 legislation to overhaul the regulation of mining on federal lands died in conference; however, the problem was not the conferees' inability to agree but the threat of a Senate filibuster of any reachable agreement. In recent Congresses fewer than one major measure per Congress on average died in conference. By the time legislation gets to conference, many people, including many of the conferees, have a stake in the legislation's enactment. Therefore, a compromise is usually found even when House and Senate versions are very different.

In the Republican-controlled 104th Congress resolving differences between the House and Senate proved to be especially difficult. The reasons illuminate the differences between the chambers in terms of their membership and rules and how those differences affect legislative outcomes. During the 1994 campaign, Republicans (House incumbents as well as House candidates) had committed themselves to enacting the Contract with America should they become the majority party in the chamber. Fueled by a large, ideologically fervent freshman class, a membership believing itself to be mandated to carrying out the Contract, and an ideologically dedicated and skillful leadership, the new majority pushed through the House in undiluted form all of the Contract's provisions except term limits and many other nonincremental policy changes as well. House rules allow a cohesive majority to work its will, and the Republicans in 1995 were certainly cohesive.

The freshmen Republican senators, at eleven a big class by Senate standards, and many of their more senior colleagues also wanted to see major policy change. The rules of the Senate, however, made the sort of swift and uncompromising action the House had undertaken impossible in the Senate. The majority leader had to keep six to eight moderate Republicans on board to pass legislation. To avoid a filibuster or to get the sixty votes for cloture, he also had to appease Senate Democrats. As a result, much of the House's "revolutionary" legislation was significantly altered in the Senate.

During the 104th, conference committees repeatedly confronted the task of reaching agreement when the differences between the two chambers' legislation were vast and the positions on both sides strongly held. On the line-item veto bill, as we saw, the two chambers took completely different approaches. On product liability and on the regulatory moratorium, the compromises necessary to enable the legislation to pass the Senate watered down broad and stringent House legislation to the point that many House Republicans no longer supported them.

Compared with many of the bills in the Contract, appropriations bills proved to be even more contentious in conference. Because appropriations bills, which fund the government, must pass, House Republicans decided to use them as vehicles to enact a host of desired policy changes quickly and to protect them from a presidential veto. Although appropriations bills are not supposed to include "legislative" provisions (called "riders"), Congress frequently uses this tactic; what was different in the 104th was the large number of riders House Republicans attached to appropriations bills and the scope and magnitude of the legislative changes they tried to bring about in that way. The bills that went to conference carried riders on highly controversial issues. The most salient riders concerned restrictions on abortion, on Environmental Protection Agency (EPA) enforcement of environmental laws, and on the right to lobby of non-profit groups that receive federal grant funds; but many others created problems between the House and Senate as well. Agreement on the Treasury-Postal Service and general government appropriations bill was held up for weeks because of an amendment by Rep. Ernest Jim Istook, Jr., R-Okla. The Istook amendment would have cut off federal grants to groups that used even a small part of their budgets to lobby. Senate conferees adamantly refused to accept the amendment, aimed as it was at liberal groups, and House conferees, concerned about passing the conference agreement in the House, just as adamantly refused to drop it. In the end House leaders agreed to drop the amendment. The bill died nonetheless, and the departments and agencies it covered were funded through continuing resolutions.

Conferees' Power and Its Limits

Conferees have considerable power over the substance of legislation. House and Senate rules specify that conferees are limited in the agreement they reach to the differences between the House and Senate versions of the legislation. However, Senate rules interpret this quite broadly in those cases, the majority, where the Senate passed a substitute to the House bill (rather than a series of specific amendments to the House bill). In the House the conferees can get around the rule by taking their conference report to the floor under a special rule from the Rules Committee that waives it. Although House members or senators can (by majority vote) instruct their conferees about the substance of the legislation, these instructions are not binding (Tiefer 1989, 780–833; Gold et al. 1992, 337–347). Since many conference committees finish their work late in a Congress when everyone works under severe time constraints, senators and representatives not on a conference committee often lack the time to study the conference report and thus be able to challenge it.

Once a majority of the House conferees and a majority of the Senate conferees have formalized their approval by signing the conference report, it is returned to both chambers, where the full membership must decide whether to accept what their representatives have done. At this point no amendments are in order; the membership votes up or down on the compromise as a package.[1] Although the overwhelming majority of conference reports are approved, occasionally one is sent back to conference, a parliamentary move only available to the chamber that acts first, or simply voted down.

In the summer of 1994, several groups of House Democrats were unhappy with the compromise conferees had reached on the crime bill. African-American members were displeased with the conferees' decision to drop language aimed at combating racial bias in death penalty sentencing; some southern and rural members were distressed with the inclusion of an assault weapons ban. When these members joined most Republicans, who opposed the bill, in voting against the rule for bringing the conference report to the floor, the rule lost, and the bill was in danger of dying. To rescue it, the Clinton administration and the House Democratic leadership made a deal with a group of moderate Republicans. Because the Senate had not yet acted on the conference report and thus the conference committee had not been officially disbanded, the conference report could be sent back to conference and changed to incorporate the compromise (Idelson 1994, 2340–2343; Idelson and Sammon 1994, 2449–2454; Kuntz 1994, 2485). That was done, and the new conference report passed the House.

---

1. The exceptions are appropriations bills on which the conferees have exceeded the scope of the differences between the two chambers' bills or to which the Senate has added amendments that constitute unauthorized appropriations or legislation and bills on which the Senate has added nongermane amendments. House rules allow separate votes on those matters (Tiefer 1980, 833–848).

In 1988 the House had added to the District of Columbia appropriations bill an amendment barring the District from using its own funds to pay for poor women's abortions; when the conference committee dropped the provision, the House voted to recommit the report and insist on its amendment. Similarly, in 1993 the House voted to cut off funding for the superconducting supercollider; the conference committee, however, included funding for the supercollider in the energy and water appropriations conference report. The House refused to accept that outcome and recommitted the report to the conference, which complied with House wishes.

In 1995 the House rejected several conference reports on appropriations bills. For example, Democrats joined by environmentalist Republicans and some deficit hawks twice recommitted the conference report on the Interior Department appropriations bill. At issue was a moratorium on the purchase by private companies of federal land for mining at very low prices. During floor consideration of the bill, an amendment extending an already existing moratorium had passed, but the conferees dropped it in conference. When the conference report was brought back to the House, the coalition that had approved the amendment held together and recommitted the bill to conference. The conferees then agreed on the moratorium but with some caveats; the coalition, however, refused to accept half measures and again recommitted the bill to conference with instructions on the moratorium and on another issue as well. This time the conferees got the message; they reinstated the moratorium, and their conference report won House approval. The bill, however, was later vetoed by the president.

The appropriations bill for the Veterans' Administration and the Housing and Urban Development Department also ran into trouble in 1995. House conferees heeded nonbinding House instructions to drop riders restricting EPA enforcement of environmental legislation. Members, however, became disgruntled about other aspects of the bill, and they recommitted the bill with instructions to increase funding for veterans' programs. In this case the conferees did not comply, but the House leadership persuaded enough Republican defectors to change their votes to pass the conference report anyway. This bill also ran afoul of a presidential veto.

These two cases notwithstanding, the recommittal or defeat of a conference report is rare. In recent Congresses the House recommitted or defeated a conference report on fewer than two major measures per Congress on average; in the Senate there was no such case.

As infrequent as the rejection of a conference report is, its occasional occurrence serves to remind conferees that they must be sensitive to the policy preferences of their chambers' membership. Conferees have very considerable discretion but only within the limits set by the full membership's tolerance.

The Final Step

After both the House and Senate have approved legislation in identical form, it is sent to the president, who can sign it, do nothing, or veto it. If he signs it or holds it for ten weekdays while Congress is in session, the legislation becomes law. However, if Congress has adjourned *sine die* (that is, indefinitely, which happens at the end of the Congress), the president can kill legislation by holding it for ten weekdays without signing it. In those cases the president is said to cast a *pocket veto*.[2]

When the president casts a formal veto, the legislation is sent back to the Congress with the president's message of disapproval and his reasons for having cast the veto. For the legislation to become law, both houses must override the veto by a two-thirds vote.

No rules require that Congress vote to override a president's veto within a specified period of time. In the past the vote tended to come fairly soon after the veto. For years this was the expectation and the practice. Recently, however, the chamber that originated the bill (which must vote to override first) has sometimes held the bill to gain political advantage. In 1996, for example, Republican leaders did not schedule veto override votes on the "partial birth" abortion bill until late September, only weeks before the elections. This was a bill that had passed both houses way back in March and had been vetoed in April.

Mustering a two-thirds vote in both chambers on a controversial matter is a formidable task. George Bush had only one veto overridden during his four years as president even though he was politically quite weak during much of his presidency. In 1995, despite being enormously weakened by the devastating 1994 elections, Clinton suffered only one override. A bill's supporters know that if they want to enact legislation, they must either satisfy the president or be prepared to amass enough support in both houses to override his veto. The former will usually seem the eas-

---

2. Recent presidents have asserted the right to pocket veto legislation when the Congress has adjourned but not *sine die* (between the two sessions, for example); Congress has contested this in court. The Supreme Court has not ruled on the central issue so the constitutional status of such a pocket veto is uncertain (Gold et al. 1992, 248–250).

ier task. Thus, the veto gives the president considerable influence in the legislative process.

Reconciling Differences: How Much Change?

Change in the legislative process within the two chambers has spilled over and affected the process of reconciling interchamber differences. Multiple referral and members' desire for broad participation have led to bigger conference delegations, especially on the part of the House. The unwieldiness of such large delegations and committees' jurisdictional concerns have prompted conferences to work in subconferences, which on the House side have authority to make decisions only on specifically delineated parts of the legislation. The coordinating problems such an undertaking entails draw the party leadership, the only central leadership in the chambers, into a process that used to be committee dominated. The party leaders' greater involvement in the legislative process within their chamber—in working out postcommittee compromises that facilitate passage, for example—leads to a greater role for them in conference as well. If it took leadership intervention to put together the compromise necessary to pass the bill, sustaining the compromise in conference and passing the resulting conference report will often require leadership involvement as well.

Omnibus Legislation, the Budget Process, and Summits

Unorthodox lawmaking is not confined to the sorts of innovations and modifications in standard procedures and practices examined in previous chapters but encompasses new forms of legislation and new ways of making decisions. The contemporary Congress now often legislates through enormous omnibus bills, something it rarely did in the past, and entirely new processes—the budget process and summits—have become prominent.

When legislative decisions are made through omnibus legislation, the budget process, and summits, decision making is more centralized than it is ordinarily; central leaders—congressional party leaders and often the president—play a more important and frequently the decisive role. These modes of legislating make it possible for Congress to enact comprehensive policy change, always a difficult task for a decentralized institution; they also may reduce the opportunities for careful scrutiny of the legislation's provisions and for broad participation by rank-and-file members.

Divided government and big deficits are the most important of the environmental factors that fostered these developments, and their persistence ensures that the major political conflicts of a Congress will continue to revolve around omnibus legislation, the budget process, and summits.

Omnibus Legislation and the Budget Process

The legislation that Congress deals with varies from the short and simple—the one paragraph "commemorative" that declares August

National Dairy Month, for example—to the extraordinarily long and complex.[1] The 1990 Clean Air Act was about 800 pages long, and nonexperts would need a translator to make sense of it; the bills enacting President Ronald Reagan's economic program in 1981 and President Bill Clinton's in 1993 were both considerably longer.

Legislation that addresses numerous and not necessarily related subjects, issues, and programs, and therefore is usually highly complex and long, is referred to as omnibus legislation. Although there is no consensus technical definition of what constitutes an omnibus bill, every Congress watcher would classify as omnibus the 1988 trade bill that spanned the jurisdiction of thirteen House and nine Senate committees and the antidrug bill passed the same year. It covered drug abuse education and prevention, treatment, punishment of abusers and sellers, big and small, and the interdiction of drugs flowing into the United States from abroad by air, sea, and land. Many of the bills generally labeled omnibus are money bills of some sort. The most common omnibus measures in the contemporary Congress are budget resolutions and reconciliation bills, both of which stem from the budget process. In recent Congresses omnibus measures have made up about 12 percent of major legislation.

The Congressional Budget and Impoundment Control Act of 1974 created an entirely new process and superimposed it on the old way Congress made spending and taxing decisions. The new budget process made omnibus measures a regular part of the annual congressional workload and influenced the legislative process in other direct and indirect ways. Although a detailed examination of the budget process and its ramifications cannot be undertaken here, a discussion of the contemporary legislative process would not be complete without some discussion of the budget process. (On the budget process see Schick 1980; Oleszek 1996; Thurber and Durst 1993.)

Congress creates and alters programs by passing authorizing legislation; the subject matter committees, such as Agriculture or Banking, report out this legislation, which authorizes the setting up of a new program (or changes in an existing one) and usually also authorizes funding up to some cap. The Constitution requires that before the federal government can spend money, it must be appropriated. This is the task of the House and Senate Appropriations committees; every year they must report out and see enacted a series of bills that appropriate money for the federal government's multitude of programs and agencies. Cur-

---

1. The House stopped considering commemoratives in 1995.

rently, each Appropriations committee is organized into thirteen sub-committees, each of which reports one general appropriations bill that funds a number of government programs and agencies. For example, the Labor, Health and Human Services, and Education Subcommittee reports a bill that appropriates funds for the programs and agencies that fall under these three cabinet departments. Appropriations bills fund their programs only for one year. Were the Congress to fail to pass the Labor-HHS-Education appropriations bill, many of those departments' programs as well as the administrative structure would have to shut down. (Programs that are funded through a mechanism other than annual appropriations, such as social security, would not be directly affected.)

The shutting down of programs that people want and depend on is sufficiently horrendous that Congress always passes appropriations bills—though in late 1995 it did so only after a hiatus of several weeks (see the case study of the 1995 budget process in Chapter 11). Frequently, Congress cannot pass all thirteen bills by the deadline—October 1, the beginning of the fiscal year; in that case it passes a continuing (appropriations) resolution, referred to as a CR, that temporarily continues funding.[2] Usually continuing resolutions cover the few appropriations bills that have not yet passed and extend for only a few days or weeks. Occasionally, however, a CR encompasses half or more of the appropriations bills and extends through the full year—a true omnibus bill.

Not all programs are funded through annual appropriations. Some of the federal government's biggest programs are entitlement programs—programs that stipulate that people who meet certain criteria are entitled to a specified benefit. Social security, Medicare, Medicaid, government pension programs, and food stamps are all entitlement programs. Funding for many of these programs is not under the control of the Appropriations committees. Some of the biggest—social security and a part of Medicare—are funded by trust funds, and some have permanent appropriations. Even in those cases, such as food stamps, where annual appropriations are required, the Appropriations committees' discretion is highly limited. If the money appropriated runs out before the end of the year, Congress must pass a supplemental appropriations bill to fund food stamps for eligible people. Cutting spending for entitlements requires changing the legislation that authorized the program, and that is in the

---

2. Funding is usually set at last year's level or at the lower of the levels proposed by the House and Senate.

jurisdiction of the authorizing committee, not the Appropriations Committee.[3]

To provide some coherence to the process of making spending decisions, the Budget Act specifies that before the appropriations bills are drafted, the Congress must pass a budget resolution setting guidelines. The budget resolution specifies how much the federal government will spend in the next fiscal year, how much it expects to collect in taxes, and how large the deficit (the difference between the two) is expected to be. It also specifies how much is to be spent in each of twenty or so broad functional categories—health or agriculture, for example. The Budget Committee report accompanying the resolution may contain detailed suggestions about policy changes that would produce the overall figures. Although it may suggest that spending on particular programs be cut in order to reach the overall spending figure, its suggestions have no binding effect.

Estimating the deficit is not a routine technical exercise and may well be the source of controversy. The deficit depends on expected expenditures and revenues, both of which depend on a number of economic assumptions. Tax receipts, for example, depend on the state of the economy; when the economy is growing, more people have jobs, wages are likely to be going up, and more businesses are making money, and thus people and business pay more in taxes. Federal expenditures depend on economic estimates as well; for example, when the economy is bad, more people will qualify for unemployment benefits and food stamps, so spending for such entitlement programs will go up. Congress relies on the Congressional Budget Office for its estimates. The Office of Management and Budget provides estimates for the president. In 1995 a dispute over which set of figures to use was at the center of the budget battle. Small differences in assumptions about the growth rate of the American economy over the next seven years made a huge difference in the estimate of how much needed to be cut from spending in order to achieve a balanced budget by the year 2002.

Drafting the budget resolution is the task of a Budget Committee in each chamber. Since the resolution sets overall budgetary policy and decides priorities, drafting it is too important and often too difficult a task for the committee to undertake on its own. Congressional party leaders are always involved, and the president often is.

---

3. Aid to Families with Dependent Children (AFDC) was an entitlement program; the 1996 welfare bill changed it from an entitlement to a block grant program that requires annual appropriations.

The legislative process on a budget resolution looks similar in many ways to that on ordinary legislation. After the committees report, each chamber must pass its version. In the House the majority party leadership always brings up the resolution under a special rule that restricts amendments; usually only a limited number of comprehensive substitutes are allowed. The Budget Act limits Senate debate to fifty hours and requires that amendments be germane. Thus, a budget resolution cannot be filibustered. A conference committee is appointed to come up with a compromise between the two chambers' versions, which must then be approved by both houses. The budget resolution, however, is not legislation; it is a concurrent resolution that does not require the president's signature.

In essence, the budget resolution is a set of guidelines that the Congress has agreed on to guide its own—specifically, its committees'—spending and taxing decisions for the year. The budget resolution serves as a framework within which the Appropriations committees make their spending decisions. The conference report on the resolution divides up total spending by committee. Since the Appropriations committees are responsible for all spending done through appropriations, they receive the largest allocation.

The resolution may—and in recent years often has—included binding instructions to other committees to bring law within their jurisdiction into conformance with the dictates of the budget resolution. For example, if the resolution specifies that $xx billion be spent on agricultural programs and current law would result in more spending, the Agriculture Committee is instructed to change legislation under its jurisdiction in such a way as to save the necessary amount of money. The budget resolution instructions do not prescribe the details of the changes, only the amount of savings. Similarly, if the resolution specifies that tax revenues need to increase over what current law would bring in, the tax-writing committees—House Ways and Means and Senate Finance—will be instructed to draft a tax bill that raises a specific amount, but they will not be told how to do it—by raising the gas tax or by increasing income tax rates, for example. Such instructions in a budget resolution are called reconciliation instructions; they instruct the various committees to reconcile legislation under their jurisdictions with the figures in the budget resolution. These instructions usually target entitlement programs. Reconciliation instructions also specify a deadline for committee compliance.

When the budget process is used as a vehicle for making comprehensive policy change, the number of committees instructed is large. The budget resolution in 1981, which carried Reagan's economic program, instructed fifteen House and fourteen Senate committees. The 1993 resolution containing Clinton's program instructed thirteen House and twelve Senate committees. The 1995 resolution encompassing the new Republican majority's economic plan instructed twelve House and eleven Senate committees.

The instructed committees draft their legislation and then send it to the Budget Committee, which packages it into an omnibus reconciliation bill. The legislation must then win approval by each chamber. In the House special rules that tightly restrict amending activity are always used to protect these big and usually controversial packages. The Budget Act protects the reconciliation bill against a filibuster in the Senate by limiting initial floor debate to twenty hours and debate on the conference report to ten hours; in addition, only germane amendments are allowed.

Conference committees on reconciliation bills are sometimes huge. All the committees with provisions in the legislation as well as the Budget committees are represented, and the totals can run into the hundreds. The conference committee on the 1981 reconciliation bill consisted of 208 House conferees from 17 committees and 72 senators from 14 committees (Tiefer 1989, 798). In 1993, 164 House members from 16 committees and 53 senators from 13 committees served on the reconciliation bill conference committee. Generally, such conferences work in subgroups; the 1981 conference met in fifty-eight subgroups (Granat 1984, 1298). Most conferees have authority to make decisions only about the provisions their committee or subcommittee drafted. Conferees from the Budget committees usually have authority over the entire bill and take on the task of coordination, a formidable undertaking. Because reconciliation bills are so substantively and politically important, the party leadership is always involved.

Unlike the budget resolution, the reconciliation bill is legislation, so the president can veto it. This possibility gives the president influence in the process of putting the bill together, even if the Congress is controlled by the other party. Unless the congressional majority party has huge majorities in both chambers, its chances of amassing a two-thirds vote to override the president on legislation that goes to the heart of the differences between the parties are exceedingly dim. If his own party is in the majority, the president and congressional party leaders are likely to work together closely on such a major piece of legislation. (See the case studies in Chapters 11 and 12 for both circumstances.)

The budget process provides Congress with a tool for making comprehensive decisions. Before the 1974 Budget Act, Congress made spending and taxing decisions in a piecemeal and uncoordinated fashion. To pass an economic program embodying a significant change in direction such as Reagan's in 1981 or Clinton's in 1993 would have required enacting a dozen or more separate bills.

Reconciliation bills make a multitude of policy decisions through an abbreviated legislative process in which many provisions receive limited scrutiny. No committee hearings may have been held on the changes included in the legislation. With the committees operating under time constraints, many provisions may have received only perfunctory attention during committee markup; as part of a much larger package, they may have been altogether ignored during floor debate. In fact, many members may not have been aware of many of them.

Yet the provisions in a reconciliation bill are very likely to become law. Simply the size of the package tends to take attention away from any but the most major provisions. In the House the bill will be considered under a special rule that prohibits most amendments. In the Senate the bill is protected from a filibuster. And a reconciliation bill is considered "must pass" legislation by the majority party.

Given these advantages, the temptation to use a reconciliation bill as a vehicle for enacting extraneous provisions that have nothing to do with implementing the reconciliation instructions is enormous. To counter that temptation, the Senate in the mid-1980s adopted the Byrd rule, named after its creator, Sen. Robert C. Byrd, D-W.Va. It prohibits extraneous matter in a reconciliation bill and requires a three-fifths vote to waive the rule (Tiefer 1989, 891–894; Gold et al. 1992, 302–303, 326). Since what is extraneous is not self-evident, a set of rules defining what does and does not fall under the Byrd rule has developed. Application of the rule can have major policy consequences; in 1995, for example, Senate Democrats managed to knock out of the reconciliation bill big chunks of the Republicans' welfare reform legislation (see Chapter 11). The rule often adds to the strains between the House and Senate; House members bitterly complain that a Senate rule dictates what can and cannot be included in reconciliation bill conference reports.

The Byrd rule is only one example of the way in which the budget process has superimposed onto the two chambers' rules another set of highly complex rules. In the House the result is that special rules from the Rules Committee, which can waive budget rules, become even more important in managing the business of the chamber. In the Senate another set of decisions that require a supermajority has been added. For example, the key decision in the Senate's approval of legislation implementing the General Agreement on Tariffs and Trade in 1994 was not the vote on passage, which required a simple majority. Before the Senate could vote on approval, sixty votes were needed to waive a Senate budget rule requiring that new legislation be "budget neutral." Since the GATT agreement reduced tariffs, a form of taxes, it did not comply with that rule.

Congress, the President, and Summitry

The veto, the president's status as head of his party, and his capacity to command media attention allow the president to play a major role in the legislative process. Many legislative proposals originate in the executive branch. Executive branch officials testify before congressional committees on most legislation; they are often present during committee markups and during conference committee deliberations. In addition, executive branch officials let committee and party leaders know through private meetings and frequent informal contacts what the president wants and will accept.

Even if the president is from the other party and has very different policy preferences, the congressional majority party must pay some attention to his wishes if it wants to enact legislation. Presidents under such conditions of divided control have become adept at veto bargaining—at threatening a veto in order to extract the maximum in terms of substantive concessions from an opposition congressional majority. Of course, if the divergence in policy preferences is very wide, the result may be stalemate rather than compromise.

In recent years the president and Congress have resorted to "summits" when normal legislative processes have been incapable of producing a bill and the costs of failing to reach an agreement have been very high. (For a somewhat similar argument, see Gilmour 1990.) Relatively formal negotiations between congressional leaders and high-ranking administration officials representing the president directly, summits have no official status; they occur when the president and the majority party leadership decide to engage in such talks. During the 1980s and 1990s, normal legislative processes often ended in stalemate because of divided control, the sharp differences in policy preferences between the president and an opposition party congressional majority, and the tough decisions that big deficits made necessary. The deficit and the budget process, especially as revised in the mid-1980s by the Gramm-Rudman automatic spending-cut provisions, often provided the sense of emergency and the statutory deadline that made inaction politically costly.

The 1990 budget summit provides a good example. A need for action and the inability of normal processes to produce agreement forced a resort to a summit on budget issues (Sinclair 1991). The policy and political stakes of budget decision making were enormous. A budget is a statement of priorities; when resources are tight, budget decisions involve painful trade-offs. The Gramm-Rudman requirement—that either the deficit be cut by a specified large amount or that "sequestration" take place—raised the stakes: the costs of the president and Congress failing to reach an agreement would be very high. Sequestration would involve automatic across-the-board spending cuts of Draconian proportions. Furthermore, estimates of the deficit were rising, and the economy showed signs of slowing. This made decisive action even more necessary.

Most independent experts agreed that a serious budget reduction package would have to include significant revenue increases. Yet in decisions about taxes, the parties saw their future electoral prospects at stake. Attempting to shake the high tax image that Republicans had successfully pinned upon them, Democrats were determined to refuse to take the initiative—and the blame—in proposing new taxes. A great many Republicans believed that their "no new taxes" stance accounted for their party's electoral success; Bush had pledged himself to that course during his 1988 campaign. As they saw it, Republicans had a great deal to lose by reneging on that promise.

Under these circumstances, normal processes were unlikely to produce results. So President George Bush invited the congressional leadership to the White House for talks. Congressional Democrats had little choice but to agree. Because the president could veto the reconciliation and appropriations bills that implement the congressional budget resolution, his assent would be necessary to avoid a sequester. Furthermore, refusing the president's request to talk would give the Democratic Party a black eye with the public.

The congressional party leaders appointed seventeen members—including chairmen and ranking minority members of Budget, Appropriations, and the tax-writing committees—as negotiators. Treasury secretary Nicholas F. Brady, OMB head Richard G. Darman, and White House chief of staff John H. Sununu represented the president. The first meeting was held on May 17, 1990, and sessions continued through much of June. Estimates of the likely size of the budget deficit continued to increase, but no progress toward a plan to deal with it was made.

Finally on September 30, the day before the beginning of the fiscal year when a new budget must be in place to keep the government functioning, the president and congressional leaders announced that a deal had been reached. Even after Bush had conceded the need for some new revenues, differences over taxes and domestic spending cuts had continued to block progress. Eventually, the congressional negotiating group was pared down to include only the top party leaders, and it was this small group of key leaders and high-ranking administration officials that forged the agreement.

Neither Bush nor the Democratic House leadership was able to sell that agreement to their troops, and it was defeated in the House. A revised version, however, was approved soon thereafter and sequestration was avoided. A summit may offer the only hope of agreement, but as a decision-making mechanism it is relatively expensive for party leaders and the institution; it not only short-circuits the normal decision-making process but also excludes most members and is therefore likely to lead to discontent.

What Is the Regular Process?

The textbook diagram of how a bill becomes a law no longer accurately describes the legislative process on major bills. In the contemporary Congress there are many variations; one can more accurately speak of legislative processes in the plural than of a single cut-and-dried set of steps through which all measures proceed.

While my step-by-step discussion of the legislative process makes the variety obvious, it does not yield any precise sense of the cumulative impact of these procedures and practices. That is best conveyed by a systematic analysis of the legislative process on recent major legislation. How many of the special process variations characterized the process on major legislation? How frequently did such legislation follow the old textbook process?

TABLE 5.1 Special Procedures and Practices in the House and Senate on Major Legislation, 1987–90, 1993–94

Number of special procedures and practices	Percentage of major measures in which the legislative process was characterized by special procedures and practices	
	House[a]	Senate[b]
0	22.2	34.2
1	28.5	27.8
2	30.4	23.4
3 or more	19.0	14.5

SOURCE: Computed by the author.

[a] The enumerated special procedures and practices that the legislation may have encountered as it worked its way through the House are multiple referral, omnibus legislation, the passage of legislation as a result of a legislative-executive branch summit, the bypassing of committees, postcommittee adjustments, and consideration under a complex or closed rule.

[b] For the Senate the procedures and practices that were counted were the same as for the House except consideration under a complex or closed rule. Also counted was whether the bill ran into filibuster trouble and whether it was subject to an amending marathon (ten or more amending roll calls).

For each of the 158 major measures in the 100th, 101st, and 103rd Congresses, I counted the number of special procedures and practices that the legislation encountered as it worked its way through the House. The procedures and practices enumerated were multiple referral, omnibus legislation, a legislative-executive branch summit, legislation resulting from the bypassing of committees, postcommittee adjustments, and consideration under a complex or closed rule.

The House legislative process on the 158 major bills of these recent Congresses displayed at least one of these characteristics in 78 percent of the cases and two or more in 49 percent (see Table 5.1). To talk about the "regular order" in the House as the absence of these characteristics is no longer accurate, at least on major legislation.

Another perspective is provided by calculating the proportion of legislation that followed the supposedly regular process: legislation that was reported by one committee, that was not omnibus nor the result of a summit, that was not subject to postcommittee adjustments, and that was considered on the floor under an open rule. In the House the legislative process on only 10 percent of major legislation in these recent Congresses meets these criteria.[4] The "regular order" is no longer the norm; on major legislation it has become the exception.

To assess the frequency of the new procedures and practices in the Senate, I counted the same characteristics as for the House, excepting, of course, the use of special rules. In the Senate these special procedures and practices are somewhat less pervasive than in the House; the legislative process on 47 percent of major bills displayed at least one special characteristic and 16 percent displayed two or more.

This measure, which parallels the one constructed for the House, excludes the most notable changes in the legislative process in the Senate: the increase in floor amending activity and the more frequent use of extended debate. When a second Senate measure of special procedures and practices is created by also counting whether the bill ran into filibuster trouble or was subject to an amending marathon (ten or more amending roll calls), 66 percent of major bills display at least one and 38 percent two or more special process characteristics (see Table 5.1). In the Senate, as in the House, the legislative process on major legislation frequently no longer conforms to what we still tend to think of as the normal process.

---

4. This figure is less than the 22 percent without any of the special process characteristics in Table 5.1 because the table includes measures that did not get to the House floor and measures considered under procedures other than rules— mostly suspension of the rules.

In both chambers, then, the legislative process on major legislation has changed; such legislation is now more likely than not to traverse an unorthodox or nonstandard course. How and why this happened is the subject of the next chapter.

Why and How the Legislative Process Changed

WHY DID THE "TEXTBOOK" LEGISLATIVE PROCESS that had seemed so routinized and entrenched change extensively? In this chapter I argue that the modifications and innovations can be seen as responses to problems and opportunities that members—as individuals or collectively—confronted, problems and opportunities that arose from changes in institutional structure or challenges in the political environment.

The story is complex and its various strands intertwined in intricate ways, but three factors can be analytically isolated as key: internal reforms that changed the distribution of influence in both chambers in the 1970s, the institution of the congressional budget process, an internal-process reform with sufficiently far-reaching effects to deserve separate treatment, and a political environment in the 1980s and early 1990s characterized by divided control, big deficits, and ideological hostility to the legislative goals of the congressional Democratic Party. I discuss each of these briefly and then analyze how the legislative process was affected by them.

From Decentralization to Individualism in the Senate

In the U.S. Senate of the 1950s and before, influence was decentralized but unequally distributed, with committee chairs and other senior members, who were predominantly conservative, exercising the lion's share. It was a relatively closed and inward-looking institution. The typical senator specialized in the issues that came before his committees and participated meagerly on the floor; he was deferential to his seniors, loyal to the institution, and restrained in the use of the powers that Senate rules confer upon the individual (Matthews 1960; Sinclair 1989).

Senate rules then as now allowed unlimited debate and, in most cases, unlimited amending activity. The restraint that characterized the Senate of that period was not a function of rules; rather it depended on norms—unwritten rules of behavior—and on a political environment in which acting with restraint was relatively costless to senators.

That began to change in the late 1950s. The 1958 elections brought into the Senate a big class of northern liberal Democrats elected from electorally competitive states and on a platform promising action; succeeding elections through the mid-1960s augmented the number of such members. These senators could not afford to wait, as the old norms had demanded, to make their mark; both their policy and their reelection goals dictated immediate and extensive activism.

An activist style based on participation in a broader range of issues and on the floor as well as in committee became attractive to more and more senators as the political environment and the Washington political community changed radically in the 1960s and 1970s. New issues and an enormous growth in the number of groups active in Washington resulted in senators being highly sought after as champions of groups' causes. These developments made the role of outward-looking policy entrepreneur available to more senators. Successfully playing that role brought a senator a Washington reputation as a player, media attention, and possibly even a shot at the presidency.

Incentives to exploit fully the great powers Senate rules confer on the individual increased immensely, and senators began to offer many more amendments on the floor and to use extended debate more often. As a result, the Senate floor became a more active decision-making arena. The proportion of legislation subject to high amending activity (ten or more amending roll calls) was tiny in the 1950s; for the 84th and 86th Congresses, it averaged 3 percent. During the 1960s and 1970s, it rose to a mean of 8 percent per Congress, and in the 1980s it averaged 15 percent (Sinclair 1989, 115).[1]

As senators became much more willing to exploit their prerogative of extended debate, filibusters, overt and covert, increasingly became a routine part of the legislative process in the Senate. As Table 6.1 shows, filibusters were once rare; in the 1950s a typical Congress saw one filibuster. By the 1970s more than ten filibusters occurred per Congress on average,

---

1. These figures are based on data for even-numbered Congresses from the 88th to the 96th Congress and for all Congresses from the 97th through the 99th.

TABLE 6.1   Filibusters and Cloture Votes, 82nd–103rd Congresses

Congresses	Years	Filibusters[a]	Cloture Votes[a]	Successful Cloture Votes[a]
82nd–86th	1951–60	1.0	0.4	0.0
87th–91st	1961–70	4.6	5.2	0.8
92nd–96th	1971–80	11.2	22.4	8.6
97th–99th	1981–86	16.7	23.0	10.0
100th–102nd	1987–92	26.7	39.0	15.3
103rd	1993–94	30.0	42.0	14.0

SOURCES: For the filibusters per Congress, "A Look at the Senate Filibuster," Special Report of the Democratic Study Group, June 13, 1994, No. 103–28, Appendix B, compiled by Congressional Research Service. For the cloture votes, Norman Ornstein, Thomas Mann, and Michael Malbin, *Vital Statistics on Congress, 1993–1994* (Washington, D.C.: Congressional Quarterly, 1994), 162. Data for the 103rd Congress are from Richard S. Beth, "Cloture in the Senate, 103rd Congress," memorandum, Congressional Research Service, June 23, 1995.

[a] Entries are per Congress.

and by the late 1980s and early 1990s filibusters were taking place at a rate of more than one a month. (See Beth 1995 for cautions about these data.) As the number of filibusters grew, so did attempts to stop them by invoking cloture; cloture votes became an ordinary part of the legislative process. While cloture was often successfully invoked, passing legislation that is at all controversial increasingly required sixty votes.

Reform and Its Legacy in the House

In the House changes in chamber and majority party rules during the 1970s transformed the distribution of influence (Dodd and Oppenheimer 1977; Sinclair 1983; Smith 1989; Rohde 1991). Even more than in the Senate, legislative influence in the House had been vested in powerful and often conservative committee leaders over whom party leaders and members had little control. Reformers who were primarily liberal Democrats objected to the conservative policy this system produced and to the limited opportunities for participation it afforded rank-and-file members.

Through a series of rules changes mostly instituted between 1969 and 1975, reformers changed the distribution of influence. Powers and resources were shifted from committee chairs down to subcommittee chairs and rank-and-file members and up to the party leadership. For example, the power to appoint subcommittee chairs was taken away from the committee chair and given to the majority party members of the committee; subcommittees were ensured adequate budget and staff. Rather than securing their positions automatically through their seniority on the committee, committee chairs had to win approval by majority vote on a secret ballot of the majority party membership. Junior members gained resources, especially staff, that enormously increased their ability to participate actively in the legislative process. The Speaker, the leader of the majority party, was given the power to select the Democratic members of the Rules Committee, a greater say in the assignment of members to other committees, and new powers over the referral of bills.

During the same period, the House adopted sunshine rules that opened the legislative process to greater public scrutiny. Recorded votes became possible—and easy to force—in the Committee of the Whole where the amending process takes place. Most committee markup sessions and conference committee meetings were opened to the public. The greater visibility of congressional decision making increased members' incentives for activism.

These reforms had far-reaching direct and indirect effects. By reducing the power and autonomy of the committees, they made legislating more difficult for the majority party. To be sure, Democratic reformers had often been unhappy with the sort of legislation conservative-led committees had produced. By the late 1970s, however, the committee chairs and the membership of the most powerful committees were more representative of the Democratic Party than they had been earlier; Republicans and dissident Democrats had become adept at using floor amendments to make political points and confront mainstream Democrats with politically difficult votes. Compromises carefully crafted in committee were being picked apart on the floor, and floor sessions were stretching on interminably.

The number of floor amendments decided on a teller or recorded vote had risen gradually from 55 in 1955–56 to 107 in 1969–70. With the institution of the recorded teller, it jumped to 195 in 1971–72, and with electronic voting it jumped again to 351 in 1973–74 (Smith 1989, 33). During the 94th Congress (1975–76), 372 such amendments were offered on the floor and, during the 95th, 439. In 1979 floor consideration of the budget resolution took nine days during which fifty amendments were offered (Sinclair 1983, 180).

Democrats began to look to their party leaders, the only central leaders in the chamber, to counter these problems. The leaders responded by innovating in ways that led to alterations in the legislative process. The leadership became more involved with legislation before it reached the floor, and this involvement increasingly took the form of negotiating substantive changes in the legislation, often at the postcommittee stage, in order to produce a bill that could pass the chamber. To respond to the barrage of amendments offered on the floor, the leadership developed special rules into powerful devices for structuring floor decision making.

Budget Reform

When President Richard Nixon aggressively challenged Congress's power of the purse, Congress responded by passing the Congressional Budget and Impoundment Control Act of 1974. Presidents had been encroaching on Congress's budgetary powers for decades; lacking a mechanism for making comprehensive decisions, Congress had long used the president's budget as its point of departure for budgetary decision making and usually altered it only marginally. However, when Nixon claimed the right to impound—that is, not spend—congressionally appropriated funds, the Congress had to respond or acquiesce in a severe diminution of its powers. Nixon argued that congressional appropriations were just ceilings and that he was not required to spend any of the money Congress appropriated. In effect, he was arguing that Congress had only negative powers: Congress might be able to prevent the president from doing something by not appropriating funds, but it could not force a president to carry out a policy he opposed.

The Budget Act went far beyond devising a procedure to control impoundments: the budget process that it established provided a mechanism by which comprehensive policy making in Congress became possible. During its first few years, however, the budget process was not used in that way. In the House the battles over budget resolutions were hard fought and highly partisan; debate did turn on the political parties' different priorities, but the resolutions themselves did not call for significant policy change (Ellwood and Thurber 1981; Schick 1980).

Reconciliation instructions that mandated committees to make changes in legislation under their jurisdiction were first included in the budget resolution in 1980 (Sinclair 1983, 18–190). Frighteningly high inflation in January 1980 convinced President Jimmy Carter and the Democratic congressional party leadership that budget cuts needed to be made and quickly. The ordinary legislative process, they decided, would take too long and be too subject to delay by interests adversely affected by the cuts. Therefore, they decided to use the budget process and to include reconciliation instructions in the first budget resolution. Doing so was highly controversial (in part because the Budget Act envisioned such instructions being included in the second budget resolution, which in this and most cases would be too late), and the committees subject to instructions objected vigorously. Nevertheless, the resolution with the instructions passed, and the committees did comply. To do otherwise was to defy the will of the Congress as expressed in its budget resolution.

Although the policy changes required by the 1980 budget resolution were modest by later standards, the experience made clear to perceptive participants that, under certain circumstances at least, the budget process was a mechanism available to central leaders for making comprehensive policy change. David Stockman, a Republican member of the House from Michigan from 1977 to January 1981, was one of those perceptive participants. As President Ronald Reagan's first head of the Office of Management and Budget, he suggested using the budget process to enact Reagan's economic program in 1981 (Stockman 1986). The administration-supported budget resolution included instructions to committees to make substantial changes in policy; supporters forced a single vote on them as a whole and then packaged the policy changes into one massive reconciliation bill where again the key vote was whether to accept or reject them as a whole. This strategy enabled Reagan and his supporters to achieve major policy change quickly in a system resistant to such change.

The budget process has had wide-reaching effects on the legislative process. In the years since 1981, budget politics have remained at center stage. The attempt to control the big deficits Reagan's economic program created has shaped our politics. The budget process has become the tool of choice for those attempting to bring about comprehensive policy change.

A Hostile Political Climate as a Force for Innovation: The 1980s and Early 1990s

Both the House and Senate entered the 1980s beset by problems resulting from changes in their internal distribution of influence. The highly individualistic Senate in which each senator was accorded extraordinary latitude was very good at agenda setting and publicizing problems, but it was less well structured for legislative decision making. The House, which had greatly increased rank-and-file members' opportunities for participation, also had problems legislating, though its central leadership had begun to develop reasonably effective responses.

The political climate of the 1980s and early 1990s exacerbated the problems of legislating, especially for the Democratic House. Ronald Reagan was a conservative, confrontational president whose policy views were very far from those of congressional Democrats, and the policy preferences of his successor, George Bush, were not much closer. In 1981 Reagan and his congressional allies ran over the Democratic House majority and enacted sweeping policy changes over futile Democratic protests. Thereafter, Reagan was never as politically strong again, but he and Bush still had the bully pulpit and the veto.

The growing ideological polarization of the parties exacerbated the conflict. Reagan's nomination had signaled the Republican Party's move to the right. The congressional party, especially the House Republican Party, had begun to change in the mid- and late 1970s. Not only were fewer moderates being elected, more hard-edged, ideological conservatives were entering the House. The elections of 1978 brought a Republican freshman from Georgia named Newt Gingrich to the House.

The Democratic Party in the 1980s became more cohesive as its southern contingent changed. Republicans won southern seats, and the southern Democrats that remained depended for reelection on the votes of African-Americans. The Republican Party's increasing conservatism also made ideological differences among Democrats seem less.

The voting cohesion of House Democrats began to increase after the 1982 elections, and in the late 1980s and early 1990s it reached levels unprecedented in the post–World War II era. For the period 1951 through 1970, House Democrats' average party unity score was 78 percent; it fell to 74 percent for the period 1971 to 1982.[2] After the 1982 elections the scores began rising and averaged 86 percent for the 1983–94 period. During this same period, the proportion of party votes also increased, averaging 56 percent compared with 37 percent during the 1971–82 period. During the 103rd Congress, a majority of Democrats opposed a majority of Republicans on 64 percent of House recorded votes (Rohde 1991; *Congressional Quarterly Almanac,* various years).

During the 1980s, then, an increasingly cohesive House Democratic majority faced a hostile president, a Republican Senate, and a more aggressive and conservative Republican minority.

After 1981 big deficits became chronic and severely restricted feasible policy options. Democrats often found themselves in the position of fighting to protect past policy successes. Not infrequently the decisions that had to be made, if not carefully managed, had the potential of pitting Democratic members against each other.

Partisan conflict and stalemate in Washington fed public cynicism about government's ability to handle effectively the problems facing the country; many people concluded that government could not do anything right. Pass-

---

2. Party votes are recorded votes on which a majority of Democrats voted against a majority of Republicans. A member's party unity score is the percentage of party votes on which he or she voted with a majority of his or her party colleagues.

ing legislation the majority Democrats considered satisfactory became very difficult in such a climate. Even enacting legislation to keep the government going was hard, both because of the ideological gulf between congressional Democrats and Republican presidents and because the legislation frequently required making unpalatable decisions. This tough climate forced further innovation in the legislative process, especially in the House.

How Internal Reform and a Hostile Climate Spawned Unorthodox Lawmaking

Internal reforms, the hostile political climate, and other lesser changes in the environment altered the context in which members of Congress functioned. As they and their leaders sought to advance their goals within this altered context, they changed the legislative process. Sometimes changes were brought about by formal revisions in chamber rules; more frequently, they were the result of alterations in practices.

Multiple Referral

As our society and economy evolve over time, the issues at the center of controversy change. In the 1950s and early 1960s, for example, environmental protection was an obscure issue, and congressional attempts to deal with it mostly entailed programs to help municipalities build water treatment plants; by the 1970s the environment had become a highly salient issue, and Congress was considering ambitious legislation to protect endangered species and to force automakers and other polluters to clean up the air. As new issues arise and old ones change, the fit between the prominent issues on the congressional agenda and the committee system becomes increasingly poor. Yet Congress, especially the House, has great difficulty in realigning committee jurisdictions. Taking away jurisdiction from a committee reduces its clout; both committee members and affected interest groups that have established good working relationships with the committee will fight the change. Since committee membership is a considerably more important basis of members' influence in the House than in the Senate, realigning jurisdictions so that they fit better with the issues of the day is harder in the House than in the Senate.

By the early 1970s committee jurisdictions that had last been significantly overhauled in 1946 were seriously outmoded; jurisdiction over a number of key issues—energy, the environment, and health, for example—was spread over a number of committees, leading to a lack of coordination and numerous turf fights. The House attempted to reform its committee jurisdictions in the mid-1970s but largely failed (Davidson and Oleszek 1977). The Senate's attempt at committee reform in the late 1970s was considerably more successful (Davidson 1981).

Unable to realign committee jurisdictions and driven by reform-minded members' desire to increase opportunities for broad participation in the legislative process, the House in 1975 changed its rules to allow multiple referral of legislation (Davidson and Oleszek 1992).[3] In the first Congress with multiple referral, 1975–76, 6 percent of the measures introduced were multiply referred. Over time and driven by the same forces that led to its institution, multiply referred legislation became an increasingly prominent part of the House workload (see Table 6.2). On average a little more than one in ten measures were multiply referred during the four Congresses between 1977 and 1984; the frequency rose to 14 percent in the 99th Congress and averaged 18 percent in the 100th and 101st Congresses (Young and Cooper 1993, 214).

If only major legislation is considered, the increase has been steeper. The congressional agenda of major legislation included 8.6 percent multiply referred legislation in the 94th Congress and 9.6 percent in the 97th, figures very close to those for all measures. Since then, however, multiply referred measures have made up a considerably greater proportion of major legislation than of all legislation. In the late 1980s and early 1990s about 30 percent of major measures were multiply referred. The partial data suggest a further increase in the 104th Congress; despite a rule change intended to rein in multiple referral, 40 percent of the major measures were referred to more than one committee.

Multiple referral of legislation has always been possible in the Senate through unanimous consent. The Senate, however, did manage to realign its committee jurisdictions during the 1970s, and because senators can more easily influence legislation outside the committee setting than can House members, they have less incentive to insist on a referral (Fenno 1973; Sinclair 1989). As a consequence, the referral of legislation to more than one committee continues to be considerably less frequent in the Sen-

---

3. Actually, even before then, something quite similar to multiple referral occurred under specialized circumstances; when legislation referred to a committee other than Ways and Means contained a revenue component, that section would be sent to the tax committee. In the 91st Congress (1969–70), for example, three bills primarily under the jurisdiction of a committee other than Ways and Means were also referred to Ways and Means for consideration of their revenue sections; thus, the Interstate and Foreign Commerce Committee was mostly responsible for the Airport Development Act, but the trust fund and tax provisions were handled by Ways and Means.

TABLE 6.2   Multiple Referral in the House and Senate, 94th–104th Congresses

Congress	Years	House		Senate	
		Percentage of all measures	Percentage of major legislation	Percentage of all measures	Percentage of major legislation[a]
94th	1975–76	6.0	8.6		5.2
95th	1977–78	10.3			
96th	1979–80	11.7		6.4	
97th	1981–82	9.6	9.6	5.0	5.6
98th	1983–84	11.6		4.4	
99th	1985–86	14.0		3.0	
100th	1987–88	17.5	33.3		6.5
101st	1989–90	18.2	30.0		7.0
103rd	1993–94		27.8		14.5
104th	1995		40.0[b]		16.7[b]

SOURCES: The data on the House for all measures are from Young and Cooper (1993, 214). The data on the Senate for all measures are from Davidson (1989, 381). Other data were compiled by the author. Major legislation is defined by the list of major legislation in the *Congressional Quarterly Weekly Report*, augmented by those measures on which key votes occurred, again according to Congressional Quarterly.

[a] Includes cases of multiple committee consideration of legislation that was not formally multiply referred.

[b] Includes 1995 only.

ate. Several committees do sometimes consider different bills on the same topic, a procedure that can create complications much like those formal multiple referral can produce.

Roger Davidson found that from the late 1970s through the mid-1980s on average less than 5 percent of all Senate measures were multiply referred and that, if there was a trend, it was toward a decrease (Davidson 1989, 381). Major measures, however, show a mild increasing trend toward multiple committee consideration in the late 1980s and early 1990s (see Table 6.2). An informed observer suggested that the frequency of multiple referral in the House was pressuring the Senate to include more committees in the process formally so that the substantive expertise and political support of these committees' leaders would be available in conference with the House.

Committees as Shapers of Legislation

By reducing the power of committee chairs and increasing the opportunities and incentives for rank-and-file members to participate in the legislative process, the House reforms of the 1970s diminished the capacity of committees to pass their legislation without change. No longer were bills protected by a powerful chair with the weapons to retaliate against members who challenged his legislation in committee or on the floor or by voting rules that prevented most recorded votes on floor amendments. Junior committee members and members not on the committee now had the staff and the access to information that made their participation feasible. The increased prevalence of multiple referral lessened committee autonomy; committee leaders were not always capable of resolving the conflicts among their committees, yet unresolved intercommittee conflicts endangered legislation on the floor. The reformers had given Democratic majority party leaders some new tools, and, as the problems the reforms had wrought became increasingly evident, the now more ideologically homogeneous Democrats began to expect their leaders to use those tools to engineer passage of legislation broadly supported by the Democratic membership.

To respond to their members' demands, the Democratic leadership became more involved in the legislative process in the period before legislation reached the floor. A bill's substance is by far the most important determinant of its fate on the floor. As it became more difficult for the committee or committees of jurisdiction to write a bill that could pass on the floor, the party leaders stepped in more often to help.

Party leaders, of course, may involve themselves informally on legislation during committee consideration; anecdotal and interview evidence indicates that such intervention is much more frequent than it used to be (Sinclair 1995). That kind of involvement is, however, impossible to document systematically across time. Substantive adjustments to legislation after it is reported—whether engineered by the party leadership or others—can be counted with more precision.[4]

Postcommittee adjustments were rare in the prereform era. In the 91st Congress there was no such instance in the House on the fifty-four major measures, though in one case the leadership was involved in making an adjustment of this kind after a veto. Committees were quite success-

---

4. I ascertained the presence or absence of a postcommittee adjustment and whether it was directed by the party leadership by doing a case study of each of the major measures for the selected Congresses. The case studies relied primarily on the *Congressional Quarterly Weekly Report* and the *Congressional Quarterly Almanac.* Thus, instances not ascertainable from the public record could have been missed; however, when I had independent information from interviews or participant-observation available, they confirmed the coding done on the basis of the written record.

TABLE 6.3   The Changing Role of Committees in the Legislative Process,
91st–104th Congresses

Congress	Years	Percentage of major legislation in which the committee with jurisdiction was bypassed		Percentage of major legislation subject to post-committee adjustment	
		House	Senate	House	Senate
91st	1969–70	2	4	0	2
94th	1975–76	2	3	4	2
97th	1981–82	8	4	23	22
100th	1987–88	21	18	37	22
101st	1989–90	18	11	39	35
103rd	1993–94	6	13	29	36
104th	1995	11[a]	27[a]	47[a]	63[a]

SOURCE: Compiled by the author.

[a] Includes 1995 only.

ful on the floor, lessening the need for tinkering after they had finished their work. Even when committees lost on the floor and when that loss was no big surprise, leaders seem to have made no attempt to head off the floor defeat by substantive adjustments in the legislation. Presumably the committee leaders had done what they could and would in committee, and the party leaders lacked the tools to get involved.

In the 94th Congress there were two clear instances of postcommittee adjustments to major measures; both cases involved the new budget process. In 1975 and again in 1976 it became clear that the budget resolution as reported by the Budget Committee would not pass. In each case the party leadership stepped in and crafted an amendment to the budget resolution to ensure passage in a form acceptable to most Democrats.

In the 1980s and early 1990s the hostile political climate made passing legislation Democrats wanted difficult. Big deficits made it harder for committee leaders to forge broadly acceptable deals; a climate of scarcity begets zero-sum politics in which one group's gain is perceived as a loss by other groups and fewer "sweeteners" to induce support are available. As committee Democrats tried to craft a bill that was passable yet as close as possible to their preferred policy position, they could easily misjudge what was passable. Furthermore, changes in the political environment after the committee had reported—in the salience of the issue or in the public's response to presidential rhetoric—could alter what would pass. Leadership counts of members' voting intentions often showed not enough support for the committee-reported bill. Therefore, major legislation frequently required substantive alterations. As important legislation increasingly involved a number of committees, the compromises that needed to be made among the committees to bring a passable bill to the floor were often beyond the capacity of committee leaders to negotiate. In such a climate postcommittee adjustments, almost always party leadership directed, became almost routine (see Table 6.3).

The increased frequency with which committees are bypassed is a result of the same forces—namely, internal reforms that decreased the power and autonomy of committees and empowered the party leaders and the hostile political climate that exacerbated the difficulties the reforms had produced. To be sure, not all instances of committees being bypassed are leadership directed; occasionally a discharge petition is successful. Most often, however, when committees are bypassed, it is the party leadership that made the decision, though not necessarily over the committee's opposition. Sometimes a committee is bypassed with its members' full concurrence simply to speed the process—when identical legislation had passed in the previous Congress, for example.

On the fifty-four major measures in the 91st Congress (1969–70), the committee was never actually bypassed in the House, though in one case the committee reported only because of a threat of discharge. (That case, an organized crime control bill forced out of a reluctant Judiciary Committee, is counted as a bypass in Table 6.3.) In the 94th Congress the committee was bypassed in one case; the leadership undertook the drafting of an internal reform measure. As Table 6.3 shows, bypassing the committee became considerably more frequent in the 1980s. The circumstances varied widely, but in most cases the decision to bypass the committee was a majority party leadership decision. In the 103rd Congress the frequency decreases; in the 104th it increases again, but the relatively low figure—based on partial data—is somewhat deceiving, as I discussed in Chapter 2; although most items in the Contract with America went through the formal committee process, they were actually drafted elsewhere.

When the party leadership decides to bypass a committee, it does so in order to move legislation. Since bypassing committee is a violation of committee prerogatives and likely to make some members unhappy, especially in the House, leaders would prefer to avoid doing so. Therefore, House leaders will bypass a committee only as a last resort and thus are more likely to do so when the political context makes legislating particularly difficult. With the same party (the Democrats) controlling Congress and the presidency in 1993–94, legislating became a little less difficult for the House, and House leaders had less need to use tactics that are relatively expensive. This explains the decline in the 103rd Congress shown in Table 6.3. The 104th Congress is discussed in the final section of the chapter.

If internal reforms had unintended consequences that made legislat-ing more difficult for the House, the Senate's individualism run rampant made the House's problems look picayune. Furthermore, the Senate unlike the House did not give its central leadership new tools for dealing with the problems.

In the Senate as in the House, one response was an increase in post-committee adjustments to legislation. They were rare in the late 1960s and 1970s; the 91st and 94th Congresses saw one case each. In the 1980s and early 1990s postcommittee adjustments became much more frequent. The Senate majority leader often engineered or at least oversaw the working out of postcommittee changes in legislation, but committee leaders and even individual senators sometimes took on the task, reflecting the wide dispersion of power in the Senate.

Although the frequency of postcommittee adjustments declined appreciably in the 103rd Congress in the House, in the Senate it crept up a bit. For the majority-rule House, united control made legislating some-what easier; at least large margins to dissuade the president from vetoing the legislation were no longer necessary. The Senate, in contrast, still needed sixty votes to pass most controversial legislation. With the return of divided control in the 104th, postcommittee adjustments became more frequent again in both chambers.

In the Senate the frequency with which committees are bypassed has also increased. Committees were seldom bypassed on major legislation before the mid-1980s; the 91st, 94th, and 97th Congresses each saw two cases. The frequency, however, increased substantially with the 100th Con-gress, remained well above its previous level in the 101st and the 103rd Congresses, and reached a new high in the 104th.

Special Rules in the House

In the prereform era most legislation was brought to the House floor under a simple open rule that allowed all germane amendments. Tax bills and often other legislation from the Ways and Means Committee were considered under a closed rule that allowed no amendments (except those offered by the committee itself); such legislation was regarded as too complex and too politically tempting a target to allow floor amend-ments. In the 91st Congress (1969–70), for example, 80 percent of the major legislation was considered under simple open rules; 16 percent— primarily bills reported by the Ways and Means Committee—came to the floor under closed rules. Only two measures were considered under rules with provisions more complex than simply allowing all germane amend-ments or barring all amendments.

The reforms, however, made legislation much more vulnerable to alteration on the floor. With rank-and-file members having greater incentives and resources for offering amendments on the floor, the number of amendments offered and pushed to a roll call vote shot up. Committee bills were more frequently picked apart on the floor, members were often forced to go on the record on votes hard to explain to constituents back home, and floor sessions stretched on late into the night.

The reformers had given the Democratic leadership the power to name the Democratic members and the chair of the Rules Committee and had thereby made the committee an arm of the leadership. In the late 1970s some Democrats began to pressure their leaders to use special rules to bring floor proceedings under control. Forty Democrats wrote Speaker Thomas P. O'Neill Jr., D-Mass., in 1979 asking that he make more use of restrictive rules in order to curtail frequent late-night sessions (Smith 1989, 40–41).

As Table 6.4 shows, as late as 1977–78, most special rules were still open rules; only 15 percent restricted amendments in some way. As Democratic members began to comprehend the costs of the wide-open amending process fostered by the reforms and to demand that their leaders do something about it, the frequency of restrictive rules increased. In the hostile climate of the 1980s and early 1990s, restrictive rules were used more and more often. Holding together compromises and protecting members from political heat became more difficult and more essential; and leaders, in response to their members' demands, developed special rules into powerful devices for shaping the choices members face on the floor. By 1993–94, 70 percent of special rules restricted amendments to some extent.

When only major measures are examined, the trend is even stronger. In the 91st Congress (1969–70) almost all rules for major legislation were simple open rules or closed rules. The frequency of simple open rules dropped steeply between the 94th (1975–76) and the 97th (1981–82) Congresses and again between the 97th and the 100th and 101st (1987–90). By the late 1980s three-quarters or more of major measures were considered under complex or closed rules. From the 97th Congress on, almost all the complex rules to a lesser or greater extent restricted amending activity.

The power and flexibility of special rules make them a useful tool under a broad variety of circumstances. Both the uncertainty that the 1970s reforms begot and the problems that majority Democrats faced in legislating during the adverse political climate of the 1980s and early 1990s stimulated an increase in the use of complex and restrictive rules (Bach and Smith 1988; Sinclair 1983, 1995). The election of a Democratic president in 1992 presented congressional Democrats with a great legisla-

TABLE 6.4   Change in the Character of Special Rules in the House, 91st–104th
Congresses

			Percentage of major legislation	
Congress	Years	Percentage of all rules that were restrictive[a]	Considered under closed or complex rules	Considered under closed rules, modified closed rules, or modified open rules
91st	1969–70	—	19	16
94th	1975–76	—	17	9
95th	1977–78	15		
96th	1979–80	25		
97th	1981–82	25	39	32
98th	1983–84	32		
99th	1985–86	43		
100th	1987–88	46	81	72
101st	1989–90	55	77	72
102nd	1991–92	66		
103rd	1993–94	70	84	82
104th	1995	49[b]	94[b]	77[b]

SOURCES: Data on all rules were compiled by Donald Wolfensberger, minority counsel, Committee on Rules, from the Rules Committee calendars and surveys of activities. The 104th Congress data are from *Congressional Record,* March 7, 1996, H1795. Data on major measures were compiled by the author.

[a] This includes all rules for initial consideration of legislation, except rules on appropriations bills, which only waive points of order. Restrictive rules include closed rules, modified closed rules, and modified open rules. These rules are defined in Chapter 2, pp. 20–23.

[b] Includes 1995 only.

tive opportunity, but it also put them under pressure to deliver under difficult circumstances. The Democratic leadership responded by intensifying its employment of restrictive rules during the 103rd Congress.

The new Republican majority in the 104th Congress had promised to pass an ambitious agenda, much of it in the first 100 days. Before the election, however, House Republicans, including prominently their leadership, had vehemently denounced restrictive rules and promised not to use them. The proportion of all rules that were restrictive did go down in the 104th, though Democrats claimed Republicans manipulated the figures by considering under open rules some noncontroversial legislation that should have been considered under the suspension procedure. Major legislation was mostly considered under complex and usually restrictive rules; the usefulness of such rules for promoting the Republicans' legislative objectives outweighed any damage from the inevitable charges of hypocrisy that their use provoked.

The Senate Floor: Amending Activity and Extended Debate

The Senate, unlike the House, has not developed effective tools for coping with the consequences of alterations in its internal distribution of influence and challenges from its political environment. The attractiveness to modern senators of rules that give the individual so much power and the difficulty of changing Senate rules make developing such tools extraordinarily difficult. Since a two-thirds vote is required to cut off debate on a proposal to change Senate rules, an oversized coalition for change must be constructed. To be effective, the tools would have to give more control to the majority party leadership as they did in the House, but minority party senators certainly have no reason to do so, and even many majority party senators are likely to be ambivalent.

The rules changes the Senate was able to make were modest. Perhaps most important, the Budget Act imposed limits on debate on budget resolutions and reconciliation bills, preventing filibusters on these important measures. In 1975 the number of votes required to invoke cloture was lowered from two-thirds of those present and voting to three-fifths of the full membership—usually sixty. (Cloture on changes in Senate rules was exempted and still requires a two-thirds vote.) In response to the postcloture filibuster that developed in the 1970s, rules concerning delaying tactics in order after cloture were tightened. In 1986 floor consideration after cloture was limited to a total of thirty hours.

None of the new rules placed limits on the amendments senators can offer on the floor, and a senator's right to offer unlimited amendments to almost any bill proved as useful to senators as individuals in the 1980s and 1990s as it had in the 1970s. The political climate of the 1970s may have been more conducive to policy entrepreneurship, and floor amendments may have been more frequently used as tools toward that end. But amendments also proved to be useful tools in the more ideological and partisan struggles of the 1980s and 1990s.

During the contentious 1980s and 1990s, major legislation was likely to encounter a barrage of floor amendments, though just how frequently varied somewhat erratically. Of the 97th, 100th, 101st, and 103rd Congresses, the frequency of amending marathons (ten or more amendments offered and pushed to a recorded vote) was highest in the 97th (45 percent) and next highest in the 103rd (38 percent). In the 100th Congress 16 percent of major measures were subject to ten or more amendments and in the 101st, 29 percent.

TABLE 6.5 Extended Debate–Related Problems on Major Legislation, 97th–104th Congresses

Congress	Years	Percentage of major legislation[a]
97th	1981–82	21
100th	1987–88	27
101st	1989–90	28
103rd	1993–94	47
104th	1995	(44)

SOURCE: Compiled by the author.

[a] Percentage of major legislation that encountered a problem related to extended debate (for example, filibuster, threat of filibuster, hold) discernible from the public record. Data in parentheses are partial and include only those major measures that were considered on the floor of the House or the Senate in 1995.

Senators continued to increase their use of extended debate during the 1980s and early 1990s. The rules changes may have made imposing cloture easier, but they did not reduce the incentives to use extended debate. Rampant individualism combined with the highly charged political climate to put an increasing share of major legislation under at least a threat of a filibuster. In 1981–82 about one in five major measures experienced some filibuster-related problem discernible from the written record (see Table 6.5). By the 103rd Congress (1993–94), almost half of major measures ran into problems related to extended debate. Passing major legislation in the Senate has come to require sixty votes.

Omnibus Legislation and the Budget Process

Omnibus legislation—legislation of great substantive scope that often involves many committees—increased as a proportion of the congressional agenda of major legislation from none in the 91st Congress (1969–70), to 8 percent in the 94th (1975–76), and to 20 percent in the 97th (1981–82) and 100th (1987–88). In the 101st, the first Congress during George Bush's presidency, the proportion decreased to 8 percent, but this figure included some of the most important legislation of 1989–90. In the 103rd, following Bill Clinton's election to his first term, 11 percent of major measures were omnibus; and in the first year of the 104th, 14 percent were.

During the 1980s, the Democratic majority party leadership sometimes decided to package legislation into omnibus measures as part of a strategy to counter ideologically hostile Republican presidents, especially Ronald Reagan, who was so skillful at using the media to his advantage. Measures the president very much wanted could sometimes be packaged with others that congressional Democrats favored but the president opposed, thus forcing the president to accept legislative provisions that, were they sent to him in free-standing form, he would veto. By packaging disparate and individually modest provisions on salient issues such as trade, drugs, or crime into an omnibus bill, Democrats sought to compete with the White House for media attention and public credit. During the 103rd Congress, congressional leaders no longer needed to coerce the president into signing their legislation, but omnibus measures remained useful for raising the visibility of popular legislation, and the device continued to be employed in that way.

Many omnibus measures are budget related. Budget resolutions, reconciliation bills, and massive continuing resolutions have constituted the preponderance of omnibus measures since the passage of the Budget Act in 1974. In both the 94th and the 101st Congresses, for example, all of the omnibus measures were budget related. The budget-related measures, however, were much more important pieces of legislation in the 101st than in the 94th. The Budget Act made omnibus measures a regular part of the congressional agenda, but changes in the political environment made budget measures the focus of controversy. In the 1980s the budget process moved to the center of the legislative process, and it has remained there. The Reagan administration's use of the budget process in 1981 to redirect government policy made its potential clear; since then it has remained the tool of choice for comprehensive policy change and was used for that purpose by the Clinton administration in 1993 and by the new Republican majority in 1995.

The budget process's centrality stems even more, however, from the impact of the big budget deficits of the 1980s and 1990s. During the 1970s, the budget resolutions did not include reconciliation instructions (that is, instructions to committees to make changes in law); the budget process, by and large, accommodated what the committees wanted to do rather than constrained them. In 1980, as I discussed in Chapter 5, the president and congressional Democratic leaders, in response to an economic crisis, used the budget process to make spending cuts; reconciliation instructions were included in the budget resolution for the first time. Then in 1981 the Reagan administration and its congressional allies not only used the budget process to make radical cuts in domestic spending; they also enacted a huge tax cut. The deficits that resulted from that tax cut have shaped American politics ever since and have kept the budget process at the center of the legislative process.

Since 1981 efforts to do something about the deficit have dominated political debate, if not always legislative enactments. The decisions made in the budget resolution and in the reconciliation bill that it usually required became the crucial legislative decisions. Decisions on other legislative issues were made within the context of scarce resources and, as discretionary domestic spending shrank, the trade-offs that had to be made among programs became increasingly tough. The Gramm-Rudman legislation, the stated aim of which was to force the Congress to balance the budget, complicated the process by adding targets and deadlines that, if missed, would result in horrendous automatic spending cuts.

The politics of big deficits thus made unpalatable policy decisions necessary. The deep policy divisions between Republican presidents and House Democrats made agreement between the branches on such decisions excruciatingly difficult. The 1980s and early 1990s saw a succession of high visibility, high stakes showdowns between congressional Democrats and Republican presidents on budget measures. Reconciliation bills, like other omnibus measures, were sometimes used to try to force on an opposition party president provisions he opposed; such attempts, of course, raised the level of conflict. The existence of the budget process at least made it possible to wrap unpopular spending cuts and sometimes tax increases into one big package—often sweetened with provisions that members wanted—and get a single vote on the package as a whole. The congressional leadership frequently could persuade its members to pass such a package because defeating it would be devastating for the party's reputation; passing the components individually would have been impossible.

Summits

In the 1980s and early 1990s the sharp differences in policy preferences between Republican presidents and congressional Democrats and the tough decisions that had to be made sometimes stalemated normal processes. When normal processes, even supplemented by the increasingly active role of majority party leaders, were incapable of producing legislation, the president and Congress had to find another way; the costs of failing to reach an agreement on budget issues were just too high, especially after Gramm-Rudman with its automatic spending cuts went into effect in the mid-1980s. The new device was the summit, relatively formal negotiations between congressional leaders and high-ranking administration officials representing the president directly. Because summits take place only when the stakes are very high, congressional party leaders have always represented their members in such talks; members are not willing to rely on committee leaders to make such decisions on behalf of the party membership as a whole.

Actually, the first instance of major legislation emerging from a process similar in some respects to the summits of the late 1980s and 1990s was the 1980 (FY 1981) budget resolution during the Carter administration. The announcement on February 22, 1980, that the consumer price index had increased at an 18 percent annual rate in January created a crisis atmosphere. In early March an unprecedented series of meetings between the Carter administration and the Democratic congressional leadership took place for the purpose of discussing budget cuts. The budget resolution approved by Congress closely followed the agreement that had been reached in those meetings (Sinclair 1983).

In the mid-1980s attempts at summit negotiations were made several times but with limited success. The 1983 deal to reestablish the fiscal soundness of the social security system emerged from a process that shows some similarities to the summits as well (Gilmour 1990, 248–250). A commission had been appointed to develop a solution, but the deal was really worked out behind the scenes by a few commission members who directly spoke for President Reagan and Speaker O'Neill.

During the 100th and 101st Congresses (1987–90), four summits took place. Three concerned budget issues. In the fall of 1987, the stock market crashed; in response, Reagan administration officials met with the congressional leadership and worked out a deal that shaped the 1987 reconciliation bill and the full-year continuing resolution. The deal also determined the major outlines of the following year's budget resolution (FY 1989). In the spring of 1989, the new Bush administration and the congressional leadership worked out a more modest deal to avert Gramm-Rudman across-the-board cuts; this agreement shaped the 1989 (FY 1990) budget resolution and the 1989 reconciliation bill, though it by no means settled all the major issues, especially on reconciliation. The need for action and the inability of normal processes to produce agreement again led to a summit on budget issues in 1990. The highly intense issue of aid to the Nicaraguan contras was the subject of the fourth summit. In 1989 the Democratic leadership met with Bush administration representatives to work out a final agreement on contra aid. (For details on these cases, see Sinclair 1995.)

An emergency and severe time pressure may create the conditions for a summit as they did in 1980, but usually when the congressional majority and the president are of the same party, normal processes supplemented by informal consultation and negotiations will suffice. Thus, there were no summits during the 103rd Congress. Normal processes are more likely to fail when policy and electoral goals are in conflict, as they tend to be under divided government when the presidency is controlled by one party and the Congress by another.

The Evolution of Unorthodox Lawmaking: A Summary

In this chapter I have sketched the story of how changes in internal structure and in the political environment created problems for and presented opportunities to members of Congress—as individuals and collectively—and how members' responses led to modifications and innovations in the legislative process. Changes in the internal distribution of influence in both the House and Senate provided opportunities to individual members to participate more fully in the legislative process. However, the high rate of activity and the uncertainty that resulted from members taking advantage of their new opportunities created problems for the chambers and their majority parties; legislating became more difficult. The adverse political climate of the 1980s exacerbated the problems of legislating, especially for congressional Democrats, who were the majority party in the House throughout the 1980s and early 1990s. Party leaders, responding to their members' demands for legislative success, sought ways of coping with the problems. They began to use omnibus legislation more frequently; summits were developed as a last resort means of reaching agreements between Congress and the president. In the House party leaders involved themselves in the legislative process on major legislation earlier and more deeply, often negotiating compromises after the committee or committees had reported legislation so as to ensure the legislation's passage on the floor. Special rules from the Rules Committee were developed into powerful tools for controlling floor consideration and sometimes for shaping floor outcomes. The Senate, in contrast, failed to develop ways of coping effectively with the problems created by internal reforms and the political environment. The enormous opportunities for influence that full use of the Senate's rules gave each senator were just too valuable to senators as individuals; senators were unwilling to curtail their power. Senate leaders also increased their involvement in the legislative process, seeking to put together deals that made legislation passable; but they did so without enhanced tools or resources. Consequently, legislating remains problematical in the Senate.

Unorthodox Lawmaking in the 104th Congress

The 1994 elections brought enormous and unexpected political change to the Congress, especially to the House of Representatives. Republicans won majorities in both chambers, taking control of the House for the first time in forty years by picking up fifty-three seats. During the campaign, House Republicans had promised to change the way

Congress works were the voters to give them control. In fact, the rules changes that constitute the reforms of the 1970s were in many cases changes in Democratic party rules, not changes in the rules of the House itself. Much of the weakening of committees and their chairs and the strengthening of the party leadership was the result of new Democratic Caucus rules concerning committee assignments and the designation of committee and subcommittee chairs.

One might thus expect that a change in party control would have brought with it major alterations in how the House functions. Yet the data on special procedures and practices presented in this chapter tend to show continuity and sometimes even an acceleration in existing trends rather than a change in direction. An analysis of why this is so illuminates the relationship between the congressional process and the broader political process in which it is embedded.

On the first day of the 104th Congress, House Republicans did, in fact, make some significant changes in House rules. Modest though not inconsequential committee jurisdiction reform was accomplished by shifting some of the Energy and Commerce Committee's immense jurisdiction to other committees and by eliminating three committees (Post Office and Civil Service, Merchant Marine and Fisheries, and District of Columbia). Republicans were able to accomplish the politically difficult task of abolishing committees by restricting themselves to committees with mostly Democratic constituencies. Committee staffs were cut by a third, another task made easier by the change in control; Democratic committee leaders had the big staffs, and these were the people let go.

Committee chairs were given control over the entire majority staff of the committee; subcommittee chairs no longer had the authority to hire one staffer on their own. New Republican party rules gave committee chairs more control over the choice of subcommittee chairs and over the assignment of members to subcommittees. These new rules that tended to strengthen committee chairs were, however, more than counterbalanced by new rules tending to weaken them. By House rule, committee chairs were subjected to a limit of three terms; proxy votes, which absent committee members could give to any other committee member to cast for them but most often gave to the chair, were banned; and sunshine rules were modestly strengthened, making it harder to close a committee meeting.

During the 1980s and early 1990s, House Republicans had in many instances imitated House Democrats by adopting rules that decreased the autonomy of their committee leaders and strengthened their party leadership. Their committee leaders (ranking minority members when the party was in the minority, committee chairs when Republicans became the majority), after being nominated by the Committee on Committees, were made subject to a secret ballot ratification vote in the Republican Conference, the organization of all House Republicans; the Republicans' top leader had been given the power to nominate Republican members of Rules and more say on the party committee that makes committee assignments.

Political circumstances, not rules changes, made Newt Gingrich a powerful Speaker. Gingrich, in the eyes of most Republicans and the media, was the miracle maker; he was seen as responsible for the unexpected Republican victory in 1994. Gingrich had worked and schemed to build a majority for many years (Connelly and Pitney 1994); he had recruited many of the House challengers who won and had helped them with fund raising and campaign advice. The Contract with America was Gingrich's idea, and he had orchestrated its realization.

Consequently, the election results gave Gingrich enormous prestige. They also provided him with a membership that was ideologically homogeneous and determined to enact major policy change. The huge freshman class—seventy-three strong—consisted largely of true believers, deeply committed to cutting the size and scope of government and to balancing the budget; with the sophomores, who were very similar in outlook, they made up over half of the Republican House membership. These members and a considerable number of more senior Republicans believed themselves to be mandated to make such policy change. Even moderate Republicans strongly agreed that, for the party to maintain its majority, Republicans had to deliver on their promises in the Contract.

The combination of an extraordinarily ambitious agenda, a new majority united behind the agenda, and a leader with enormous stature made the exercise of strong leadership both necessary and possible. Without strong central direction, passing the agenda would have been impossible. Without a membership united in its commitment to swift and drastic policy change, no Speaker could have exercised such strong, central direction of the legislative process.

Relying on his immense prestige with House Republicans, Gingrich, in the days after the 1994 elections, exercised power well beyond that specified in Republican Conference rules. He designated Republicans to serve as committee chairs, bypassing seniority in several instances. According to the rules, the party committee on committees nominates chairs and the Conference approves them. Gingrich preempted that process, assuming correctly that his stature would prevent anyone from challenging his choices. Gingrich did not, however, bypass moderate Republicans; he selected chairs for energy, aggressiveness, and media savvy—not for ideology. He also engineered a rules change to increase the party leadership's voice on the committee on committees and used that new influence to reward junior Republicans who were his strongest supporters with choice assignments.

The 104th Congress, especially in 1995, saw enormous party leadership involvement and oversight on major legislation; committee leaders were clearly subordinate to party leaders on Contract with America bills and on much of the major legislation that went into the Republicans' attempt to balance the budget (see Chapter 11). Because most senior Republicans had signed the Contract, Gingrich had a strong tool for persuading committee leaders to report legislation without making major changes and to do so quickly; the new Republican chairs did not all agree with all elements of the Contract, and most would have liked more time to work on their bills, to take care of substantive problems, and to put their own stamp on them. The Republicans' leadership reminded them: "We promised to do it in 100 days; we must deliver." In early 1995, and later when balancing the budget was at issue, the chairs knew that the leadership was backed up by the freshmen's strong support.

The attempt to deliver on the ambitious promises House Republicans had made took the full set of procedural tools available to the majority party leadership. The need for speed and flexibility, and occasionally the political delicacy of the issues involved, dictated that the leaders sometimes bypass committee. The leadership made extensive use of member task forces on legislative issues ranging from agriculture policy to gun control to immigration reform. By and large, committees were not bypassed on the issues task forces worked on, but the task forces did have the purpose and the effect of keeping the pressure on committees to report legislation satisfactory to the party majority and in a timely fashion.

Even though political circumstances made committee leaders unusually responsive to the wishes of the party leadership and the party membership, party leaders frequently found it necessary to make postcommittee adjustments in legislation. Multiple referral, the need for speed, and the ambitiousness of the agenda all contributed to producing circumstances where the legislation as reported had to be altered in order to engineer passage in a form that would accomplish the party's objectives.

As developed by Democratic leaders in the 1980s and early 1990s, special rules had become powerful and flexible tools of the leadership. Given the task Republicans had set themselves, their leaders could hardly eschew using restrictive rules, despite their preelection promise to do so. In working to pass their ambitious agenda, House Republican leaders continued the trend toward creative use of restrictive rules.

If passing the Republicans' agenda in the majority-rule House was a big task, getting it through the Senate was an even more difficult, and sometimes impossible, endeavor. Having had the filibuster wielded against them so effectively in the previous Congress, Democrats made full use of their prerogatives under Senate rules; major legislation frequently encountered extended debate–related problems.

Senate Republicans had not signed the Contract with America, but the House's actions put great pressure on the Senate to follow suit; clearly the media would judge Republicans by their success in getting the Contract, and then the balanced budget legislation, through both houses. Furthermore, the Senate majority leader was running for president and touting his ability to get things done. Senate Republicans, Bob Dole especially, had a stake in passing the legislation. In their attempt to do so, the Republicans, with Dole often playing the lead role, used all the special procedures available to them; committees were frequently bypassed, and great effort went into postcommittee adjustments to bills in the attempt to craft legislation that could amass the sixty votes Senate passage usually requires. The tools available to Senate leaders often proved insufficient, and much of the Contract legislation died in the Senate.

Republicans could get their agenda through the House and sometimes even through the Senate without worrying about President Clinton. Enacting their bills into law was a different matter altogether. As Democrats had when facing a hostile Republican president, Republicans made use of omnibus bills to try to force the president to accept provisions he disliked by linking them to must-pass legislation or to provisions he favored. On the critical budget legislation in the 104th Congress that strategy failed (see Chapter 11). The Republican leadership and the president then resorted to a summit.

The change in party control of Congress as a result of the 1994 elections did not disrupt the trend toward unorthodox lawmaking for two reasons. First, key conditions did not change: internal rules were not altered very much (certainly strong, autonomous committees were not resurrected); the budget process continued to dominate congressional decision making; and the congressional majority faced a hostile opposition-party president. Second, the trend toward more frequent employment of these special procedures and practices continued because, whatever their origins, they have become flexible tools useful to members and leaders under a variety of circumstances.

c h a p t e r   s e v e n

National Service Legislation: (Mildly) Unorthodox Lawmaking

THE LEGISLATIVE PROCESS IN THE CONTEMPORARY Congress is better conceptualized as plural rather than singular; there are now many paths from introduction of a bill to enactment. This chapter and the next two illustrate some of the variety through case studies of the 1993 national service bill, regulatory reform legislation in 1995, and an omnibus drug bill in 1988. The process in these three cases ranges from mildly to extraordinarily unorthodox. The process by which national service became law in 1993 is similar in many respects to the old standard process, though with some unorthodox elements; the legislative process on the regulatory overhaul bills in 1995 was much less like the "textbook" process; the 1988 drug bill became law through a radically unorthodox "designer" process. Examining the process on specific legislation also illuminates how and when the various special procedures and practices are employed and with what effects. Often leaders use those under their control to solve political problems, sometimes problems created by individual members' exploitation of those that they control.

Why National Service? Origins and Prospects

A national service program under which young people would perform needed services in communities across the nation and, in return, receive financial assistance for their education was a central element of newly elected President Bill Clinton's agenda in 1993. He had highlighted it during the 1992 campaign; in a press conference the day after the election, he listed it as one of his priorities along with health care and economic recovery. He called for a "season of service" in his inaugural address, and, in his first address to a joint session of Congress on February 17, 1993, he urged the program's swift enactment.

As Clinton and his advisors saw it, a correctly structured national service program could accomplish several important objectives beyond the obvious. Needed services of all sorts—from teaching children to refurbishing parkland to bringing meals to shut-in senior citizens—would get performed. Young people would earn needed financial aid for college. In addition, however, Clinton and other national service advocates in the administration believed the program could give young people from all parts of American society the opportunity to work with and get to know each other, thus fostering understanding across racial and class divides and, like the Peace Corps, foster in these young people an ethic of service (Waldman 1995, 24–29, passim).

On April 30, 1993, the Clinton administration unveiled its bill, and on May 6 it was introduced in both houses of Congress. Passing the legislation was clearly important to the new administration and to the majority congressional Democrats, who after twelve years of divided control needed to show they could govern. Democratic party leaders did not expect any real problems; the idea of national service was broadly popular, and the bill neatly fit into the jurisdiction of only one committee in each house, making for a simpler process than on much major legislation. Passing the legislation, however, proved to be a more complicated undertaking than its supporters anticipated; the zero-sum budget game that big deficits had induced pitted popular programs against each other for funding, and the highly partisan climate encouraged Republicans to oppose the program so as to deprive the Clinton administration of a victory.

Committee Action

After a day of hearings held jointly by the Subcommittee on Select Education and Civil Rights and the Subcommittee on Human Resources of the House Education and Labor Committee, the full committee met to mark up the legislation. There it ran into a blizzard of Republican amendments. Attempting to split Democratic support, Republicans argued that money for the new program would come at the expense of other education programs such as Pell grants and work study; since eligibility for the latter but not the former was based on need, the result would be switching funds from poor to middle-class students. This was an argument that resonated with the liberal Democrats who make up much of the Democratic membership of the Education and Labor Committee. Thus, the biggest test came on an amendment by Rep. Bill Goodling, R-Pa., the committee's ranking minority member, to means-test national service; under the amendment only the financially needy could receive the educational awards. The administration strongly opposed the amendment because it would negate one of the major goals of the program. With committee chairman William Ford, D-Mich., George Miller, D-Calif., another influential liberal on the committee, and the administration working against it, the Goodling amendment was defeated on a 12–29 vote.

On June 16, 1993, after a single day of markup, the Education and Labor Committee reported the bill, HR2010, by a voice vote. The Republican attacks, however, had put supporters on notice that this legislation would not get a free ride on the House floor.

The Senate Labor and Human Resources Committee also marked up the legislation on June 16. Sen. Nancy Landon Kassebaum of Kansas, ranking minority member of the committee, attacked the program, saying it took away resources from other education programs. Still the bill was reported out on a 14–3 vote; Sen. Orrin G. Hatch, R-Utah, and Sen. Strom Thurmond, R-S.C., voted with Kassebaum, but a number of other conservative Republicans supported the bill.

The Special Rule and House Floor Action

In the House the next step toward passage was obtaining a rule for floor consideration. Although the national service bill was important legislation (as its swift movement through committee indicated), it had to compete for floor time with other major legislation, including the must-pass appropriations bills. On June 29, 1993, the Rules Committee granted a rule for general debate only; the next day a Rules Committee member announced on the floor that the rule regulating amending activity would require amendments to be printed in the *Congressional Record* at least a day before they were offered.

General debate on national service took place on July 13. By a 239–159 vote, the House adopted the rule; Democrats supported the rule unanimously, all but three Republicans voted against it. Despite the generous three hours of general debate the rule provided, Republicans complained about the separation of general debate and the amending process, about the preprinting requirement the second rule would impose, and about the bill itself.

On July 14 the Rules Committee on a party-line vote reported out the rule governing the amending process. It stipulated that, to be in order, an amendment had to be printed in the *Congressional Record* by July 20. Thus, members had been given three weeks altogether to prepare their amendments. Nevertheless, when the rule came to a vote on July 21, most Republicans voted against it; it passed on a 261–164 vote.

The decision on the character of the special rule has become an important part of legislative strategy. Legislation in this issue domain has traditionally been considered under an open rule. Neither the substance nor the politics of this particular bill justified a truly restrictive rule; it was certainly not in enough political trouble to warrant such a move. The Rules Committee and the party leadership, however, could and did help the bill's supporters by requiring the preprinting of amendments. Supporters thus could plan their strategy without worrying about an unanticipated amendment that might wreak havoc with the bill. Eventually, eighteen amendments would be introduced. The rule also specified that Chairman Ford could offer a group of amendments that would be voted on as a package.

Chairman Ford offered his "nondivisible en bloc amendments," and after a short debate they were adopted on a voice vote. Included were some modifications he had worked out with members of the committee minority and a number of the amendments proposed by House members not on the committee. By rolling these noncontroversial changes into a package, Ford saved floor time and bolstered support for the bill; the members whose amendments were incorporated in the bill had, as a result, an added incentive to support the legislation.

Republicans' arguments that the program would consist of "make work" and that it would add to the bureaucracy did not worry supporters. Some Republicans, however, focused on the contention that the program took from the poor to give to the better off. Rep. Dick Armey of Texas called it "a welfare program for the aspiring yuppies of America," and Representative Goodling intoned, "Immoral is the only term I can use, because it is Robin Hood in reverse" (Waldman 1995, 187–188). This argument could split the Democratic coalition. On the floor the supporters of the bill countered by pointing out the benefits that diversity in the program could yield.

The most important work, however, had already been done. Because they knew which amendments would be offered, supporters—including the White House—had been able to mount an effective information and persuasion effort before the bill hit the floor. As an important part of their campaign to pass the bill, the White House and congressional proponents made sure that members were aware of the broad range of groups that supported it; the informational packets they distributed included letters of endorsement from the National Governors Association, the Girl Scouts, police and firefighters unions, major companies such as Dow Chemical and Ford Motor Company, and the Red Cross (headed by Elizabeth Dole, the wife of bill opponent Bob Dole of Kansas, the Senate's minority leader at the time). Most persuasive with liberals, who were a special target, was a letter from Marian Wright Edelman, the highly respected head of the Children's Defense Fund, a liberal advocacy group; she endorsed the program without means testing.

Amendments identical to those advocated by Republicans in committee—for means testing and for fully funding other education programs first—were defeated on largely party-line votes. Other Republican amendments were defeated or amended to make them acceptable to the bill's supporters. One amendment passed over supporters' objections, but it was of a technical nature and relatively minor.

One Republican amendment confronted supporters with a serious problem. Arguing that those who defended the country and perhaps risked their lives doing so deserved more than civilian volunteers, Rep. Bob Stump, R-Ariz., proposed reducing the education benefit to 80 percent of that provided by the GI bill. The ranking minority member of the Veterans' Affairs Committee further argued that equal benefits would make recruiting for the all-volunteer army much harder.

The administration adamantly opposed the Stump amendment. Clinton had already compromised on the size of the educational benefit. A whip count, however, persuaded the Democratic leadership that the Stump amendment could not be defeated on an up-or-down vote. The veterans' groups that supported Stump were too powerful a lobby. An administration proposal to compromise on 95 percent would also not fly, Majority Whip David Bonior, D-Mich., determined; a more significant compromise would have to be made.

By July 28, when the House returned to consideration of national service, a deal had been worked out. Working through G. V. "Sonny" Montgomery of Mississippi, the Democratic chairman of the Veterans' Affairs Committee, Ford had gotten Stump to agree to 90 percent. As Ford said on the floor:

> I am pleased to have had the help of the chairman of the Committee on Veterans' Affairs and the ranking member of the Committee on Veterans' Affairs who are working with us to try to resolve this matter in a satisfactory way. I understand that language has been worked out and is at the desk [at the front of the House chamber], and I am prepared to accept the language that was worked out and is at the desk.
>
> Mr. Chairman, if the gentleman will ask for unanimous consent to modify his amendment by the language at the desk, we will accept the gentleman's amendment (*Congressional Record*, July 28, 1993, H5392).

The Stump amendment as modified was accepted by voice vote.

Later the same day the House passed the bill. Members had cast eleven recorded votes on amendments and had decided a number of others by voice votes. After rejecting Goodling's motion to recommit the bill by voice, the House voted for passage 275–152; twenty-six Republicans supported it, five Democrats voted against it. The result was a victory for the administration and for House Democrats, especially for Education and Labor Committee Democrats and the party leadership. They had passed a major Clinton initiative largely intact.

Senate Floor Action

On July 15, 1993, the Senate agreed by unanimous consent to take up S919, the national service bill reported a month earlier by the Labor and Human Resources Committee, immediately after disposing of a bill to revise the Hatch Act, and on July 20 debate began. As in the House, opponents argued that the new program would take money away from existing education programs. Sen. Pete V. Domenici, R-N.M., offered an amendment requiring full funding for a number of existing programs before national service could receive any funds; it was tabled and thus killed on a largely party-line vote of 55–44. Senator Kassebaum offered two amendments altering and scaling back the program; both were rejected on near party-line votes.

On July 22 debate took an unexpected and dramatic turn when Sen. Jesse Helms, R-N.C., offered an amendment to extend a congressional design patent for the insignia of the United Daughters of the Confederacy; the insignia included the Confederate flag. Even though the amendment had absolutely nothing to do with national service, it was in order because Senate rules do not require amendments to most legislation to be germane. Carol Moseley-Braun, D-Ill., the Senate's only African-American, moved to table the Helms amendment, but her motion failed on a 48–52 vote, with twelve Democrats joining all but four Republicans in voting against her. Vowing to filibuster "until this room freezes over" to reverse the vote, Senator Moseley-Braun gave a passionate speech:

> The issue is whether or not Americans such as myself who believe in the promise of this country . . . will have to suffer the indignity of being reminded time and time again that at one point in this country's history we were human chattel. . . . We were property. We could be traded, bought and sold. [The Confederate flag] is something that has no place in our modern times . . . no place in this body . . . no place in our society" (quoted from Zuckman 1993, 1960).

Other senators rose to support Moseley-Braun. When Sen. Howell

Heflin, D-Ala., said he would switch his vote, it was clear the tide had turned. A conservative southerner whose ancestors had fought for the Confederacy, Heflin made clear that he would not knowingly contribute to divisions between the races. By a 76–24 vote, the Senate agreed to reconsider its initial vote and then voted 75 to 25 to table and thus kill the Helms amendment. The Senate then returned to debating national service and voted down several more Republican amendments.

On the same day, July 22, Senate Republicans decided to filibuster national service (Waldman 1995, 201–203). They clearly lacked the votes to change the legislation significantly via amendments, but by their attacks they had made the legislation sufficiently vulnerable, they believed, to maintain a filibuster. The word quickly spread; senators continued to debate and to attempt to amend the bill, but everyone knew a filibuster was on. That evening Majority Leader George Mitchell, D-Maine, and Minority Leader Dole put the situation on the record with this exchange:

> Mitchell: I would like, if I might at this moment, to inquire of the Republican leader whether under the circumstances we will be permitted to get a final vote on the bill or whether under the current circumstances it will be necessary for us to file a cloture motion to terminate debate.

> Dole: I think if I were majority leader, I would suggest maybe filing a cloture motion (*Congressional Record*, quoted from Waldman 1995, 212).

Mitchell filed a cloture petition that night.

Mitchell pulled the bill off the floor and negotiations began. Republicans said they were most concerned about the program's costs; the original bill authorized $394 million in fiscal 1994 and unspecified sums for the next four years. Labor Committee chair Edward M. Kennedy, D-Mass., offered to decrease the authorization to three years, to scale back the fiscal year 1994 authorization to $300 million, and to specify figures for the two subsequent years—$500 million for fiscal year 1995 and $700 million for fiscal year 1996. Republicans responded that a two-year authorization was the maximum they would support. The administration called that unacceptable, pointing out that, given a six-month start-up period, a two-year authorization would make it impossible to guarantee participants their full two years of service. On July 26 Mitchell filed a second cloture motion on the bill, and on July 28 he filed two motions to invoke cloture on the Kennedy substitute amendment.

Continuing negotiations could not break the impasse, and on July 29 Mitchell moved to close debate on the Kennedy substitute amendment. The motion failed on a 59–41 vote; only three Republicans had joined all

the Democrats in voting to cut off debate, leaving national service supporters one vote short.[1]

Senate Republicans had won the battle but their cohesion was getting
shaky. Moderate Republicans were under increasing pressure to defect.
The Kennedy substitute had alleviated many of the concerns on which
they had based their opposition. The blocking of national service had
become a big news story, and Republicans were being blamed. The White
House had worked hard to persuade the media to pay attention and to
adopt their spin (Waldman 1995, 214–215, 223–225). Headlines such as
"Petty Politics on National Service" and "Senate GOP Stalls National Service Bill" began to appear. After cloture failed, moderate Republicans who
had voted to support the filibuster found themselves under direct press
attack at home. The largest paper in Oregon headlined an editorial "Oregon's Obstinate Obstructionists: Hatfield and Packwood Engage in Filibuster Abuse." The *Philadelphia Inquirer* wrote, "Sen. Arlen Specter chose
his party over his principles yesterday" (Waldman 1995, 237–238). Knowing he no longer had the votes to maintain the filibuster, Dole met with
Mitchell and agreed on a unanimous consent agreement for bringing the
bill to a vote.

On July 30 Mitchell presented the unanimous consent agreement to
the Senate. It specified that consideration of S919 would resume immediately (interrupting consideration of an appropriations bill), that the listed
amendments be the only first degree amendments in order, and that at 10
a.m. on Tuesday, August 3, the Senate vote on passage. Dole rose to
endorse the agreement, saying:

> I think we have a satisfactory arrangement. Let me just make the record
> clear, we did not have the votes to prevent cloture. We had five of our col-
> leagues who would have voted for cloture today, and we would have been one
> vote short. . . . I still hope before they finish the debate this afternoon there
> can be some adjustment on funding (*Congressional Record*, July 30, 1993,
> S9938).

Although the unanimous consent agreement made fifteen amendments—and amendments to them—in order, only three were pushed to
a roll call, and all were defeated. On August 3 the bill as modified by the
Kennedy substitute passed the Senate 58–41; fifty-one Democrats and

---

1. Under normal procedures the vote would have occurred on July 30 because the
rules require a day to elapse between the day the cloture petition is filed and the
day of the vote. However, reflecting the curious combination of conflict and
accommodation that characterizes the contemporary Senate, Mitchell asked and
received unanimous consent for the vote to take place on July 29.

seven Republicans voted in favor, thirty-seven Republicans and four Democrats opposed the bill.

The Final Steps

Congressional Democrats rushed the bill to conference hoping to finish the process before the summer recess scheduled to begin at the end of the week. Although the legislation had been considered by only one committee in each chamber, Senate conferees were appointed from two committees: sixteen from the Committee on Labor and Human Resources and three from the Committee on Governmental Affairs. The thirty House conferees were appointed from six committees. Amendments to the legislation had extended its scope.

Despite the conference committee's relatively large size and diverse makeup, agreement was quickly reached. The Senate's three-year $1.5 billion framework was kept; supporters feared another filibuster were they to move appreciably toward the House's higher funding level. Informal negotiations preceded the formal meeting of the conference committee, so the formal meeting on August 5 required only about fifteen minutes.

The House approved the conference report the next day on a 275–152 vote. Time ran out on the Senate; it was not until September 8 after the recess that the Senate voted 57–40 to adopt the conference report. The president signed into law the National Service Trust Act of 1993 on September 21, a little less than five months after he unveiled his bill. (See Table 7.1 for a chronology of House, Senate, and postpassage action.)

The Legislative Process on National Service Legislation: A Little Bit Unorthodox

The legislative process by which the national service bill became law differed from the textbook process only moderately. The legislation had high priority for the president and the Democratic leadership. Since it was basically a widely popular idea and it fell into the jurisdiction of only one committee in each chamber, no big problems were expected. The leaders saw no need to come up with a special legislative process to ensure the bill's passage.

By and large, the special procedures the leaders employed were responses to problems that arose as the bill made its way through the chambers. In the House postcommittee adjustments were made to facili-

TABLE 7.1   National Service Trust Act of 1993: A Chronology

Date	House Action	Date	Senate Action	Date	Postpassage Action
		Clinton administration unveils its bill on April 30, 1993.			
5/6	HR2010 introduced in the House; referred to the Committee on Education and Labor.	5/6	S919 introduced in the Senate; referred to the Committee on Labor and Human Resources.		
5/19, 5/20, 5/25	Committee and its subcommittees hold hearings.	5/11, 5/18, 6/8	Committee and its subcommittees hold hearings.		
6/16	Education and Labor Committee marks up HR2010 and orders it reported.	6/16	Committee on Labor and Human Resources marks up S919 and orders it reported.		
6/29	Rules Committee holds hearing and grants rule for general debate only.				
7/13	House approves rule and completes general debate.				
7/14	Rules Committee grants modified open rule for further consideration; requires preprinting of amendments.	7/15	Senate agrees by unanimous consent to take up S919 on July 20.		
7/21	House approves second rule and begins amending process. Chairman Ford offers modified en bloc amendments, and they are approved. The amending process proceeds; *Democratic leaders realize they cannot defeat the Stump amendment.* Leadership pulls bill from floor.	7/20	Senate begins consideration of S919.		
		7/22	Helms offers nongermane amendment; Moseley-Braun moves to table amendment but Senate rejects motion. Moseley-Braun threatens to filibuster; Senate reverses itself and votes to table (and thus kill) the Helms amendment. *Republicans decide to filibuster S919.* Mitchell files cloture petition and pulls bill from Senate floor.		
	Negotiations continue over the Stump amendment.				

7/28	HR2010 again considered on the House floor. Stump modified amendment (compromise version of the Stump amendment) agreed to by voice vote. House passes measure as amended.

	Negotiations begin; Kennedy proposes a compromise version.
7/26	Mitchell files a second cloture petition.
7/28	Senate resumes consideration of S919. Kennedy offers his compromise as an amendment. Mitchell files two cloture petitions to close debate on the Kennedy amendment.
7/29	Senate votes on motion to close debate on the Kennedy amendment; the motion fails 59–41.
	Mitchell and Dole negotiate.
7/30	Senate accepts Mitchell's unanimous consent request (which he negotiated with Dole) for consideration of S919.
8/3	Senate passes bill as modified by the Kennedy amendment.

8/3	Senate conferees named.
8/4	House conferees named.
8/5	Conferees agree to file conference report.
8/6	House agrees to conference report.
9/8	Senate agrees to conference report.
9/21	President signs bill, and the National Service Trust Act of 1993 becomes law.

NOTE: Official actions are in roman type; behind-the-scenes, unofficial actions are in italics.

tate passage; the committee chairman built some added support by offering a number of amendments as a package on the floor, a tactic made possible by the rule. A more major change was the compromise version of the Stump amendment, which the leadership determined had to be accepted for the bill to pass without greater change.

In the Senate that body's unique rules, and senators' willingness to exploit them fully, left their mark on the process and on the resulting legislation. The nongermane Helms amendment had the potential to derail the bill had the vote approving it not been reversed. The majority party was forced to make significant postcommittee concessions because it could not muster sixty votes to overcome a Republican filibuster of the original bill. Although the Republican leadership tried, after Senator Kennedy's compromise was offered, the minority party could not maintain its filibuster; under pressure from the press in their home states, moderate Republicans broke ranks, and the compromise was approved. Public opinion, actual and anticipated, influences senators' willingness to use extended debate to hold up specific legislation.

Senate rules and practices influenced conference deliberations as well. Because supporters feared another filibuster, the conference agreement simply incorporated the concessions that Senate supporters had made in the Kennedy substitute.

Regulatory Overhaul:
The Pitfalls of Unorthodox
Lawmaking

THE JOB CREATION AND WAGE ENHANCEMENT ACT of 1995, a component of the Republicans' Contract with America, was introduced in the House on January 4, the first day of the 104th Congress, and assigned the number HR9 to signify its priority status. Ambitious and far-reaching legislation, it proposed vast changes in the federal regulatory process, compensation for private property owners whose property had been reduced in value by federal government action, and major tax cuts, most prominently a 50 percent reduction in the capital gains tax rate.

Referral and Committee Action in the House

The bill's broad scope dictated a complex pattern of committee referral. Eight House committees received a part of the bill, in some cases exclusively, in others in concert with other committees. For example, the revenue sections—Titles I and II—were referred exclusively to the Ways and Means Committee. (They were eventually reported out as HR1215 and never rejoined with the rest of the bill, which we follow here.) Title III, Risk Assessment and Cost-Benefit Analysis for New Regulations, was referred to three committees—Science, Commerce, and Government Reform and Oversight, with Science designated as the lead committee. The Judiciary Committee received the property rights section by itself and several other titles in concert with other committees.

During the 1994 campaign, House Republicans had promised to bring all the items in the Contract to a floor vote within the first 100 days of the 104th Congress. Under pressure from their party leadership and the Republican membership to meet scheduling targets, the new Republican committee chairs quickly pushed the legislation through their committees. Despite the complexity and importance of the legislation, only minimal hearings were held, and the markups were so rushed that effective participation was difficult for minority party members. Democrats complained bitterly about the process on the risk assessment provisions. "This is a bill which makes extremely far-reaching changes in the Federal regulatory process. Yet the Science Committee, which has principal jurisdiction over the bill, dispensed with subcommittee hearings and markup entirely, and held just 2 days of hearings at the full committee level," Rep. George E. Brown Jr. of California, ranking minority member of the committee, objected. "Initially, the chairman proposed a single day of full committee hearings, to be composed of a single panel of witnesses sympathetic to the bill. Administration requests to testify were rejected until we were forced to ask for a second day of hearings, as provided by the House rules, to ensure a more balanced hearing process" (*Congressional Record,* February 27, 1995, H2235). "In the Science Committee markup of this bill, members were not given the bill text until an hour after the markup was scheduled to start," another committee Democrat protested. "Members were then given less than 2 hours to redraft their amendments to a bill that bore little resemblance to the original draft of title III of HR9. We then spent the ensuing 10 hours marking up title III, at the same time that the Commerce Committee was marking up the same title" (*Congressional Record,* February 27, 1995, H2235).

According to Democrats, the process in the other committees of jurisdiction was no more deliberative or fair. "Commerce also dispensed with subcommittees hearings and markup, and held just 2 days of hearings at the full committee level. The committee began markup 5 days after the hearings, without giving minority members a copy of the markup vehicle until the day before they began amending the bill. That left members on that committee, as well, without sufficient opportunity to prepare amendments" (*Congressional Record,* February 27, 1995, H2235).

When Democrats complained about the pace of action on the private property provisions in the Judiciary Committee, Chairman Henry J. Hyde, R-Ill., made it clear that, on the schedule at least, the party leadership was calling the shots. "I'm the subchairman of the committee," Hyde said (Benenson 1995b, 520).

On February 8, 1995, both the Commerce Committee and the Science Committee approved their versions of risk assessment legislation. The bills would require federal agencies to perform highly detailed scientific analyses of the risks addressed by proposed health, safety, and environmental regulations; the risks would have to justify the costs imposed on the private sector by the regulations (Benenson 1995a, 450). Commerce approved the legislation on a 26–16 vote; Science approved its version on a voice vote that belied Democrats' considerable dissatisfaction with the substance of the bill as well as the process by which it was considered.

On February 16 the Judiciary Committee approved HR925 to compensate owners when federal government actions have reduced the value of their property by 10 percent or more. Conservatives for a number of years had contended that when federal environmental law reduced the value of private property—by, for example, barring development in a wetlands area or mandating preservation of an endangered species' habitat, this constituted an illegal "taking" under the Fifth Amendment to the Constitution, which prohibits the government from taking private property for public purposes "without just compensation." Drafted by the chairman of the Constitution Subcommittee, Charles T. Canady, R-Fla., based on the "takings" provisions in the Contract and HR9, HR925 initially specified that the loss in value would have to be one-third or more. Canady had increased the threshold from 10 to 33 1/3 percent to increase the bill's chances of passage, but the full committee reversed him and restored the 10 percent threshold that the Contract had specified.

On the same day, February 16, Judiciary approved HR926, which would require federal agencies "to undertake an elaborate analysis and reporting process to prove that the benefits derived from proposed regulation outweighed the costs the rule would impose on individuals and society" (Benenson 1995b, 521). The day before the Small Business Committee had approved similar legislation for small businesses.

The administration opposed the legislation but had little influence on its course in the House. Officials testified that the regulatory reform provisions were unworkable and would gridlock the regulatory system. Republicans were in no mood to pay attention. "It's your credibility that doesn't exist anymore," freshman Brian P. Bilbray, R-Calif., told administration officials at a hearing. "The people are saying that rather than the government doing something for me, it's doing something to me" (Kriz 1995, 419).

Interest groups played a substantially greater role in the process. Because the new Republican majority and business groups strongly agreed on regulatory overhaul issues, Republicans gave such groups unusually intimate access to the legislative process at the pre-floor stage, even allowing lobbyists to draft provisions of the legislation. After the 1994 elections, Rep. Tom DeLay, R-Texas, had founded Project Relief, a coalition of over 300 business groups and other interests dedicated to rolling back what they regarded as burdensome federal regulations. As majority whip, DeLay worked with the coalition extensively. Every Thursday morning Rep. John A. Boehner of Ohio, chair of the Republican Conference, met with a large group of lobbyists, including representatives of Project Relief and of the Alliance for Reasonable Regulation, another similar coalition. The purpose of the meetings was to coordinate the groups' lobbying and grass-roots campaigns for the Contract (Drew 1996, 114–116). The wealth of the interests involved—energy, tobacco, construction, and drugs, among others—and their immense financial stake in regulatory legislation made them highly effective allies for House Republicans.

Postcommittee Adjustments in the House

Several problems faced these bills' proponents before they could take their legislation to the floor. First, the Science and Commerce committees' risk assessment provisions, while similar, were by no means identical. To increase the legislation's prospects of emerging unscathed from floor consideration and to speed up floor action, the party leadership wanted the committees to settle their differences before they went to the floor. Intense negotiations between the chairs of the two committees yielded an agreement that was introduced as HR1022 on February 23. This bill was never approved by either committee. As Rep. John D. Dingell of Michigan, ranking minority member of Commerce, complained:

> The legislation we have before us was never the subject of hearings, there has been no open discussion amongst the Members. What has happened is that the chairmen of the two committees, the gentleman from Virginia [Mr. Bliley] and the gentleman from Pennsylvania [Mr. Walker], have had a series of meetings somewhere, where they have quietly, without attention or notice to any individual, come up with changes to the bill . . . they never consulted with the members of the committee on both sides of the aisle (*Congressional Record*, February 27, 1995, H2237).

A second problem was that the "takings" legislation as reported faced formidable opposition. Some Republicans were concerned about potential unintended consequences of the legislation; by requiring the federal government to compensate owners under specified conditions, the bill seemed to be creating a new entitlement program that might cost billions. Fifteen Republicans wrote to Hyde on February 14, "We find it difficult to justify the creation of a new entitlement program whose potential costs are unknown and undeterminable" (Benenson 1995b, 520). Furthermore, Rep. W. J. "Billy" Tauzin, D-La., a prominent long-time supporter of private property protection legislation, believed HR925 was unworkable and extreme.[1] With some Republicans and natural Democratic allies like Tauzin opposed, the bill was in real trouble.

However, Tauzin, like the Republicans, wanted a bill. After Judiciary had reported the bill, he and Canady negotiated changes in the legislation that, they agreed, Tauzin would offer as an amendment on the floor. The Tauzin amendment would limit the reach of the law to regulations resulting from the Endangered Species Act, wetlands provisions of the Clean Water Act and the 1985 farm bill, and several laws pertaining to western water rights (*Congressional Record*, March 2, 1995, H2540). To alleviate concerns about creating a costly new entitlement, Canady crafted substitute language specifying that compensation payments would have to come out of the rule-making agency's regular budget. The Republican party leadership signed off on the deal and circulated a "Dear Colleague" letter expressing their support.

House Floor Action

Because of the number and complexity of the issues involved, the Republican party leadership had decided to bring the parts of HR9 to the floor as separate bills and repackage them after passage.

HR1022: Risk Assessment

On February 27 floor consideration of HR1022, the risk assessment bill, began with debate on the rule. The rule reported by the Rules Committee provided two hours of general debate "equally divided among and controlled by the chairman and ranking minority members of the Committee on Commerce and the Committee on Science" and limited time for amendments to a maximum of ten hours (*Congressional Record*, February 27, 1995, H2234).

Democrats vigorously protested the rule. Rep. Anthony C. Beilenson of California, the minority floor manager of the rule, argued:

> Mr. Speaker, we are opposed to this rule because it limits the amount of time allowed for considering amendments to the bill. . . . This is a very complex bill which many Members believe is seriously flawed, and the rule for its consideration ought to ensure that Members have an adequate amount of time to offer amendments which would improve it.
>
> Mr. Speaker, we understand the desire of the majority to have HR1022 con-

---

1. Later in the 104th Congress Representative Tauzin switched parties, becoming a Republican.

sidered in a timely manner. However, based on our experience during the last 2 weeks considering four bills which were also subject to a 10-hour limit on the amendment process, we can realistically expect that the actual amount of time spent debating amendments will be much less than 10 hours—somewhere between 6 and 8 hours. . . .

As I said, the majority's desire to have a time limit on the offering of amendments is understandable, but their insistence on including in that limit the time it takes to hold recorded votes is not (*Congressional Record,* February 27, 1995, H2235).

The rule passed on a largely party-line vote of 253 to 165; twenty-seven Democrats did vote with all Republicans in support.

Republicans argued that the current regulatory process is badly defective; as Rep. Robert S. Walker of Pennsylvania, chairman of the Science Committee, expressed it, "The fact is something has gone terribly wrong in our regulatory structure, and we need to do something about it . . . . The regulatory system in this country has become a nightmare, and we have done nothing. . . . It is time to use good science to ensure that the regulatory burden we impose on the American people provides them with the protection from real hazards, not the exaggerated risks of the zero-tolerance crowd"(*Congressional Record,* February 27, 1995, H2237). HR1022 is a responsible and effective remedy, he argued:

It is the hope of its sponsors that by its enactment the bill will usher in a new era of rationality in the imposition of regulations implementing safeguards for human health, safety and the environment.

This bill will require the use of sound science and sound economic principles to determine if there is a rational basis for imposing new and costly regulations on the American people. It will, for the first time, establish a consistent basis by which disparate laws can be measured and integrated. It will, for the first time, communicate to decision makers and the public the nature and magnitude of risks they face in an objective and unbiased way (*Congressional Record,* February 27, 1995, H2243).

The opposition, mostly Democrats, criticized both the process and the product. Representative Dingell warned, "This legislation drips unintended and unforeseen consequences. No one here knows or understands what are going to be the consequences of this legislation." He went on to blast the legislative process, calling it "careless, sloppy, slovenly, partisan and irresponsible. . . . It is done in a way which has precluded intelligent participation on the part of all the Members" (*Congressional Record,* February 27, 1995, H2237).

Another Democrat summed up opponents' arguments against the legislation:

The bill before us is an ill-considered piece of legislation that will have widespread unintended consequences and make legitimate regulation much more difficult. In its present form, it would: Set up a cumbersome and costly procedural maze which is likely to require more Federal employees and agency costs at a time we are trying to downsize the Federal bureaucracy—by imposing a whole new set of regulatory requirements on top of existing ones which are already too complex; invite massive amounts of new litigation; establish a nonscientific process of comparative-risk analysis; permit peer review panels to be dominated by scientists who have financial conflicts of interest; and impose an inflexible and unrealistic requirement that agencies certify that benefits outweigh costs before issuing final rules (*Congressional Record*, February 27, 1995, H2235).

Opponents offered a series of moderating amendments, but all were voted down; most Republicans and a group of about twenty-eight Democrats opposed such changes. Then Rep. Joe L. Barton, R-Texas, offered an amendment that would complicate the risk assessment process even further; it would allow citizens and businesses to petition federal agencies to review and possibly revoke existing regulations. Walker opposed this amendment, fearing its passage would lend credence to charges that Republicans were out to destroy all health, safety, and environmental regulations. Even so, the Barton amendment was barely defeated on a vote of 206 to 220; almost three out of four Republicans voted for it. On February 28 the House passed HR1022 on a 286–141 vote with all but two Republicans and sixty Democrats supporting it.

HR926: Cost-Benefit Analysis

Because of the tight schedule required by the Republicans' pledge to pass the Contract within the first 100 days of the 104th Congress, the House took up the rule for consideration of HR926 on the same day it passed the risk assessment bill. HR926 would require federal agencies to undertake an elaborate analysis and reporting process to prove that the benefits derived from a proposed regulation that had an annual effect on the economy of over $50 million outweighed the costs. The rule provided for ninety minutes of general debate, "with sixty minutes equally divided and controlled by the chairman and ranking minority member of the Committee on the Judiciary and thirty minutes equally divided and controlled by the chairman and ranking minority member of the Committee on Small Business" (*Congressional Record*, February 28, 1995, H2373). Although an open rule allowing all germane amendments, it did advantage those amendments that had been printed in the *Congressional Record* before consideration began. The rule stated that "during consideration of the bill for amendment, the Chairman of the Committee of the Whole may accord priority in recognition on the basis of whether the Member offering an amendment has caused it to be printed in the . . . *Congressional Record*" (*Congressional Record*, February 28, 1995, H2373). By including this "preprinting" provision, the Rules Committee could report an open rule and still help the bill's supporters; the provision, of course, encourages members to print their amendments and thus reduces uncertainty for supporters, making it easier for them to plan strategy. Because the rule did allow all germane amendments, it was not controversial and passed on a voice vote.

When the House met on March 1 to debate HR926, the arguments were similar to those on HR1022. Republicans contended that the bill was a reasonable response to an enormous problem:

> [W]e in this Congress must change the philosophy of the Federal Government to regulate every facet of our lives. Throughout our deliberations we must be conscious of the small businessman. . . .
>
> HR926 will help free the small businessman from these kinds of burdensome, job-killing regulations and direct the President to enact a citizen[s'] regulatory bill of rights, something he does not appear to want to do (*Congressional Record*, March 1, 1995, H2376).

Opponents, mostly Democrats, expressed support for the intent of the legislation but argued that it went too far:

> I am concerned about the broad nature of this legislation, and I want to explore its actual impact on the regulatory process before casting my vote on the bill itself. I am well aware of the need to make the regulatory process more sensitive to the reality of running a small business. I was a small businessman myself and can sympathize with the overwhelmingly difficult task of conforming to government requirements. Certainly reform needs to be taken and the regulatory process simplified.
>
> However, I am troubled by the fact that this bill makes no attempt to identify specific problem areas and correct them. Rather, it utilizes a blanket approach by requiring complicated, costly and time-consuming studies on any major rule with an annual effect on the economy of $50 million. For the past 20 years, every Administration, Republican and Democratic alike, has defined a major rule with a $100 million benchmark. Lowering the threshold in this way will only create more work and paper for the bureaucracy at a time in which we are reducing government.
>
> Another problem with this legislation is that it is very costly. EPA alone estimates it will cost taxpayers up to $1.6 million for each Regulatory Impact Analysis and risk assessment. In addition, regulations could be delayed for up to 2 years. While a delay of this length may not be harmful in some areas, it is not acceptable for rules that pertain to true health and safety—drinking water, airplane safety, disaster assistance, food protection, and many others (*Congressional Record*, March 1, 1995, H2376).

Although the legislation actually had much broader reach, supporters sold it as a small-business relief bill. Still traumatized from their disastrous showing in the 1994 elections, few Democrats were willing to take on such an important constituency. The ranking minority member of the Judiciary Committee subcommittee most responsible for the legislation did offer an amendment raising the threshold from $50 to $100 million, but it was defeated on a 159–266 vote, with only two Republicans supporting the amendment and forty-one Democrats voting against it. The House passed the bill by an overwhelming vote of 415 to 15.

HR925: Property Rights

The House then moved right to HR925, the property rights bill. It was already evening but the leadership, working to meet its 100-day deadline, was determined to begin the debate. To that end the majority leader asked for unanimous consent to employ an unusual procedure. (If all members agree, a legislature can choose to ignore any of its rules.) Although the House had not as yet passed the rule for the consideration of HR925, the House would debate the rule and then proceed to general debate on the bill as if the rule had been passed but would put off the vote on the rule until the next morning. That would avoid further roll call votes that evening and so allow members to go home if they wished to do so. As Dick Armey of Texas, the majority leader, explained:

> Let me say, again, it is an unusual request. It is an unusual procedure, not something that we would expect to be a habit in the future. But certainly it is something that by the minority's agreement, we were able to do so folks can get home tonight. We will then begin with a vote on the rule tomorrow, and I would remind Members who want to participate either on the debate on the rule or HR925, the private property bill, that those debates will take place tonight (*Congressional Record,* March 1, 1995, H2459).

The rule for HR925 was more complex by far than the rule for either the risk assessment bill or the cost-benefit analysis bill. The first part included some fairly standard provisions: it provided one hour of general debate to be divided between the chair and ranking minority member of the Judiciary Committee, allowed a maximum of twelve hours for the amending process, and required that all amendments be printed in the *Congressional Record* before consideration. Problems with the legislation and the postcommittee attempts to fix them required complex procedures. A number of Budget Act rules were waived because the Judiciary Committee bill could be read as violating those provisions in several respects, including by creating a new entitlement. The Canaday substitute, which was intended to fix that problem, was made in order despite problems of germaneness, and the Tauzin amendment was given priority over all other amendments.

Section 2 of the rule specified that "after passage of HR925, it shall be in order to consider in the House the bill (H.R. 9)." Section 2 continued:

> All points of order against the bill and against its consideration are waived. It shall be in order to move to strike all after section 1 of the bill and insert a text composed of four divisions as follows: (1) division A, consisting of the text of H.R. 830, as passed by the House; (2) division B, consisting of the text of H.R. 925, as passed by the House; (3) division C, consisting of the text of H.R. 926, as passed by the House; and (4) division D, consisting of the text of H.R. 1022, as passed by the House. All points of order against that motion are waived. The previous question shall be considered as ordered on the motion to amend and on the bill to final passage without intervening motion except one motion to recommit with or without instructions (*Congressional Record*, March 1, 1995, H2459).

In other words, the rule specified that the parts of HR9 that had been considered and passed as separate bills be rolled back together and passed as HR9.

Democrats objected to the rule on the same grounds that they had criticized other rules with limits on amending time. They also had a field day taking the Republicans to task for waiving budget rules.

Even more than the risk assessment bill, HR925 exposed major philosophical differences among members of the House, differences that only partially followed party lines. Republicans argued that the legislation was necessary to rein in an out-of-control federal government. As Rep. Enid Greene Waldholtz, R-Utah, one of the very conservative members of the freshman class, contended:

> . . . [F]or too long the Federal Government has trampled on the rights of private property owners. Federal agencies have made rules and taken actions that have severely impacted private citizens, drastically reducing the value of their homes and property. Yet because of restrictive interpretations by the Courts of the "takings" clause of the Constitution, these citizens have had no means of redress to be compensated for their losses.
>
> This bill will change that and protect the interests of private citizens where the government restricts the use of their property. HR925 requires that the Federal Government compensate a property owner when a limitation placed on the use of their property by a federal agency action causes the fair market value to be reduced by 10 percent or more (*Congressional Record*, March 1, 1995, H2460).

Opponents' responses evinced a quite different set of premises about government. One Democrat claimed that HR925 "would impose, without regard for the Government's important role in protecting the general welfare, an arbitrary compensation requirement for reductions in property values attributable to regulatory or other actions by Federal agencies. This is unacceptable and an extreme requirement." The member continued:

> First, it seriously undermines the Federal Government's ability to protect the general welfare. Second, it imposes an almost unlimited fiscal burden upon the American taxpayer. Third, it creates a potentially costly new direct spending program as well as a new and costly Federal bureaucracy to evaluate compensation claims. Fourth, it supplants 200 years of constitutional jurisprudence under the fifth amendment (*Congressional Record*, March 1, 1995, H2465).

Another opponent argued more colorfully:

> Mr. Speaker, the only people being "taken" by this taking bill are the American people. This bill will be a massive raid on the Treasury. . . . And what bothers me most is the likelihood that many of these claims could be fraudulent ones. This bill sets up the possibility that greedy land speculators could make false claims on the United States saying that actions deprived them of the use of property that they never intended to use in the stated fashion (*Congressional Record*, March 1, 1995, H2465).

On March 2 consideration continued with a vote on the rule that was easily approved 271–151, with forty-six Democrats joining all but one Republican in support. Since general debate had been concluded the night before, the amending process began immediately. The Tauzin amendment was up first and passed by a wide margin—301–128.

Opponents made a number of attempts to moderate the bill. Although most of the opponents were Democrats, most of the meliorating amendments were offered by one of the small band of Republican opponents; for opponents from both parties, it made sense to have a majority party member take the lead. Republican supporters and their Democratic allies beat most such amendments handily, but a proposal by Rep. Porter J. Goss, R-Fla., to increase the threshold from 10 to 30 percent was rejected by only one vote—210–211, with fifty Republicans defecting from the party position. That close vote indicated to supporters that the 10 percent threshold was not viable, and when Goss offered another amendment to raise the threshold to 20 percent, most Republicans supported it, and it passed 338–83.

On March 3 HR925 passed 277–148; twenty-three Republicans voted against it, but seventy-two Democrats crossed the aisle to support the bill. Then, as the rule stipulated, the House packaged the bills that had passed separately back into HR9 and passed that on a 277–141 vote.

Senate Committee Action

Unlike House Republicans, Senate Republicans had not signed the Contract with America and did not necessarily feel bound to that agenda. Most, however, did agree that an overhaul of the federal regulatory process was necessary and that the 1994 elections in which they had taken control of the Senate constituted a mandate for making such changes. Nevertheless, Senate Republicans disagreed among themselves about how drastic the overhaul should be much more than House Republicans did.

Since there was no "official" Republican bill in the Senate as the Contract had provided in the House, a number of senators introduced their own proposals for regulatory overhaul. On January 27, 1995, Sen. William V. Roth, Jr., R-Del., chairman of the Senate Committee on Governmental Affairs, one of the committees with jurisdiction in the area, introduced S291. By the standards of HR9, the Roth bill was moderate; it required elaborate risk assessment and cost-benefit analysis, but it would apply only to regulations with a gross annual effect of $100 million or more and would not allow suits over how the cost-benefit and risk assessment analyses were conducted.

On February 2 Majority Leader Bob Dole of Kansas introduced S343, saying: "Last November, the American people sent us a message. . . . Stop micromanaging our lives through burdensome and costly regulations. We are responding to that message" (quoted in Cloud 1995, 1219). Dole's bill was similar to HR9 and much more radical than Roth's. Lobbyists for business interests affected by the legislation played a major role in drafting Dole's bill (Cloud 1995, 1219–1222). Running for president in an increasingly conservative Republican Party, Dole seems to have singled out regulatory reform as an issue on which he could display his conservative bono fides and his ability to get things done.

The same day Sen. Frank H. Murkowski, R-Alaska, chairman of the Senate Energy and Natural Resources Committee, introduced S333, a measure that in stringency fell between the Roth and Dole measures. The two chairmen's bills were referred to their own committees; Dole's was sent to the Judiciary Committee and also to Governmental Affairs.

On March 14 the Administrative Oversight Subcommittee of the Senate Judiciary Committee approved the Dole bill in a somewhat amended but not moderated form. The Governmental Affairs Committee was scheduled to mark up the Roth bill on March 23. Supporters of an overhaul knew that agreeing on one bill would increase their chances of successfully passing legislation, so during the week of March 13 senators and staff members from the committees worked to reconcile the differences between the two bills. No mutually agreeable compromise could be found.

Thus, on March 23 Roth brought his bill to markup and, working with committee Democrats, fashioned legislation that garnered strong bipartisan support. "We can pass something that is doable and workable," Ohio senator John Glenn, the ranking Democrat on Governmental Affairs, said, contrasting the committee's bill with Dole's. "Or we can pass something that looks tough but is unworkable" (quoted in Benenson 1995c, 867). The committee vote was 15–0.

Attempting to guard against the Dole bill being given priority over its measure, the Governmental Affairs Committee, after approving the amended version of S291, voted to strip out the original text of S343 and replace it with the text of S291. The notion was that if Dole brought S343 but not S291 to the floor, both versions of S343 would be considered on the floor.

On March 29 the Energy and Natural Resources Committee approved S333 on a 10–9 party-line vote. Senator Murkowski had attempted to put together a bipartisan compromise but failed, losing even the ranking minority member who was an original co-sponsor of the legislation.

The Judiciary Committee meanwhile was having more serious problems. Democrats complained bitterly that the chairman was trying to rush the legislation through and not providing enough time for the consideration of amendments; Republicans complained that Democrats were filibustering. The problem was that on the Dole bill very little common ground between committee Democrats and Republicans existed.

The Judiciary Committee began markup on April 6 but only worked its way through two amendments. "There's a lot of pressure on me to get it out," acknowledged Chairman Orrin G. Hatch, R-Utah, as he pushed for final action before the April 7 recess. Democrats objected but eventually did agree to a unanimous consent request to finish markup on April 26. The Senate was not in session on April 26, but the markup reconvened on April 27. Bipartisan staff negotiations during the intervening period had slightly modified the bill but had left all the major issues open. Democrats had many amendments they wanted to offer and asked Senator Hatch to be flexible about time since the leadership did not intend to bring the bill to the floor before June. Bob Benenson recounts what happened next:

> Hatch said that if Democrats did not join in a unanimous consent agreement to conclude by 1 p.m., he would revert to the original agreement that deemed the bill to be approved on April 26. But Edward M. Kennedy, D-Mass., strongly objected, saying there would not be enough time to sufficiently debate his and other amendments.
>
> The squabble, which lasted for about 20 minutes, ended abruptly. Hatch invoked the original unanimous consent agreement and declared the

markup over. "When you make an agreement, stick to it," he exclaimed. . . . Hatch then rose, forcefully gaveled the committee meeting to a close and slammed two notebooks to the committee table before departing (Benenson 1995d, 1174).

Postcommittee Negotiations in the Senate

On June 21 Majority Leader Dole announced on the floor of the Senate:

> I have been working with Senator Johnston for some time to produce a strong regulatory reform package, in order to ensure that Congress answers America's call for relief. I am pleased to say that I think Senator Johnston and I have reached an agreement on at least a discussion draft, a package that we believe will enjoy broad support (*Congressional Record*, June 21, 1995, S8792).

Dole knew that a regulatory overhaul bill lacking broad support, including some support from Democrats, was likely to run afoul of Senate debate rules; the way in which his bill had been reported out of committee did not bode well for floor success. So Dole had commenced negotiations; he chose to work with J. Bennett Johnston of Louisiana, a Democrat and ranking minority member of the Energy and Natural Resources Committee, because Johnston supported far-reaching changes and because his support might win over enough conservative and moderate Democrats to avoid a filibuster.

After several weeks of talks, Dole and Johnston agreed on a draft bill. Dole consented to alter the judicial review language. Suits based on the risk and cost-benefit procedures used by federal agencies would not be allowed; because experts disagree on those procedures, allowing such suits would make challenging rules much easer and would enormously expand the potential for litigation under the legislation. Only final rules could be challenged in court, though the procedures used would be part of the record. Provisions that would make it possible to challenge current rules were also weakened.

Roth took part in the negotiations and signed on to the resulting legislation, abandoning S291, his own bill. But, as Dole and Johnston well knew, many senators still had concerns. Thus, rather than presenting their compromise as a finished product, they explicitly labeled it a draft and invited suggestions for improvements. The draft, Johnston explained,

> has been arrived at after extensive conversations, negotiations and writing, and we have worked in over 100 amendments to the underlying text. I hope my colleagues like the result, and I have reason to suspect that they will.

> I would like to emphasize ... that this is, in fact, a discussion draft, and that we invite input from all of our colleagues. By filing this to be printed, it is simply a matter of giving notice to colleagues of what is in the discussion draft. It is not the filing of the bill or the filing of an amendment. But it is a filing of notice, so that all of those who have meaningful input can work through the process and, hopefully, we will be able to improve the bill, so that by the time a bill or an amendment is filed, it will contain the suggestions of our colleagues, if we can agree upon those suggestions. Am I correct on that? (*Congressional Record,* June 21, 1995, S8794).

Although a bit more cautious, Dole essentially agreed and invited his colleagues to negotiate:

> The Senator is correct. I will underscore that this is a very significant effort.... I do not want to suggest we are going to rewrite the whole thing.... [H]opefully, we can continue discussions tomorrow and Friday and again on Monday, so that on Tuesday we might be prepared to take the bill up with fairly broad bipartisan support (*Congressional Record,* June 21, 1995, S8794).

Negotiations with Democrats and moderate Republicans in the days following the unveiling of the draft failed to produce a compromise. The sides were simply too far apart. Moderate Republican John H. Chafee of Rhode Island called the Dole-Johnston bill a "prescription for litigation and bureaucratic gridlock" (Benenson 1995e, 1836). Senator Glenn, a supporter of S291, was not won over; he and Chafee decided to offer a slightly modified version of S291 as a substitute to the Dole-Johnston compromise.

Lacking better alternatives, Dole sent S343 to the floor June 28; the Dole-Johnston compromise was to be offered as a substitute for the original bill; Glenn would offer the slightly modified version of S291 as the Democratic alternative.

The tide was beginning to shift. During the early months of the 104th Congress, the media focused primarily on the Contract scorecard—on how many items Republicans had passed and on whether they would meet their 100-day goal; arcane and complex Contract bills such as regulatory reform and their potential real-world effects received almost no attention. Groups and interests that favored radical regulatory reform were well organized, well financed, and working hard and effectively in Congress and at the grass-roots level to promote the legislation. In the late spring environmental and consumer groups began to mount an effective counterattack, and the Clinton administration began to speak out more strongly in opposition. Media coverage increased and began to focus on the likely effects of the legislation. Business lobbying in the Senate was intense, but now there was some counterveiling pressure.

Senate Floor Action

Debate began after the July 4 recess, and the bill quickly ran into trouble. Rather than debating regulatory reform at an abstract level, opponents focused on specific regulations they argued the bill would endanger. For example, they highlighted proposed Agriculture Department rules that required slaughterhouses to institute better procedures to prevent contamination; they also cited regulations to tighten equipment quality and personnel training requirements for mammography practitioners. Put on the defensive by media coverage of these attacks, the bill's supporters gave ground. Dole himself offered an amendment specifically to include food safety threats among the emergencies for which regulations could be provisionally issued without meeting the elaborate risk assessment and cost-benefit requirements. Dole attempted to kill the mammography amendment by Sen. Barbara Boxer, D-Calif., but she threatened to filibuster. Every year 46,000 women die of breast cancer, Boxer pointed out: "I will stand on my feet for 46,000 minutes or 46,000 hours or whatever it takes" (Benenson 1995f, 2051). The bill's supporters gave in and the Boxer amendment was adopted on a 99–0 vote.

Bennett Johnston had never agreed with the provision in both Dole's bill and the House bill applying the new regulatory review procedures to any rule with an annual effect on the economy of $50 million or more. As he had said he would do, he offered an amendment to increase the threshold from $50 to $100 million. In a significant blow to Dole and other supporters of a stringent bill, the amendment passed on a 53 to 45 vote, with seven moderate Republicans joining all the Democrats in support.

Debate dragged on; dozens of amendments were offered and brought to a vote, but the end seemed no closer. Dole decided to file a cloture petition. On July 17 the Senate rejected the motion to invoke cloture and thus close debate by a vote of 48 to 46; five Republicans voted against cloture, three Democrats supported it.

The next day the Glenn substitute was brought to a vote and failed by a narrow margin—48–52; again five Republicans and three Democrats defected from their party's position. Later the same day Dole brought a second cloture petition to a vote, and it failed on a 53–47 vote; five moderate Republicans still refused to vote to cut off debate. On July 20 Dole made one last try to invoke cloture; he had made a last-minute deal to accept some of the moderate Republicans' provisions and thereby picked up their votes. Although all Republicans voted in favor of cloture, it nevertheless failed, 58–40.

Regulatory Overhaul Dies

After eleven days of debate during which twenty-six amendments were offered and twenty-one accepted, Dole pulled the bill off the floor. He had failed to craft a compromise that could command sixty votes. Dole accused Democrats of sinking the bill; Democrats claimed they wanted a bill but a workable and reasonable one. Both sides talked of reviving legislation at some later date. The prospects did not, however, look promising. As Dole made more and more changes to placate moderates, conservatives in his party became increasingly restive and concerned that Dole was watering down the legislation unacceptably. Yet the changes he made were never sufficient to alleviate the concerns of most Democrats.

In November of 1995, House Republicans made an attempt to revive S343 by attaching its provisions to a bill raising the debt limit temporarily. The tactic offered a chance—though not a good one—of bypassing all the internal Senate problems and forcing the president to accept a bill he disliked. Clinton vetoed the legislation as he had indicated he would.

The Senate Judiciary Committee in mid-December 1995 approved on a 10–7 vote a property rights bill with an even broader reach than the one that had passed the House (Freedman 1995, 3884). Because a filibuster was a certainty, Dole, a strong supporter, never brought it to the floor. (See Table 8.1 for a chronology of House and Senate action on regulatory reform legislation.)

The Hazards of Unorthodox Lawmaking

An extensive package of alterations in the federal regulatory process was a part of the Contract with America, so the problem House Republicans faced was how to pass within the promised 100-day period extremely complex and controversial legislation that fell under the jurisdiction of many committees. To reduce somewhat the jurisdictional problems, the party leadership decided to split the legislation. To meet the strict schedule, the party leaders pressured Republican committee leaders to report their legislation quickly. The committee leaders knew the Speaker could impose stringent reporting deadlines on their committees should he choose to do so. More important, however, they knew that the Republican membership fully backed the leadership. Furthermore, most agreed that future Republican electoral success rested on the party keeping its promises.

Jurisdictional complexity and political considerations forced post-committee adjustments in the two major bills. Under leadership instruc-

TABLE 8.1   1995 Regulatory Overhaul: A Chronology

Date	House Action	Date	Senate Action
1/4	HR9, the Job Creation and Wage Enhancement Act of 1995, introduced in the House and referred to eight committees; Title III, Risk Assessment and Cost-Benefit Analysis for New Regulations, referred to the committees on Science, Commerce, and Government Reform and Oversight; provisions of Titles VI–VIII on cost-benefit analysis and the property rights section referred to the Committee on the Judiciary.	1/27	Roth, chair of the Committee on Governmental Affairs, introduces S210, the Regulatory Reform Act of 1995. S210 referred to Committee on Governmental Affairs.
1/31, 2/3	Science Committee holds hearings.		
2/1, 2/2	Commerce Committee holds hearings.	2/2	Murkowski, chair of the Committee on Energy and Natural Resources, introduces S333; this bill referred to the Committee on Energy and Natural Resources. Majority Leader Dole introduces S343, the Comprehensive Regulatory Reform Act of 1995; S343 referred to Committee on the Judiciary.
2/3, 2/6	Judiciary Committee holds hearings.	2/3	S343 referred to Committee on Governmental Affairs.
2/7	Government Reform and Oversight Committee holds hearings. Commerce Committee marks up Title III.		
2/8	Commerce Committee continues markup and orders Title III reported; Science Committee marks up Title III and orders it reported.		
2/16	Judiciary Committee marks up and orders reported HR926 (Regulatory Reform and Relief Act) and HR925 (Private Property Protection Act).		
	The chairmen of the Commerce and Science committees negotiate a compromise version of their committees' risk assessment bills.		
	Canady and Tauzen negotiate changes to HR925 that will be offered as an amendment; Republican party leadership endorses the deal.		
2/23	Compromise on risk assessment (Title III provisions) introduced as HR1022.	2/22, 2/24	Judiciary Committee holds hearings.
2/24	Rules Committee grants modified open rule placing ten-hour time limitation on the amendment process for HR1022.		
2/27	Rules Committee grants open rule for HR926. House approves rule for HR1022 and begins consideration.		
2/28	House passes HR1022, approves rule for HR926. Rules Committee grants modified open rule placing twelve-hour time limitation on amendment process and granting Tauzin amendment priority for HR925.		

3/1	House considers and passes HR926. House begins general debate on HR925 under unanimous consent.
3/2	House approves rule for HR925 and begins consideration. Tauzin amendment approved.
3/3	House passes HR925. As specified by the rule, HR925, HR926, and HR1022 are inserted back into HR9 and the House passes HR9.
3/6	Energy and Natural Resources Committee holds hearings.
3/14	Judiciary subcommittee approves S343 for full committee action. *Supporters of S343 and S210 negotiate to try to come up with one bill; they fail to reach an agreement.*
3/17	Judiciary Committee holds hearings.
3/23	Governmental Affairs Committee marks up and orders reported S210 and S343 (which it has amended to be identical to S210).
3/29	Energy and Natural Resources Committee marks up and orders reported S333.
4/5, 4/6	Judiciary Committee marks up S343.
4/27	Judiciary Committee completes markup and orders reported S343. *Dole negotiates with Johnston on compromise package.*
6/21	Dole and Johnston announce their package on the floor and invite other senators to negotiate. *Negotiations proceed but fail to produce consensus package.*
7/10	Senate begins debate on S343. *Negotiations continue.*
7/17	Motion to invoke cloture fails, 48–46. *Negotiations continue.*
7/18	Motion to invoke cloture fails, 53–47. *Negotiations continue.*
7/20	Motion to invoke cloture fails, 58–40. Dole pulls S343 off floor; bill is effectively dead.

NOTE: Official actions are in roman type; behind-the-scenes, unofficial actions are in italics.

tions, the chairmen of the Commerce and Science committees worked out the differences between the risk assessment bills reported by their committees so that a single bill could be taken to the floor. The compromise Tauzen amendment to the property rights bill produced the support needed to pass it.

The bills were brought to the floor under special rules that ensured speedy consideration but still allowed Republicans to claim they were abiding by their promise to allow all germane amendments. The complex rule for the property rights bill was tailored to the specific problems facing that bill on the floor; it included a number of special provisions for the consideration of the postcommittee adjustments. It also provided for the repackaging of the various bills into HR9, its original Contract number. In the House, then, the process was complex but orderly and swift.

In this case, however, the speed was bought at a cost. These were enormously complex bills that dealt with enormously complex problems. The lack of deliberation that such a swift process necessitated resulted in flawed legislation; in the views of many experts, the procedures for risk assessment and cost-benefit analysis that the legislation prescribed would be extremely costly and would increase bureaucratic gridlock, delay, and litigation (Benenson 1995a, 1995b).

Interest groups with views opposed to those expressed in the Contract were cut out of the process. While business lobbyists actually drafted key parts of the House legislation, environmental interests were shut out, as were in reality their Democratic allies on the committees. By rushing the legislation through the House before opponents had a chance to mobilize, the House leadership ensured that the bill would pass in the Republicans' preferred form. That manner of proceeding, however, made it more likely that the legislation would run into significant problems later in the process.

The legislative process in the Senate reflected that body's more informal character and the necessity of building broad support that its rules and practices impose. There were a number of bills; Senate Republicans did not give their majority leader's bill much precedence. The need to build a supermajority coalition forced Dole to make a series of major postcommittee adjustments to his bill. The floor colloquy between Majority Leader Dole and Senator Johnston about their openness to further modifications in their bill makes clear the extent to which passing legislation in the Senate requires accommodating senators as individuals. Despite their efforts to make the bill palatable to their colleagues, it was subject to an amending marathon and eventually killed by a filibuster. Opponents were able to force supporters to go on record on all sorts of tough amendments and then were able to muster the votes necessary to prevent debate from being cut off. Public pressure can persuade senators to acquiesce in the passing of legislation they strongly oppose, but in this case that never materialized. To the contrary, as media coverage increased, significant public opposition appeared and bolstered Senate opponents.

The Omnibus Drug Bill: A "Designer" Legislative Process

IN LATE APRIL 1988 SPEAKER OF THE HOUSE Jim Wright, D-Texas, decided Congress should pass comprehensive antidrug legislation. The drug problem was becoming an increasingly salient issue in the early months of 1988 as Jesse Jackson, running for the Democratic presidential nomination, focused attention on it and struck a chord with audiences of all sorts. Responding to public concern, members of both chambers were introducing bills and offering amendments aimed at the drug problem. Thus, Wright saw an opportunity to accomplish something useful, and he knew that he had to act quickly if the Democratic party leadership wanted to control the legislative process on the issue. On a hot-button issue such as drugs, some proposals that are Draconian, unworkable, or both are always offered; strong and early involvement would allow the leaders to exert a measure of quality control. Furthermore, in a presidential election year and with an opposition party president in the White House, Speaker Wright wanted the Democratic Party to receive credit for passing antidrug legislation.

Speaker Wright decided Congress should pass an omnibus bill. The drug problem is multifaceted; members and experts alike agreed that education, treatment, interdiction, prosecution, and punishment were all necessary parts of an effective antidrug strategy even if they disagreed about how much emphasis should be given to the various approaches. In addition, the Speaker knew that an omnibus bill would garner much more media attention than would a group of narrower bills and thus yield more credit. In 1985, the Speaker explained, the Democratic House had passed a series of antidrug bills; Republicans, who then controlled the

Senate, put the bills together into one package in the Senate, called it the Republican drug initiative, and got all the press attention. That, he said, had taught Democrats a lesson.

Passing an omnibus bill would not be easy. Many committees would have to be involved, and time was short; less than half a year remained till adjournment, and much other business needed to get done. Furthermore, while almost everyone in Congress—Democrats and Republicans, liberals and conservatives—wanted to pass a drug bill, many of the specific provisions would be highly contentious.

Putting Together the House Bill

The procedure the Speaker chose was designed to ameliorate these problems. Wright asked Majority Leader Tom Foley, D-Wash., to oversee the process of putting together a bill and to do it in concert with Minority Leader Bob Michel, R-Ill. The need for speed and the subject matter dictated a bipartisan effort. Partisanship would slow the process down. What is more, a fierce partisan battle between Democrats advocating more money for education and treatment and Republicans supporting more severe punishment of users and dealers would not benefit the Democrats' image with the electorate. Passing a balanced bill would.

On May 2 Wright, Foley, and Majority Whip Tony Coelho, D-Calif., met with the chairs of eleven committees—ten with relevant jurisdiction and the Select Committee on Narcotics Abuse and Control (which, as a select committee, could not report legislation)—to discuss what might be included in the bill. The Speaker asked the chairs to make it a bipartisan effort. "I don't want a bidding war," he said. He told them that the target date for reporting out their legislation was June 21, and they promised to comply.

On May 9 Speaker Wright announced the initiative at his daily press conference, explaining both the procedure to be used and the deadline. His primary purpose, of course, was to publicize the effort. A not unwelcome byproduct of making the deadline public was to increase the pressure on the committees to produce their legislation in a timely fashion.

By mid-June committees began to report their legislation, and by the end of the month, all the committees with jurisdiction had reported. The issue had continued to increase in saliency; on June 15 Vice President George Bush, who by then had wrapped up the Republican nomination for president, appeared on Capitol Hill with Republican House leaders as they unveiled their drug legislation, a package put together by the Republican Leadership Task Force on Drugs, chaired by Bill McCollum, R-Fla.

Republicans, too, wanted credit for the legislation. Furthermore, in the Democrats' eagerness to pass a bill, they saw opportunities to enact provisions they favored. Republicans worked in the committees with mixed success to incorporate their provisions into the legislation reported. Some Republican amendments provoked sharply partisan battles within committees; others found bipartisan support. In the end all of the committees reported their legislation on a bipartisan vote.

Taken together, the legislation reported by the ten committees constituted a comprehensive attack on the drug problem; interdiction, education, treatment, and penalties were each addressed from a number of different angles. There were many widely ranging provisions—making it more difficult for drug kingpins to launder money (reported by the Banking Committee), establishing new drug awareness and education initiatives (reported by Education and Labor), authorizing more money for Coast Guard drug interdiction (reported by Merchant Marine and Fisheries), increasing penalties for drug offenses and devising controls to prevent the flow of solvents used to refine cocaine (reported by Judiciary), and creating programs for treatment and rehabilitation (reported by Energy and Commerce).

It was Majority Leader Foley's job to take these provisions, and the myriad others in the ten measures reported, and meld them into a coherent whole. From the beginning of the process, Tom Foley and senior leadership staff had monitored the committees. They had worked to spot problems and to try to work them out and had pushed the participants to move quickly and settle their disputes expeditiously. Periodic meetings of the chairs had been held to keep the pressure on. To maintain as much bipartisanship as possible, Foley had conferred regularly with Minority Leader Michel.

In putting together the bill to take to the floor, Foley faced two sorts of problems: jurisdictional and political. One of the problems, an aide explained, is that "a lot of committees did each other's work." In other words, they invaded each other's jurisdiction. The Ways and Means Committee complained that six major provisions drafted by other committees trespassed on its jurisdiction. For example, the Merchant Marine and Fisheries Committee had drafted an "innocent owner" provision to limit the ability of the Customs Service and the Coast Guard to seize boats on which small amounts of drugs were found if the owner of the vessel knew nothing about the drugs; because Ways and Means has oversight jurisdiction over the Customs Service, it considered this an invasion of its turf. A number of committees complained that the Judiciary Committee had overstepped its bounds. "[The committees have] been told to work it out by the deadline, or we'll do it for them or work it out on the floor," a leadership aide asserted.

The second problem was how to handle numerous highly contentious issues, many of which were not simply partisan but split Democrats as well. The Democratic leadership had hoped to take a broad consensus vehicle to the floor and handle "the controversial stuff" through floor amendments. The legislation reported by the committees made that largely though not completely possible.

By the time the committees had finished their work, the issues that would provoke the most heated conflict had become clear. A Republican proposal on "user accountability" that would deny federal benefits of various sorts to those convicted of drug use was voted down on a largely party-line vote in the Education and Labor Committee; a different version was approved by the Judiciary Committee. Judiciary turned down a provision allowing the death penalty for drug kingpins, another Republican priority, but adopted one requiring a seven-day waiting period before the purchase of a handgun. The adamant opposition of the powerful National Rifle Association (NRA) to a waiting period ensured a battle on that provision.

Designing the Rule

The process of putting together the legislative vehicle to take to the floor merged into that of crafting the rule for floor consideration. Despite intense lobbying by the NRA, the seven-day waiting period was left in the omnibus bill. Amendments to weaken it, however, would be made in order by the rule. A number of the jurisdictional problems were solved by removing the offending provisions from the base bill but allowing them to be offered as amendments on the floor; the Judiciary Committee's user accountability and drug czar provisions were handled in this way. Foley and Michel, in lengthy negotiations, decided which of the hot-button amendments would be allowed on the floor. Foley agreed to votes on the Republicans' top priority amendments—on user accountability, the death penalty, and the exclusionary rule—in return for their limiting the number of amendments they would offer.

Liberal Democrats particularly would have preferred a rule that disallowed Republican amendments on those hot-button issues; such votes confronted members with a choice between "trashing the Constitution" by voting for punitive provisions contrary to the Bill of Rights and casting a vote very hard to explain to constituents right before an election, they believed. However, the price of Republican cooperation was allowing votes on some of these controversial amendments, and the Democratic leadership knew that it could not pass a rule that barred such votes. Too many of its own members would defect. The Democratic leadership could and did give their liberals opportunities to attempt to counter Republican amendments they believed pernicious; eight amendments aimed at ameliorating the Republicans' death penalty amendment were made in order.

At about 11 p.m. on August 10, after three days of deliberation, the Rules Committee reported out a rule for consideration of HR5210, the Omnibus Drug Initiative. Members had proposed over 150 amendments; the Rules Committee, under leadership guidance, decided to allow thirty-five—nineteen to be offered by Republicans, sixteen by Democrats.

A long and complex rule, it carefully structured floor consideration. After three hours of general debate equally divided between the majority and minority leaders, the thirty-five amendments were to be debated under varying time limits adding up in total to another twelve and a half hours of debate. In the words of the rule:

> No amendment to the bill shall be in order except the amendments specified in the report of the Committee on Rules accompanying this resolution, or those amendments offered by the majority leader in the manner specified herein. The amendments printed in the report of the Committee on Rules shall be considered only in the order and in the manner specified in the report. . . . Each amendment may only be offered by the Member designated for such amendment in the report of the Committee on Rules, or his designee. . . . Debate on each of said amendments shall not exceed the time specified in this resolution or in the report of the Committee on Rules, to be equally divided and controlled by the proponent and a Member opposed thereto. . . . No amendment shall be subject to amendment, except as specified in the report of the Committee on Rules (*Congressional Record*, August 11, 1988, H6846).

Two pairs of amendments were to be considered under a king-of-the-hill procedure. A death penalty amendment by Rep. George W. Gekas, R-Pa., and a life imprisonment alternative by Rep. Charles B. Rangel, D-N.Y., were paired. The Gekas amendment was given the advantaged last position; the Democratic leadership did not believe this was a winnable fight. Two amendments on establishing a drug czar were to be brought up under the same procedure; in this case the version offered by the chair of the Government Operations Committee was to be voted on after the Republican alternative and thus adopted should both receive a majority.

House Floor Action

On August 11 the House approved the rule on a vote of 363 to 41. The leaders had succeeded in crafting a rule that most members considered fair but that nevertheless structured and limited debate. Although swift by congressional standards, the process had dragged on long enough that consideration of the bill could not be completed before the August recess. To cement the agreements that had been reached, the Democratic leaders decided to bring up the rule before the recess; especially in an election year, members at home campaigning might be tempted to toughen their stance.

The House took up the drug bill when it returned from its August recess and, after six days of consideration, approved it on a 375–30 vote. The Gekas death penalty amendment passed but so did some of the mitigating amendments. The relatively moderate Judiciary Committee version of the user accountability amendment was approved, as was the Republicans' exclusionary rule amendment. The seven-day waiting period was struck from the bill, but Democrats defeated a Republican attempt to delete the innocent owner provisions. The Democrats' drug czar amendment prevailed.

Putting Together the Senate Bill

If the legislative process in the House deviated from the textbook model in a number of important respects, the legislative process in the Senate on the drug bill bore almost no relationship to the textbook model. In response to the growing saliency of the issue, both of the Senate parties formed working groups and charged them with formulating a package of antidrug proposals. Individual senators, taking advantage of the Senate's permissive rules on amendments, had been offering their own proposals on the floor; on June 10 Sen. Alfonse M. D'Amato, R-N.Y., proposed legislation allowing the death penalty for drug kingpins, and it passed on a 65–29 vote. He had threatened to attach the death penalty measure as an amendment to the defense authorization bill and, in return for withdrawing it, was given a floor vote on the free-standing measure.

The Senate Democratic working group, chaired by Sam Nunn of Georgia and Daniel Patrick Moynihan of New York, unveiled its proposals in the last week of June. The Senate Republican task force followed on July 7. Both packages were comprehensive, covering the same broad range from education to interdiction as the House measure. The two parties' packages differed, however, not only in details but also in emphasis. The Democrats focused 60 percent of the resources on reducing the demand for drugs through education and treatment, while the Senate Republicans, like their House colleagues, proposed strict user accountability provisions and the death penalty for drug kingpins.

If the normal process had been followed, and these proposals had been sent to the committees with jurisdiction, antidrug legislation almost certainly would not have been enacted in 1988. Given the many commit-tees that would have had to be involved and the number and contentious-ness of the issues, the time left before the 100th Congress adjourned per-manently was just too short. Yet most senators wanted to pass a bill. They not only wanted to respond to public demand; they also knew that, if the House passed legislation and the Senate did not, they would look terrible.

To solve the problem, the joint party leadership—Majority Leader Robert C. Byrd, D-W.Va., and Minority Leader Bob Dole, R-Kan.—decided to forgo committee consideration altogether and appoint a bipartisan work-ing group to negotiate a bill. This group of about twenty senators, most of whom had worked on their party's task force, "had literally hundreds of hours of meetings," as Sen. Warren Rudman, R-N.H., one of its most active members, reported (*Congressional Record*, October 12, 1988, S15636). Other senators with an interest in any aspect of the problem were invited to present their proposals to the working group. After several months of tough negotia-tions, the group produced a consensus core bill. Included were the provi-sions on which this politically diverse group managed to reach full agree-ment. Several highly controversial issues were left to be decided on the floor.

Getting the Bill to the Senate Floor

On October 3, 1988, Senator Nunn introduced S2852, the core bill, on behalf of the bipartisan working group and the joint leadership. Because of its scope and importance but also because it would likely be one of the last major bills to clear during the 100th Congress, S2852 immediately attracted scores of amendments. If all these and possibly other amendments were debated on the floor, time would run out, and all the hard work would be for naught. To get the bill to a passage vote, a unanimous consent agreement limiting debate would have to be negoti-ated. Yet to get all senators to agree, senators' rights had to be preserved.

Democratic leader Byrd and Republican leader Dole agreed on a complex procedure that they hoped would yield such an agreement. Amendments would be classified into three categories: those on which the working group could agree, mostly noncontroversial ones; a limited num-ber of highly contentious amendments that would be debated and voted on individually on the floor; and an intermediate group for which some other procedure would have to be worked out. Byrd and Dole sent the most active members of the working group back to work, examining and classifying the 100 or so amendments that had been filed.

Over the course of several days of intensive meetings, the working group identified more than thirty amendments on which they could agree. Eight amendments—on the death penalty, user accountability, and other contentious issues—warranted individual floor debate, the working group decided. Another eighteen or so amendments—later called the purgatory group—fell into neither of these categories: they were too controversial for the working group to accept but not important enough to warrant scarce floor time.

The unanimous consent agreement that Byrd and Dole presented to their membership on October 12 specified that the first group of amendments would be packaged together and jointly offered by the two leaders and the co-chairs of the working group. Together with the original bill developed by the working group, these amendments would constitute the new core bill. There would be a single vote up or down on this package.

The eight hot-button amendments would be debated under specific time limits; any amendments to those amendments would have to be germane. The fate of the purgatory amendments, Byrd and Dole agreed and the unanimous consent agreement specified, would be determined by a special four-person task force they set up. The task force—Nunn, Moynihan, Rudman, and Phil Gramm, R-Texas—would review the amendments, giving their sponsors an opportunity to defend them. If the four agreed on the amendment, it would go into the package; if not, Byrd and Dole would act as a court of appeal. The amendments turned down by both the task force and the leaders could not be offered.

"[A] single objection, of course, will mean we have no agreement, and a single objection may mean that we will have no drug bill," Majority Leader Byrd said pointedly as he presented the unanimous consent agreement (UCA) on the floor (*Congressional Record*, October 12, 1988, S15633). William Armstrong, R-Colo., complained vehemently about the restraint on senators' rights. He argued that the Senate had set up its own Rules Committee and that it was "a bad practice and a bad precedent," but in the end he did not object (Lawrence 1988a, 2978). Unwilling to be responsible for the demise of the bill, he and other senators who disliked the UCA delayed it for a day but ultimately acceded.

The UCA made it possible for the Senate to complete the bill after two days of debate and only nine roll call votes. On October 14 the Senate passed the bill 87–3.

Reconciling House-Senate Differences: The Initial Phase

Well before Senate passage, House and Senate majority party leaders had begun discussing how to resolve the differences between the chambers. By a September 22 meeting to coordinate the two chambers' end-of-the-session schedules and to discuss problem legislation, the leaders had begun to conclude that sending the legislation to conference would kill it. Given the number of issues and the number of committees involved, a conference would not be able to produce a compromise bill in the limited time left before adjournment. A less formal process would have to be used.

To be ready to start working out agreements between the chambers as soon as the Senate passed its bill, the House leadership began preparations. On Thursday, October 13, the Speaker and Majority Leader Foley met with the committee and subcommittee chairs involved. They informed the chairs that the Senate expected to finish the bill late Friday and urged them to begin working out their differences with their Senate counterparts over the weekend. The chairs complained about the Senate process: "Who do we talk to? There's a 'core group' over in the Senate who are putting the bill together. It doesn't necessarily include the committee people," groused one. "There's no one to talk to," lamented another, reflecting the consensus view. The leaders commiserated with their members and tried to soothe them. "We can't solve [the Senate's] process problems," the Speaker responded to the chairs' complaints. "After the Senate gets a bill, they will have to talk," the majority leader pointed out. Both the Speaker and the majority leader urged the chairs to focus on getting an agreement. "If you're leaving town this weekend, designate a staff person to start the process," the Speaker said. "Please have your staff monitor Senate action and keep in touch with leadership staff," prompted the majority leader.

When the Senate passed its bill about 4 p.m. on Friday, the two chambers' leadership staffs were ready. At 5 p.m. the House and Senate Democratic leadership staffs met to figure out the differences between the two bills and to identify where the problems were likely to be. The House leadership staff distributed the Senate package to all relevant House committees "so they [the staff] could spend the weekend looking over the differences between the two bills." A number of the most contentious issues fell into the jurisdiction of the Judiciary Committees; their House and Senate staffs worked Saturday afternoon and all day Sunday to get a head start.

Monday and Tuesday were devoted to negotiations at the staff level. "One of the problems," a leadership staffer explained, "is that we are doing it by committee, and the Senate is doing it by subject matter." House committee staff did not know with whom to deal on the Senate side. House leadership staffers identified for the House committee staffs the Senate staff aides working on issues within their jurisdictions. Shifting groups of staffers worked through their sections of the bill, clarifying differences, trying to resolve minor ones, and identifying "member issues"—those important and politically delicate enough that members would have to resolve them.

By Wednesday morning staff had done what it could do; the minor and the easy issues had been resolved. Members had also been meeting with their counterparts from the other chamber, trying to reach agreements on the more difficult issues. The Senate's unorthodox procedure continued to annoy the House chairs who complained to their party leadership about senators who did not show up for scheduled meetings, and others that lacked expertise because they did not serve on the committee of jurisdiction. At a 2 p.m. meeting of the House Democratic leadership and the chairs, many also charged that getting agreements to stick was a problem. "It is all independent contractors over there [in the Senate]. If you come to an agreement with one of them, others may not go along," a powerful chair complained. Our staff negotiated with Orrin Hatch's staff for several hours, another chair recounted. And then in came the staffs of Gramm and Sen. John Danforth, R-Mo., who said, "Hatch can't speak for the Republicans on that; we refuse to accept anything that has been done." Called to assess progress, the meeting made clear that substantial headway had been made but that reaching an overall agreement would require a more assertive leadership role.

At 4 p.m. the top Democratic and Republican party leaders of the House and Senate met in the Speaker's Capitol office and agreed upon a procedure for resolving the remaining differences. Byrd and Dole designated Nunn and Rudman as lead negotiators for the Senate. Foley and Michel would mediate for the House. Sections of the bill on which there were unresolved problems would be taken up one by one, the members involved called in, and a compromise worked out. Staff drew up a schedule; the process was to begin at 6 p.m. and continue the following day until all outstanding differences had been ironed out.

The marathon meeting began in a large room on the House side of the Capitol. When their issues were called up, House members and some senators briefly stated their case. Many of the affected senators were represented by staff or were consulted by phone by Nunn and Rudman. The two senators and Foley were the most active participants, Michel often having business elsewhere. They pressed members to compromise and sometimes suggested provisions or even legislative language to that end. Some problems were resolved entirely; on others agreement was reached in principle, and the affected members were sent off to work out the details; on still others, no progress was made, but the members were exhorted to go back and try again.

By late Thursday afternoon, October 20, this process had accomplished what it could. Many differences had been resolved. However, others, which had seemingly been resolved, emerged again as tentative agreements fell apart. The time pressure under which members negotiated sometimes led to disagreements about what actually had been agreed to; the process of transforming verbal agreements into legislative language sometimes revealed disagreement; and sometimes negotiators found they could not sell a deal they had made to their interested colleagues. On still other disagreements, the opponents refused to give any ground. Late in the day the issue of random drug testing of transportation workers, an issue on which House and Senate were adamant and split, came up again. Foley in jest suggested trial by combat. Not long after, Dole came in and, after being briefed, concluded that the testing issue was "one of those issues that will have to go to the Supreme Court" of top leaders. "Is it the only one?" he asked hopefully. No, Nunn told him, there are seven or eight.

Resolving the Tough Ones: The "Supreme Court" Decides

At 7 p.m. in the Speaker's office, the "Supreme Court" gathered: Speaker Wright, House Majority Leader Foley, House Minority Leader Michel, Senate Majority Leader Byrd, Senate Minority Leader Dole, and Senators Nunn and Rudman. An amendment by Sen. Jesse Helms, R-N.C., lifting diplomatic immunity for diplomats who deal in drugs, drive drunk, or commit a violent crime was the first order of business. The Reagan administration opposed the amendment as did many House Foreign Affairs Committee members; the senators were not willing to fight for it, and it was tentatively dropped. The related issues of drug testing and tough new certification standards for labs that do drug tests were discussed. Democratic representative John D. Dingell of Michigan, chair of the committee that had drafted the certification provisions, came by to report that some seemingly hopeful talks had gotten nowhere. Finally, the leaders decided to drop the provisions altogether.

Senate Democrats "had problems" with the House's user accountability provision; they believed it unworkable. Dropping that provision was not, however, a viable option; both chambers had voted for a version, and there was too much support for it, especially in the House. After lengthy discussion a compromise was worked out between the House and Senate versions that included the Senate's provision making the denial of benefits discretionary for the judge. The "innocent owner" provision was still a problem; the Customs Service, Rudman reported, was strongly opposed to the change: "they keep coming back at us like the Mongolian hordes."

Working from the various proposals that had been made on the issue, the leadership group came up with a hybrid compromise: if someone is caught with a small amount, forfeiture of the boat or other vehicle could occur only if the owner displayed "willful blindness"; on the other hand, if someone is caught with a large amount, the owner must show that he did everything reasonable to prevent the use of his boat or vehicle for the purpose of drug running.

A nongermane provision in the Senate bill, a far-reaching proposal on child pornography and obscenity, proved to be the single most difficult issue. Language allowing the federal government to seize property used to commit or promote the commission of an obscenity offense was so broad, opponents claimed, that innocent retailers might have their bookstores or video rental businesses seized because a federal prosecutor determined that a book or video in the store's inventory was "obscene" (Lawrence 1988b, 3032). Judiciary Committee negotiators believed they had reached an agreement to drop the obscenity language late October 19. However, when the Moral Majority learned of the deal and began to put pressure on members, the agreement fell apart. Thus, this provision fell to the top leaders to resolve as well.

Florida representatives Bill McCollum and E. Clay Shaw Jr., Republican Judiciary Committee members deeply involved in the issue, stopped by the leadership meeting; although they had not been invited, their presence provided the leaders with an opportunity to pressure them. Foley began by saying he had heard disturbing rumors that Republicans planned to violate any agreement reached and to try to defeat the previous question on the rule; their aim, he believed, was to make obscenity a major political issue right before the election. McCollum explained that the provision was a hot political issue with church groups and Women For, a conservative women's group. He conceded that "some guys would like to defeat the previous question." Minority Leader Michel quickly spoke up, saying he knew nothing about such a plan.

The leaders, Democratic and Republican, argued at length that the obscenity language as written was badly flawed and probably unconstitutional. McCollum and Shaw, to a large extent, indicated they agreed with their substantive arguments but that "the political forces behind this are too strong for any of us to stop"; if the obscenity language were dropped from the bill there was nothing they could do to stop right-wing members from trying to defeat the previous question and, in fact, they would have to join in the attempt. After considerable pressure from the combined leaders—with Democrats letting Republicans take the lead—McCollum and Shaw did agree to rewrite the language to decrease the Draconian effect of the forfeitures on people who do not produce but sell or show "obscene" materials. McCollum promised to work out the details of the language with his House and Senate Democratic counterparts.

By the next morning the obscenity provisions were still a problem; Judiciary Committee members were working on language but had not yet come to an agreement and the chair of House Judiciary still wanted to drop the provision entirely, a course of action House party leaders were convinced could not be sold to their members or sustained on the floor. Only days before the election few Democrats would be willing to cast a vote that an opponent could characterize as pro-obscenity. A usually reliable Democrat warned Foley on the floor that a deal on the obscenity provision had to be worked out; if it came to a vote, he would have to vote with the revolters. The innocent owner provision was causing problems again as well. Because he had been out of town, New Jersey Democrat Bill Hughes, chair of the House Judiciary subcommittee with jurisdiction, had not been a party to the most recent negotiations and objected strenuously to some aspects of the agreement reached by the leaders.

After spending much of the day working on other legislation, most importantly a tax bill, the Speaker, Foley, Majority Whip Coelho, Byrd, Michel, and Dole met for a final time at 5:30 p.m. on October 21. Foley, who had continued his task of monitoring, reported on the six or so problems that remained. Hughes was called in, and an agreement on the innocent owner provision was reached. A number of other issues were discussed, in several cases ones that had seemingly been resolved earlier. This time everyone knew there would be no tomorrow, and final decisions were made, sometimes after checking by phone with the administration or affected members.

The obscenity provision remained unresolved. Hughes and McCollum were called in and reported that they had agreed on "85 percent" but were at loggerheads on the remaining issues. Foley had a staff aide call Senator Rudman, hoping he could persuade McCollum to compromise. He was being besieged by the religious right, McCollum claimed, and could not give in any more than he already had. After a long discussion, Hughes suggested a compromise by which the stringent forfeiture provisions would apply only to those "engaged in the business" of selling pornography, thus exempting the inadvertent store owner. Under intense pressure from everyone in the room, with Rudman taking the lead, McCollum agreed to take the compromise proposal to the members threatening to try to defeat the previous question and "see if I can sell it."

At 9:50 p.m. Hughes and McCollum found the Speaker in the House dining room having a quick dinner and reported they had a deal. Even then getting McCollum's religious right colleagues to sign off on the exact wording took more time. The tax bill was finally ready for floor consideration at 10 p.m. Negotiations on that bill had been going on simultaneously with those on the drug bill and the party leaders, especially the Speaker and Dole, had to divide their time between the two. At 11 p.m. the Speaker, Foley, and Michel left the floor of the House and went to the Speaker's ceremonial office to place the traditional call to the president, informing him that Congress was about to adjourn. Although the leaders usually make the call after adjournment, they decided the president would really rather not be called in the middle of the night.

The tax bill was completed and the drug bill called up on the House floor about midnight. At 1:20 a.m. the House cleared the drug bill on a 346–11 vote. The House actually voted to agree to Foley's motion to concur in the Senate amendment to HR5210 with an amendment—this "amendment" being the product of the lengthy negotiations. At 3:15 a.m. the Senate concurred in the House amendment by voice vote, thus clearing the Omnibus Drug Initiative Act of 1988 for the president. Both chambers adjourned sine die immediately after their vote, thereby bringing the weary 100th Congress to an end.

The 1988 omnibus drug bill was enacted through a "designer" process; abandoning the orthodox, leaders by plan and by improvisation devised a process to cope with the specific problems this piece of legislation presented. Little about this process—from the majority leader's supervisory role in the House, to the bypassing of committees and use of task forces to craft legislation in the Senate, to the informal multistage process culminating in the "Supreme Court" of top party leaders to resolve differences between the chambers—would have been familiar to members who served in the Congress of the 1970s or even the Congress of the early 1980s.

Unorthodox Lawmaking in the House and Senate: Lessons from Three Cases

The legislative process in the U.S. Congress is much more varied than it used to be; as the three cases in Chapters 7, 8, and 9 illustrate, the path from introduction to enactment (or legislative death) can differ radically from one bill to another.

The net impact of the new procedures and practices differs substantially for the House and the Senate, as these cases also suggest. In the House the procedures by and large are under the control of leaders who use them to further the legislative goals of their members by facilitating the passage of legislation. On balance, the party leadership in the House has gained considerable control over the legislative process and

TABLE 9.1 Omnibus Drug Initiative Act of 1988: A Chronology

Date	House Action	Date	Senate Action	Date	Postpassage Action
April	*Speaker Wright decides Congress should pass drug bill; asks Majority Leader Foley to oversee process of putting together a bill.*				
5/2	*Democratic leaders meet with chairs of eleven committees to discuss what to include.*				
5/9	*Wright announces initiative at his press conference.*				
5/9–late June	*Committees work on legislative language; Foley rides heard.*	June	*Party working groups craft drug proposals.*		
Mid-June–August 11	*Foley works with committees to put bill together; works with Minority Leader Michel on rule for its consideration.*	July	*Majority Leader Byrd and Minority Leader Dole appoint a bipartisan working group to negotiate a bill.*		
		July–September	*Bipartisan working group negotiates.*		
8/10	Rules Committee grants rule for consideration of omnibus drug initiative.				
8/11	Foley introduces HR5210, the Omnibus Drug Initiative Act of 1988; House agrees to rule.				
9/7– 9/8, 9/14– 9/16	House considers HR5210.				

9/22   House passes HR5210.

10/3   Senator Nunn, leading Democrat on the working group, introduces S2852, the core bill agreed on by the working group; S2852 is placed directly on the Senate's legislative calendar.

Unanimous consent agreement for considering S2852 is negotiated by the working group leaders and the party leadership.

10/12   Senate accepts unanimous consent agreement.

10/13   Senate considers S2852.

10/14   Senate considers and passes bill: it strikes all after the enacting clause of HR5210 and inserts in lieu thereof the text of S2852; then passes HR5210 as amended.

10/14– *House and Senate members and*
10/21   *leaders negotiate informally and reach an agreement.*

10/21   House concurs in the Senate amendment (Senate bill) with an amendment (bill negotiated between the chambers). Senate agrees to House amendment to Senate amendment.

11/18   President signs Omnibus Drug Initiative Act of 1988 and it becomes law.

NOTE: Official actions are in roman type; behind-the-scenes, unofficial actions are in italics.

is often now able to tailor the process to the problems specific legislation raises.

In contrast, because of senators' willingness to push their prerogatives to the limit, passing legislation in the Senate requires that all interested senators be accommodated or super majorities mustered. In trying to promote the passage of legislation his members need and want, the Senate majority leader often becomes a key negotiator. In working out postcommittee adjustments to legislation and in other negotiations, he does not, however, operate from a position of strength; unlike the House Speaker, the Senate majority leader has few tools for facilitating the passage of legislation. Because of his scheduling responsibilities and his central location in the chamber's information network, the Senate majority leader is often more likely than anyone else to be able to put together an agreement on highly contentious legislation. That does give him some leverage but only with those senators who want legislation. On the 1988 drug bill the Senate party leaders in concert were able to exert extraordinary control over the process because most senators ardently desired legislation and none wanted to be responsible for killing the bill. On national service and especially on regulatory reform, the majority leader's leverage was much more limited. With senators who prefer no bill, the majority leader's leverage is minimal.

The Budget Process as an Instrument for Policy Change: Clinton's Economic Program

DURING THE 1992 CAMPAIGN, CANDIDATE BILL CLINTON advocated making major changes in the direction and priorities of the federal government. In 1993 the problem confronting President Clinton and the congressional Democratic leadership was how to get such comprehensive—and sometimes painful—policy change through Congress. The usual difficulty of enacting major policy change would be exacerbated, they knew, by the highly charged partisan atmosphere and the growing ideological gulf between the parties. Two years later the new Republican congressional majorities faced the same problem in even starker terms; in their Contract with America House Republicans were advocating considerably more far-reaching changes in policy direction, they confronted an opposition party president, their margin was narrower, and the atmosphere had become even more intensely partisan.[1]

In both cases, as this and the next chapter show, the procedural solution to the problem was the congressional budget process. Through the budget process many changes in policy can be made in one piece of legislation rather than in a number of separate bills, so fewer battles have to be won. By custom, budget measures are considered on the House floor under tight rules restricting the number of amendments that may be

---

1. I thank Edward Artinian and Chatham House Publishers, Inc. for permission to reprint in this chapter in considerably rewritten form parts of pages 102–109 from my essay "Trying to Govern Positively in a Negative Era: Clinton and the 103rd Congress," in *The Clinton Presidency: First Appraisals,* edited by Colin Campbell and Bert Rockman, published in 1996.

offered, thus further reducing the fights that must be waged. Senate rules prohibit extended debate on budget measures, a huge advantage to those endeavoring to enact legislation. The deadlines in the Congressional Budget and Impoundment Control Act of 1974 (hereafter the Budget Act) exert a pressure to action that can also work to the advantage of those attempting to pass a bill.

The congressional budget process is, however, a complex process even when it is not used to attempt to enact comprehensive policy change. Its deadlines can present problems as well as exerting salutary pressure for action. Successful completion of the budget process depends upon supervision and coordination by the congressional majority party leadership; when the process is used to make major policy change, leadership involvement must be continuous and intense. Adroit use of the full set of procedural strategies that the new legislative process makes available to leaders is necessary but, as the next chapter shows, still does not guarantee success.

Budget Policy Making and Politics:
The Context in 1993

Because the economy was the 1992 campaign's dominant issue, the success of Bill Clinton and the Democratic Congress in enacting an effective economic program became a key test of whether the Democratic Party could govern.[2] Democrats had been out of the White House for twelve years, and Jimmy Carter, the last Democratic president, was remembered as ineffective. Could a Democratic president provide effective leadership, and would congressional Democrats, accustomed to going it alone, work cooperatively with the new president?

As a newly elected president who had run on the issue, Clinton set the economic policy agenda. The approach Clinton had outlined during the campaign was complex: it involved an immediate stimulus to jumpstart a sluggish economy, major long-term investment spending in areas such as education and infrastructure, and deficit reduction through tax increases on the wealthy and spending cuts in less essential programs. The news media, however, painted the election as primarily a public call for deficit reduction, in part because of Ross Perot's surprisingly strong showing in the 1992 presidential election. A sizable number of congressional

---

2. At the beginning of the 103rd Congress, there were 258 Democrats, 176 Republicans, and 1 Independent in the House; the Senate consisted of 57 Democrats and 43 Republicans.

Democrats, including many of the large freshman class, believed they would be judged in terms of how much they cut spending and reduced the deficit. In contrast, Democrats from core Democratic districts tended to emphasize the stimulus and investment spending.

On February 17, in his first address to a joint session of Congress, Clinton outlined an economic program containing the three basic elements: economic stimulus, investment spending, and deficit reduction. In response to the political climate and strong economic growth in the fourth quarter of 1992, the direct spending part of the stimulus program was reduced to $16.3 billion. The revenue component included tax increases for corporations, the wealthy, and upper-income social security recipients, and it contained a broad-based energy tax (the Btu tax).

Congressional Democrats, by and large, reacted favorably, though they knew passing it would not be easy given the ambitiousness of the package. Republicans immediately went on the attack, blasting the proposal for being tax heavy (Hager 1993, 355–359). Opposition to any new taxes has become a core tenant of Republican ideology, and many congressional Republicans believed George Bush's reneging on his "no new taxes" campaign pledge had cost him reelection to the presidency in 1992. Understandably, the public never wants to pay more taxes, and, in a period of pervasive distrust of government, no politician will damage his reelection prospects by opposing them.

The lack of incentives for Republicans to support Clinton's economic program made it clear from the beginning that Democrats would have to pass it on their own. Rep. Dick Armey of Texas, a Republican leader in the House, expressed his party's hard-line opposition: "They wanted to lead, now they've got to live with the accountability. Why should we give them cover?" (Fessler 1993, 380).

Although the stimulus package would be enacted as a supplemental appropriations bill, most of the rest of the program would be enacted through the budget process. That would require Congress to pass a budget resolution with instructions to the substantive committees to bring law in their areas of jurisdiction into conformity with the budget resolution and then enact a massive reconciliation bill incorporating all those changes.

Committing to the Clinton Plan: Crafting and Passing the Budget Resolution

On March 10 the House Budget Committee approved a budget resolution that closely followed Clinton's plan. However, the Congressional Budget Office's estimate of how much deficit reduction the Clinton plan accomplished had showed a shortfall of about $66 billion from the administration's estimate and, to get the support of "deficit hawk" Democrats, Democratic Budget Committee leaders had had to add $63 billion in spending cuts to the resolution. With this change committee Democrats held firm and voted down every Republican amendment, frequently on straight party-line votes. The committee approved the resolution on a vote of 27 to 16 with every Democrat supporting it and every Republican opposed.

The next day the Senate Budget Committee approved a similar resolution on a 12–9 party-line vote. Despite the Senate committee's much narrower partisan margin, Senate Democrats maintained sufficient unity to vote down every Republican attempt to alter the resolution.

The House Democratic leadership brought the budget resolution to the floor on March 17. Such early consideration was the result of a problem that developed with the stimulus package. Republicans' attacks made many Democrats nervous about voting for spending increases before they voted for spending cuts. To alleviate those members' concerns and ensure their votes, Clinton and the congressional leadership decided on a schedule change: action on the budget resolution would be accelerated, and it would be brought to the floor before the stimulus package.

On March 17 a rule for general debate on the budget resolution was approved. This rule, which provided for ten hours of general debate, allowed the House to begin consideration while the rule covering the amendment process was still being worked out. The next day the second rule was brought to the floor and approved by a strictly party-line vote. That rule allowed votes only on four comprehensive substitutes; crucially, no narrow amendments aimed at particular unpopular provisions were allowed. The substitutes were not amendable and were to be voted on in the order specified using the king-of-the-hill procedure under which the last one approved prevails. A substitute by Rep. John R. Kasich, R-Ohio, then ranking minority member on the Budget Committee, was placed first; it proposed deeper spending cuts and no tax increases. Another Republican substitute, offered by Gerald B. H. Solomon of New York, was placed second; the Solomon substitute added to the Draconian spending cuts in the Kasich proposal some of the tax increases in the Democrats' plan to achieve much deeper deficit reduction. The Black Caucus substitute, placed third in order, was a liberal plan that increased taxes more and made greater cuts in defense spending in order to make fewer domestic spending cuts. Last, in the advantaged position, was the "substitute consisting of the text of the concurrent resolution as reported by the Budget Committee"—that is, the Democratic leadership's proposal.

The House voted down all three substitutes by wide margins; even the Kasich substitute garnered only 135 votes; about a quarter of Republicans voted against it. Only nineteen Republicans (and one Democrat) voted for the Solomon substitute, showing again the central place that opposition to all new taxes had come to occupy in Republican Party doctrine. The Black Caucus substitute attracted eighty-seven votes. The budget resolution was then approved by a vote of 243 to 183; no Republicans voted for it, only eleven Democrats voted in opposition.

In the Senate Democratic leaders had to pass the budget resolution without the help of a restrictive rule to protect their members from tough votes. To keep the plan intact, Democrats had to vote down a plethora of amendments, most offered by Republicans to cause Democrats maximum pain. Thus, Republicans forced votes on amendments to delete the tax increase on high-income social security recipients, to reduce or delete the new energy taxes, to exempt certain small businesses from the increase in corporate taxes, and to cut the Congress's own operating funds by 25 percent. Democrats stuck together and voted down every substantive change Republicans attempted to make. To make it a little easier on their members, Democratic leaders offered a number of "sense of the Senate" resolutions, which allow senators to go on the record but have no binding effect. Sen. Edward M. Kennedy, D-Mass., for example, offered an amendment to express the sense of the Senate that the Btu tax should not apply to fuel used for home heating. On March 25, after six days of floor debate and forty-five roll calls, the Senate approved by a 54–45 vote a budget resolution very similar to the one that passed the House; no Republican supported the economic blueprint, all but two Democrats voted for it. Because budget resolutions are considered under special Budget Act rules that limit debate, Republicans could stretch out the process and make Democrats take a series of tough votes, but they could not block action.

The differences between the House and Senate versions were not large, and the conference committee quickly came to an agreement. The House on March 31 and the Senate on April 1 approved the conference report. The votes were largely along party lines and almost identical to the initial passage votes. (See Table 10.1 for a chronology of action on the budget resolution and on the reconciliation bill that followed.)

Delivering on Promised Policy Change: Reconciliation

Passing a budget resolution that reflected Clinton's priorities was an important first step; the crucial next step of enacting a reconciliation bill would, Democrats knew, be much harder. The budget resolution is a blueprint for future congressional decisions. It does not become law and does not actually make any changes in policy; the detail about policy that it, or

TABLE 10.1   1993 Budget Process: A Chronology

		Budget Resolution			
Date	House Action	Date	Senate Action	Date	Postpassage Action
	President Clinton outlines economic program in an address to a joint session of Congress on February 17, 1993.				
2/23–3/5	House Budget Committee holds hearings.				
3/10	House Budget Committee marks up the budget resolution, H.Con. Res. 64, and orders it reported.	3/12	Senate Budget Committee marks up the budget resolution, S.Con. Res. 18, and orders it reported.		
	House Democratic leadership negotiates postcommittee adjustments.				
3/16	Rules Committee grants rule for general debate only.				
3/17	House approves rule and completes general debate. Rules Committee grants second rule allowing votes on four substitutes.				
3/18	House approves rule, considers resolution for amendments, and passes resolution, 243–183.	3/25	Senate passes budget resolution, 54–45.	3/25	House and Senate name conferees.
				3/31	Conferees agree to file a conference report. House approves conference report, 240–184.
				4/1	Senate approves conference report, 55–45.
					Budget resolution having been approved by both chambers is now in effect.

			Reconciliation Bill		
Date	House Action	Date	Senate Action	Date	Postpassage Action
3/31–5/13	House committees instructed by reconciliation instructions in budget resolution hold hearings and mark up their recommendations.				
5/6	Budget reconciliation recommendations are ordered reported by the Banking, Finance, and Urban Affairs Committee.				
5/11	Budget reconciliation recommendations are ordered reported by the Energy and Commerce Committee and the Veterans' Affairs Committee.				
5/12	Budget reconciliation recommendations are ordered reported by the Armed Services, Education and Labor, Merchant Marine and Fisheries, and Natural Resources committees.	6/9–6/18	Senate committees instructed by reconciliation instructions in budget resolution consider and mark up their recommendations.		
5/13	Budget reconciliation recommendations are ordered reported by the Agriculture, Ways and Means, Post Office and Civil Service (with a provision approved by Foreign Affairs), and Public Works and Transportation committees.	6/9	Budget reconciliation recommendations are ordered reported by the Energy and Natural Resources, Banking, Housing and Urban Affairs, and Governmental Affairs committees.		
5/20	Budget Committee marks up reconciliation bill, HR2264, and orders it reported.	6/10	Budget reconciliation recommendations are ordered reported by the Armed Services, Veterans' Affairs, Judiciary, Foreign Relations, Environment and Public Works, and Labor and Human Resources committees.		

TABLE 10.1 (Continued)

			Reconciliation Bill		
Date	House Action	Date	Senate Action	Date	Postpassage Action
	Majority Leader negotiates postcommittee changes in bill to pick up support.				
5/26	Rules Committee grants rule with self-executing provision and allows only the Kasich substitute.	6/15	Budget reconciliation recommendations are ordered reported by the Commerce, Science and Transportation Committee.		
5/27	House adopts rule. House considers and passes reconciliation bill, 219–213.	6/18	Budget reconciliation recommendations are ordered reported by the Finance Committee.		
		6/22–	Budget Committee orders		
		6/24	reported the reconciliation bill, S1134. Senate begins consideration of bill.	6/24	Senate conferees are named.
				7/14	House conferees are named.
		6/25	Senate considers and passes bill, 50–49 (with the vice president voting 'yea').	7/15	Additional House conferees are named.
				8/3	Conferees agree to file conference report.
				8/5	House considers and approves conference report 218–216.
				8/6	Senate considers and approves conference report 51–50 (with the vice president voting 'yea').
				8/10	President Clinton signs HR2264, the Omnibus Budget Act of 1993, and it becomes law.

NOTE: Official actions are in roman type; behind-the-scenes, unofficial actions are in italics.

the report accompanying it, may contain is just advice to committees. To enact into law policy changes meeting the budget resolution's deficit reduction targets, the Congress must pass a reconciliation bill. In the Senate particularly, Democratic leaders had persuaded some of their members to vote for the resolution and against Republicans' attempts to change it by reminding them that the policy detail in the resolution was not binding. Once work on the reconciliation bill began, that argument could no longer be made. As Minority Leader Bob Dole of Kansas put it, "We start shooting with real bullets from here on" (*Congressional Quarterly Almanac 1993*, 106).

The political climate had also become more difficult for Democrats. Although the scheduling change had facilitated easy passage of the stimulus package in the House, a Republican filibuster in the Senate eventually killed it. Republicans had won the media battle, successfully portraying the stimulus bill as wasteful spending on pork barrel projects. The consequent lack of public demand for the bill allowed Republicans to kill it without great fear that they would pay an electoral price (Sinclair 1996).

Reconciliation in the House

The 1993 budget resolution contained instructions to thirteen House committees and twelve Senate committees to make changes in law under their jurisdiction so as to meet specific deficit reduction targets assigned to them. By Budget Act rules the committees are free to ignore any specific recommendations for policy change contained in the budget resolution or the report accompanying it, but they are bound to meet the total amount of savings assigned to them. For example, the tax-writing committees could ignore any budget resolution recommendations about what sorts of taxes to raise; they were only required to make changes in law sufficient to produce their deficit reduction figure. In its policy recommendations the 1993 budget resolution largely followed Clinton's economic program. Only if the resolution's recommendations were followed at least in broad outline could the end result of the process be considered a victory for the president and his supporters.

The Btu tax was shaping up as a particular problem. The administration favored it because it was a broad-based tax on all energy sources and thus seemed fair and because it would improve the environment by promoting more efficient use of energy. The tax's broad reach, however, proved to be a serious problem: it stimulated a broad range of interests to lobby against the tax. The big umbrella business organizations, such as the National Association of Manufacturers and the U.S. Chamber of Commerce, opposed it; many affected industries—for example, the oil industry, which was especially heavily taxed by the plan, and the aluminum industry, which is a heavy energy user—worked feverishly to get changes or kill the Btu tax altogether.

The House Ways and Means Committee and the Senate Finance Committee were responsible for by far the single biggest chunk of deficit reduction; not only do these committees write tax legislation, but they also have jurisdiction over Medicare, from which the Clinton plan proposed extracting a significant amount of savings. Because the Constitution specifies that tax legislation must originate in the House, the Ways and Means Committee began work first. Its chairman, Rep. Dan Rostenkowski, D-Ill., vowed to produce legislation close to Clinton's proposal. To put together a coalition that could withstand Republicans' continuing attacks on the Clinton plan, he met behind closed doors with committee Democrats, working out agreements that brought them on board. Much of the negotiations concerned the Btu tax; members sought to protect their regions and crucial industries in their districts. A number of exemptions were written into the legislation. The chairman made it clear that Democrats who were accommodated were then expected to support the bill actively. On May 6, when committee markup began, Democrats immediately voted to work on the bill in closed session; Rostenkowski knew that holding his coalition together would be easier away from the press and the legion of interested lobbyists. Democrats voted down every Republican amendment and, on May 13, approved the legislation on a 24 to 14 party-line vote.

The legislation that Rostenkowski had put together and that the committee approved largely followed Clinton's blueprint. It raised income taxes on the rich and on high-income social security recipients, it included a Btu tax (though one with some exemptions), it increased the earned-income tax credit for the working poor, and it extracted significant savings from Medicare. To lessen the opposition of business and thus gain the votes of conservative Democrats, Rostenkowski significantly cut the increase in the corporate tax rate that Clinton had proposed.

All thirteen House committees met their May 14 deadline for reporting and met the deficit reduction targets assigned to them; although a multitude of smaller compromises were made to get the necessary majorities, the major features of Clinton's economic program were preserved. The Budget Committee packaged the provisions from all the committees into one bill and ordered it reported on May 20.

Clinton and the Democratic leadership faced a formidable task in passing the bill. Ambitious deficit reduction targets had been met, which meant that inevitably many committees had made unpopular decisions. Not only would Democrats have to pass the legislation without any help from Republicans, they would have to contend with the Republicans' loud and repeated charge that the program consisted mostly of taxes on the middle class.

The job of passing the bill in the House became immeasurably harder when, on May 20, Sen. David Boren, D-Okla., an ally of his home state's gas and oil interests, and three colleagues (two moderate Republicans and another conservative oil-state Democrat) proposed an alternative reconciliation package that eliminated the Btu tax and imposed a cap on entitlement spending. A few days later Boren formally announced that he would vote against the Btu tax in the Senate Finance Committee, which would have to approve the tax law changes. Since the party ratio on the committee was only 11 Democrats to 9 Republicans, his opposition made the survival of the Btu tax, and even of the broad package, appear doubtful. House Democrats were leery of voting for the unpopular Btu tax only to see it die in the Senate. "We don't want to be in a position of walking the plank and then have them go over and make a compromise in the Senate," Rep. Charles Wilson, D-Texas, explained (Hager and Cloud 1993a, 1278). Boren's high profile opposition also gave impetus to a push by conservative House Democrats for a cap on entitlement spending, which was in Boren's plan as well.

A deal on the entitlement cap, intimations of changes in the Btu tax in the Senate, adept procedural strategy, and an intense lobbying campaign by the House Democratic leadership and the administration produced a close win on the House floor.

Majority Leader Richard A. Gephardt of Missouri brokered a compromise on entitlements that satisfied conservatives without alienating liberals. Throughout the budget process two deficit hawk Democrats— Charles W. Stenholm of Texas and Timothy J. Penny of Minnesota—had advocated placing a tight cap on entitlement spending; they wanted a mechanism by which, if such spending exceeded the cap, cuts would automatically occur. This was a proposal that neither the White House nor Democratic leaders liked. Stenholm had been pressuring the Speaker to allow him to offer such an amendment on the floor, threatening to lead a revolt by conservative Democrats against the rule if his amendment were barred. When shortly before floor action was planned, Democrats still lacked enough votes to pass the rule, the Speaker instructed the majority leader to try to work out a deal. Less than twenty-four hours before the floor vote, an agreement was reached; rather than automatic cuts if the entitlement cap were exceeded, the president would have to propose a way of paying for the overspending, or he would have to raise the cap. Congress would have to vote on whatever the president proposed.

The administration got some energy-state Democrats back on board by acknowledging what was becoming inevitable: the Btu tax would be altered in the Senate.

The House leadership brought the bill to the floor under a rule that allowed only a vote on a comprehensive Republican substitute; amendments to delete various unpopular elements of the package—the Btu tax and the tax on social security payments to high-income recipients—were barred. The rule also prohibited the minority from offering a motion to recommit with instructions, which is another way of amending the bill. The rule thus gave Republicans an opportunity to offer a comprehensive alternative to the Democratic plan, and it gave the whole House a choice between two distinct approaches. The rule, however, made it impossible for Republicans to use the amendment process to unravel the Democratic package by narrowly targeting the least palatable provisions, and it also protected Democrats from having to cast some excruciatingly difficult votes. A vote for a deficit reduction package would be easier for Democrats to explain to their constituents than a stand-alone vote for higher taxes.

In addition to these provisions, the rule contained what is called a "self-executing" provision by which adoption of the rule simultaneously results in adoption of certain legislative language. In this case the deal on the entitlement cap, as well as some other language about enforcement of the budget agreement that was worked out after the bill was reported from committee, was thereby incorporated into the bill without requiring a separate vote.

Whip David E. Bonior, D-Mich., personally headed up the whip task force set up to pass the bill. Starting work several weeks before the bill got to the floor, members of the task force, and later the top leaders, unrelentingly pursued every House Democrat. Anyone who might have influence with an undecided or recalcitrant member—state party chairmen, governors, union officials, personal friends—was enlisted to help in the persuasion effort. The administration was very much engaged in the drive to build support for the bill. Cabinet secretaries called and visited Democrats; Secretary of the Treasury Lloyd Bentsen, for example, attended the Texas delegation's regular lunch meeting to sell the bill. Two days before the vote, President Clinton invited about seventy-five House members to the White House; he personally called close to sixty members—some of them repeatedly.

Given the level of effort, no Democrat could fail to understand that how he voted on the bill would affect his future in the House. As Rep. Barney Frank, D-Mass., said, "Nobody got a pass on this" (Hager and Cloud 1993b, 1341). At a Democratic caucus meeting the day before the vote,

some members made clear that this was a litmus test vote, that future decisions on committee and subcommittee chairmanships would be influenced by how members voted. Just before the vote, freshmen circulated a
petition demanding that any committee or subcommittee chair who voted
against the party be stripped of his or her position by the caucus. Within
hours, more than eighty Democrats, including several influential committee chairmen, had signed (Hager and Cloud 1993b, 1345).

The rule was adopted by a vote of 236 to 194, with all but nineteen
Democrats and no Republicans supporting it. Republicans were much
less united on their substitute; as with the budget resolution, many
Republicans believed attacking the Democratic plan without giving
Democrats anything on which to attack them was the politically smarter
course. The Kasich substitute received only 138 votes; forty Republicans
opposed it.

Because of the character of the rule, the key vote would be on passage. The Speaker himself closed floor debate for his party, acknowledging that this was indeed a tough vote: "We seldom do important, valuable
and lasting things by taking easy votes, comfortable votes, politically popular votes." He challenged members, saying "this is a time to stand and
deliver; this is a time to justify your election" (Hager and Cloud 1993b,
1341). On May 27 the House passed the legislation, 219–213; again, not a
single Republican voted in support; thirty-eight Democrats opposed their
party's position.

Reconciliation in the Senate

Although twelve Senate committees were under instructions to report
reconciliation provisions, the Finance Committee had by far the most formidable task; the fate of Clinton's economic program depended largely
on Finance Committee action. Boren's opposition to the Btu tax and the
committee's narrow partisan margin meant that significant changes would
have to be made. Some strategists suggested that the Democratic leadership bypass the Finance Committee altogether and bring the tax and
other provisions within its jurisdiction to the floor directly. Majority
Leader George Mitchell of Maine decided not to do so, evidently convinced that such a course would only make a hard job harder.

Committee chairman Daniel Patrick Moynihan, D-N.Y., and Mitchell,
who was a member of Finance, took on the task of putting together a
package that could pass the committee and the chamber. Given the hard-
ening of the Republicans' antitax position, they knew they had to form
their majority from Democrats only. It took "two weeks of grinding negotiations" to craft a compromise package (Cloud, Hager, and Rubin 1993,

1542). As had been expected from the beginning of the negotiations, the Btu tax was jettisoned; that, however, produced a huge revenue shortfall. Eventually, a gas tax, sharper cuts in Medicare, and a host of minor changes were agreed to. Republicans offered a multitude of amendments during markup, but once the deal was struck, Democrats held together and defeated them all.

On June 18 the Finance Committee reported its crucial part of the reconciliation bill on a straight party-line vote of 11 to 9. The other committees had already complied with their instructions and reported their provisions. On June 22 the Budget Committee ordered the reconciliation bill reported.

On June 23 Tennessee Democrat James Sasser, chairman of the Senate Budget Committee, began floor debate on the reconciliation bill by reminding his colleagues what was at stake and thanking the committees for doing their job:

> Mr. President,[3] the Senate today begins consideration of the budget reconciliation bill. The reconciliation bill is really the centerpiece of the President's economic proposal and economic plan. What this reconciliation bill includes is all of the spending cuts that have come from all of the committees stretched across the Senate . . . along with enhanced revenues also coming from the Committee on Finance. All across the Senate the committees and the committee chairmen have done their duties.
>
> I want to express my appreciation to 12 of the Senate committee chairmen for their stalwart work in producing this record reconciliation bill. . . . This was not an easy task. Deficit reduction never is. . . . Everyone is for reducing the deficit in the general sense. But when you get down to the specifics, no one seems to want to do the specifics that are required to actually reduce the deficit. . . . So, deficit reduction is something everybody likes to talk about but no one really wants to do much about it. I think literally hundreds of Academy Awards would be in order for some of the posturing and play acting that I have witnessed over the past few years. . . .
>
> So, the President of the United States and the committees of the U.S. Senate looked the deficit squarely in the eye and they made some very difficult, some very tough, and some very painful choices in developing this reconciliation bill. The fruits of their labor are before us today. We have produced $347 billion in savings over the next 5 years. And a landmark $516 billion . . . in deficit reduction in this total bill when we are through with it (*Congressional Record,* June 23, 1993, S7662).

---

3. Because the Constitution designates the vice president of the United States as the president of the Senate, the presiding officer of the Senate is always addressed as "Mr. President," even though the vice president seldom presides.

Republicans responded by calling the bill "the largest tax increase in history" and charging that it was a "job killer." As Sen. Phil Gramm, R-Texas, expressed it:

> I oppose this bill because you cannot create more investment by taxing investors. You cannot create more savings by taxing savers. You cannot create more jobs by taxing job creators. Hundreds of thousands of Americans will lose their job because of this bill. Bill Clinton will be one of those Americans, but he will deserve to lose his job (*Congressional Record,* June 23, 1993, S7672).

Democrats argued that, while the bill did raise taxes, most of the new taxes would be paid by the very well off. Yes, it was a tough bill, but a fair and responsible one; it really cut the deficit and did so in a way that spread the pain according to citizens' capacity to pay.

Many acknowledged that they did not like numerous provisions in the bill: "Supporting this bill is a hard choice," admitted Sen. John Glenn, D-Ohio, explaining his vote in favor of the legislation. "I do not like every page, every provision, every punctuation point" (*Congressional Record,* June 23, 1993, S7940). As Sen. Howell Heflin, D-Ala., noted, "there is one thing that is far worse than even the most distasteful provision in this bill. And that is inaction." He continued:

> It is time to act. And it is high time for honesty here in this town. It is time to come clean about what needs to be done. It is no fun voting for taxes. It is much easier to oppose them.
>
> And it is not easy to vote for spending cuts that will hit the elderly, that will hit retirees, that will hit farmers, that will hit Federal workers. It is much easier to oppose these cuts. But I am not here to take the easy way out.
>
> I am here to make the hard choices. To do what is right for my State and for the Nation. And, Mr. President, that is why I am going to vote for this bill (*Congressional Record,* June 23, 1993, S7944).

The debate was heated and sometimes nasty. Sen. David Durenberger of Minnesota, a moderate and not usually a highly partisan Republican, said:

> I rise today in opposition to this reconciliation package. I do so because it represents a breach of faith with the American people—the voters who last November took a chance for change. . . . [I]t is a budget buster and a job killer.

To get the bill out of Finance, Mitchell and Moynihan had deleted provisions intended to provide incentives for investment that small business highly prized. This made a number of moderate Democrats unhappy. As Joseph I. Lieberman of Connecticut, one of these senators, explained, "[Some of] us . . . felt that the bill, as reported out of the Finance Committee, was a good deficit-reduction package, but if it was only that and if it is only that, we have not done our job. We must also do something to stimulate the economy"(*Congressional Record,* June 23, 1993, S7697). When scoring of the Finance Committee bill by the Congressional Budget Office indicated the bill actually exceeded the deficit reduction target by a few billion, Majority Leader Mitchell decided to use that money to ensure those senators' votes. Along with Dale Bumpers, D-Ark., chair of the Senate Small Business Committee, he crafted an amendment that provided a capital gains tax cut targeted at small business, and he increased the amount small business could write off for new equipment.

The Mitchell amendment was the first amendment offered. Support fell primarily along party lines. A few Democrats opposed it as ineffective; most Republicans simply did not want to make the reconciliation bill easier to pass. Budget Act rules impose a strict germaneness requirement on amendments, a test the amendment did not meet. If any senator made a point of order, budget rules would have to be waived to allow consideration of the amendment, and that requires sixty votes. After debate on the amendment, Republicans did raise the point of order; the motion to waive budget rules failed on a 54–44 vote, so despite a majority in support, the amendment was ruled out of order.

Mitchell made another attempt the next day with a revised amendment. This one raised to $20,500 the amount small businesses could deduct for equipment and machinery. This amendment was germane. Since it was clear it would pass, few senators saw any benefit in voting against it; the vote was 93–5.

Budget Act rules protected the bill against a filibuster and made successfully amending it more difficult than with other legislation. Republicans, however, were free to offer all sorts of amendments that would put Democrats in a difficult political position. And that they did. Republicans forced Democrats to vote on all the tough provisions by offering amendments to strike them. Some of the votes were agonizingly close—the amendment to strike the gas tax increase failed by only two votes—but Democrats held together and defeated every significant change.

In the wee hours of June 25, after two long and intense days of floor consideration, the time for the vote came. The majority and minority leaders closed debate. "Mr. President," Senator Mitchell began, "in every human endeavor, there comes a time for action, a time when the words must end and the deeds begin. For those who have so loudly endorsed making real spending cuts and making real deficit reductions, that time is now." Senator Dole responded, "The choice tonight could not be more clear. Senators can vote for President Clinton's record-breaking tax increase or they can cast a vote for America's taxpayers and send a wake-up call to the White House and to the Congress. The President has tried to make this a defining moment of his Presidency. He is right. It is and will be for years to come. He has already earned his place on Mount Tax-more." Senator Mitchell closed:

> For 12 years we have laughed as the national debt has gone up. We have had jokes, not deeds. We have had talk, not action. It is now time for action.
>
> This Chamber has been filled to overflowing with speeches about the need to reduce the deficit and there is only one way to reduce the deficit and that is to vote for this package. There is no other alternative. No other serious or credible alternative has been presented in either Chamber. If you mean to reduce the deficit you must vote for this package.
>
> Mr. President, I ask for the yeas and nays (*Congressional Record,* June 25, 1993, S7986).

At about 3 a.m., the Senate passed the bill on a 50–49 vote, with Vice President Al Gore, as president of the Senate, casting the deciding vote. Every Republican and six Democrats opposed passage.

Resolving House-Senate Differences

Changes made to pass the bill in the Senate and the narrowness of the vote to pass the bill in the Senate and House guaranteed that reaching a conference agreement on a version passable in both houses would be a delicate and difficult task. House liberals—especially members of the Black Caucus—were dismayed with the cuts in benefits for the poor and cities made to compensate for the revenue lost when the Btu tax was replaced by a gas tax. Many deficit hawk Democrats in the Senate had voted for the package without enthusiasm, believing it did not do enough; they might well defect if significant changes were made. A number of western Democrats refused to support a gas tax higher than the 4.3 cents in the Senate bill.

Because so many committees had played a role in drafting the bill, the conference committee was huge: 164 House members from 16 committees and 53 senators from 13 committees. The House delegation was formally composed of twenty-seven subgroups, each with specifically delineated jurisdiction; although the Senate designated no formal subgroups, it was understood that Senate conferees would also work on the provisions from their own committees. Most of the work of crafting a compromise proceeded in subconferences made up of members from the committee that had drafted the legislation and of Budget Committee members; Budget Committee leaders, including House Majority Leader Gephardt, the majority party representative on Budget, took part in all of the subconferences.

The most crucial decisions fell within the jurisdiction of the taxing committees. As other subconferences worked out their differences outside the media's glare, Chairmen Rostenkowski and Moynihan, under intense pressure and scrutiny, began their negotiations. Democratic party leaders and representatives of the Clinton administration also participated. Although the conflicting priorities of the various groups of Democrats who had voted for the bill often made it seem impossible, a compromise package was worked out.

Out of the media's spotlight, Democratic staff worked to protect the bill from Byrd rule attacks.[4] Before the bill had passed the Senate, Pete V. Domenici of New Mexico, ranking minority member on the Budget Committee, had put Democrats on notice. If and when the bill returned from conference, he would invoke the Byrd rule to try to knock many provisions out of the bill as "extraneous matter." Any senator can make a point of order that a provision violates the Byrd rule; if the parliamentarian agrees, sixty votes are required to waive the rule and save the provision. With solid Republican opposition, Democrats knew they could not muster the sixty votes. Therefore, as the conference proceeded, they tried to persuade the parliamentarian that their provisions did not violate the rule, or they tried to work out language that would pass the test. In many cases Democrats were forced to remove provisions; the review mechanism for entitlement spending that had been instrumental in getting deficit hawk Democrats to support the bill in the House fell victim to the Byrd rule.

Already tense relations between House and Senate Democrats were made even worse by the dictates of the Byrd rule. Senate Democrats' individualism, the willingness of many to pursue their own interests and agendas at the expense of those of their party, and Senate rules that encouraged such behavior had infuriated House Democrats all year; they did the responsible thing and took the hard votes and then someone like Senator Boren negated their efforts for narrow selfish gain, they believed. Now, with the Byrd rule, Senate rules were forcing decisions on the House and making House Democrats jettison policy changes dear to their hearts. The animosity of House Democrats for the other body would make the difficult task of passing the conference report even harder, as a House Democrat's complaints about "the insidious influence of the so-called Byrd rule on the conference agreement" make clear:

> In our small section of the conference agreement the Byrd rule was invoked twice and several important provisions were arbitrarily removed from the

---

4. The rule, named after its creator, Sen. Robert C. Byrd, D-W.Va., prohibits "extraneous matter" in reconciliation bills (see Chapter 5).

agreement text of the bill. This occurred after agreements were reached on the basis of many hours of long and intricate negotiations. The House should never enter into negotiations with the other body with our hands tied behind our backs as has happened in this process. We can't let the nameless, the faceless Members of the Senate, treated as a star chamber, dictate at their whim what is extraneous and what is not in the reconciliation process. Mr. Speaker, if this Parliamentary procedure persists it will debilitate the ability of the Congress to do its job. I would suggest our problem is that we are too often barred by archaic rules and procedures of the Senate already, without new impediments being put in place in 1993 (*Congressional Record*, August 5, 1993, H6251).

The End Game: Passing the Conference Report

With a conference agreement in hand, the task of selling it, already under way, intensified. Methodically and relentlessly, the House leadership pursued every Democrat. "There was whip meeting after whip meeting," a participant explained. "Members were getting really sick of being beat on, they would run when we came. But we kept after them." Clinton met personally with almost every organized group of Democrats. His meetings with House groups ranged from the Black Caucus to the Conservative Democratic Forum. He also met with women, freshmen, and even gym users. Many senators and some House members were courted individually as well (Cloud and Hager 1993, 2023–2028; Hook 1993, 2025–2026).

The president and the Democratic leadership argued that the reconciliation bill should be approved because it was good public policy and because Democrats needed to show they could govern. When essential to pick up needed votes, they made deals. Liberals had been mollified by the conference restoring a significant part of the social spending the Senate had cut. On August 4 Clinton by executive order set up an entitlement review process similar to that deleted from the bill because of Byrd rule problems. A last-minute agreement to allow a vote on further spending cuts in the fall satisfied some deficit hawks.

When the mercurial Boren announced he would switch and vote against the conference report, a replacement "yes vote" had to be found. "After four days of feverish wooing" by the administration and Senate leaders, Dennis DeConcini, D-Ariz., agreed to switch his vote; in return he received several policy concessions, including a lessening of the tax bite on social security recipients (Hager and Cloud 1993c, 2122–2129). With every vote essential in the Senate, some erstwhile supporters took advantage of their bargaining position to extract benefits for their constituents; freshman senator Russell D. Feingold, D-Wis., cut a deal on regulation of bovine growth hormone. A tête-à-tête at the White House and a promise of a commission on entitlements finally induced Sen. Bob Kerrey, D-Neb., to declare his support after he had very publicly criticized the package and indicated he might defect.

On August 5 the House began consideration of the reconciliation bill conference report under a rule that allowed six hours of debate. Through a self-executing provision, the rule made the entitlement review process a part of standing House rules; this was done to mollify deficit hawk Democrats.

The debate was highly charged, even for the partisan House. "We oppose this plan because it's a giant tax on the American dream and on America's future," staunch Republican Dick Armey said. "This plan is . . . a recipe for disaster. Democrats may give your President a political victory today, but it's a defeat for our economy and the well-being of the American people." A California Republican charged that "the Clinton tax bill will drive a stake into the heart of California's economy" and another Republican called it "a ship of fools" and urged the House to "sink it." Georgia Republican Newt Gingrich, then the minority whip, predicted the plan would cause "a job-killing recession" (*Congressional Record*, August 5, 1993, H6267–6269).

Democrats defended the plan and accused Republicans of being unwilling to make the hard choices. "Let me tell you what a 'no' vote on this budget means," said a freshman Democrat bluntly, "no action; no growth; no hope; no guts" (*Congressional Record*, August 5, 1993, H6229). Some also charged that their opponents had waged a war of misrepresentation about the bill. Majority Whip Bonior summed up the arguments Democrats were using:

> [W]e are approaching the closing moments of a long and wrenching national debate. This vote is about just one thing—do we have the courage to stand up and take control of our economic future and to get our Nation's house in order? . . . I know this isn't an easy decision. We in public life are often asked to do difficult things. And this is one of those difficult times. There's no easy way to make record reductions. . . . The last two Presidents have just passed the buck, passed the buck to the next generation. . . .
>
> This is the first plan in 12 years that uses real numbers to achieve real results. It's a fair plan, it's responsible, and it deserves a chance to work. We know the bold details of this plan: A record $496 billion deficit cut that will create jobs; over 200 specific spending cuts; 80 percent of the new taxes paid by the wealthiest 1 percent; and 90 percent of small businesses eligible for tax reduction, to name a few.
>
> But we have to remember that there are faces behind these numbers and stories behind these statistics. Real lives of real people.
>
> Deficit reduction will create jobs that will move autoworkers from the unemployment lines to the assembly lines. Low interest rates will put an extra

$175 a month in the pockets of working families able to refinance their homes. The earned income tax credit will give millions of working parents dignity and respect. And small businesses will use tax credits to buy new plants and equipment that will make them more competitive.

That's what this plan will do. That's what it will do for America. That's what it will do for working people. . . .

Let's tell it like it is: [The Republicans] don't have an alternative. . . . And now the choice has come down to our plan or no plan. The American people want change, they voted for change, and it's time we get on with that change. That is what we were sent here to do. . . .

When America's economy is standing tall again, historians will look back to this day and this vote, and say, "that is where it started. That is where it turned around. That is where America's renewal began."

So say "no" to gridlock. Say "no" to the status quo. Don't pass the buck— pass the plan (*Congressional Record*, August 5, 1993, H6254).

The Republicans' responses to Bonior's passionate remarks showed just how far apart the parties were in their beliefs about what constituted good economic policy. Closing debate for the Republicans, Minority Leader Bob Michel said:

The differences here are philosophical, they are real, profound, differences over fundamentals that transcend partisanship.

We will concede, with all the pressure brought to bear by the present leadership on the Democratic side, that you will probably have your way for this day, but we will be back another day to remind you of your folly. . . . [T]his package will not create any new jobs . . . because you are taxing away the incentives of the small entrepreneurs who create three-fourths of all the new jobs that are created in this country. You have been so obsessed with this $500 billion figure that you have lost your marbles attempting to achieve it.

Mr. Speaker, I strongly urge a vote against this harmful, ill-conceived conference report that taxes today or taxes yesterday, taxes today and, yes, taxes tomorrow (*Congressional Record*, August 5, 1993, H6270).

Majority Leader Dick Gephardt, speaking shortly before the vote, talked about the hard work and hard choices putting the package together had entailed:

I have been heartened by seeing all of the parts, all of the beliefs in our Democratic Party come together to work on this plan. I have seen liberal members of our party and moderate members and conservative members give and take, compromise, sacrifice, be willing to take positions that they did not know or think they could take, but took them because they knew the common good of the country was at stake.

And each who has voted for this plan in committee or on the floor has done it knowing that there is no way in the world that we can attack this great deficit without making tough, hard choices that no one really wants to take.

> And I am proud of the members of my party who have come together, taken the choices, made the decisions, and risen to the occasion.

He implicitly acknowledged that the leadership was still uncertain it had the votes to pass the bill when he alluded to the undecided:

> To Members here tonight who are still undecided, let me say this is a challenge, this deficit; this plan is a challenge to our generation that we must meet. . . .
>
> Ladies and gentlemen of the House, . . . surely tonight we can take the responsibility ourselves to see that the country we hand to the next generation is not as good but is better than the country that was handed to us (*Congressional Record*, August 5, 1993, H6270).

Speaker Tom Foley closed debate:

> This is not an easy bill. We have all noted that. . . . The Republican Party will march in lockstep, so we on this side of the aisle must bear the burden of responsibility. We are ready to do it. We are anxious to do it, and we will do it.
>
> The Bible says that there is a time for everything. Tonight is the time to decide. Tonight is the time for courage. Tonight is the time to put away the old easy ways. Tonight is the time for responsibility. Tonight is the night to vote.
>
> Let us not break faith with our people. Let us pass this plan. Let us move forward to a better day for our country (*Congressional Record*, August 5, 1993, H6271).

At the end of an exhausting day of feverish, one-on-one lobbying and combative floor rhetoric, the House passed the conference report by a vote of 218 to 216; only a vote switch by Rep. Marjorie Margolies-Mezvinsky, D-Pa., saved the package. When working to put together a majority on a high-profile, contentious bill, congressional party leaders often accumulate "pocket" or "if you need me" votes; these are promises of votes from members who would rather not support the legislation, usually for reelection-related reasons, but who do not want to be responsible for its demise. Margolies-Mezvinsky, a freshman from a Republican district, had promised her constituents she would vote against any tax increase and had opposed the reconciliation bill initially; she was not willing, however, to grievously wound the Clinton presidency, so she switched her vote.[5]

The next day, August 6, the Senate passed the conference report— also by a hair. The vote was 51 to 50, with Vice President Gore casting the

---

5. Representative Margolies-Mezvinsky was defeated in 1994. Given how badly Democrats did in that election, it is unlikely that voting differently on the conference report would have saved her.

deciding ballot as he had on passage of the reconciliation bill. No Republican in either chamber voted for the legislation. Speaker Foley had been right. The Republicans had marched in lockstep, but the Democrats had held together enough to prevail.

Unified Government, Procedural Control, and Policy Success

Passing the economic program represented a major legislative victory for President Clinton and congressional Democrats. Although many alterations and compromises were made during the long, complex process, the final product followed the outlines of the plan Clinton had laid out in February 1993 and, within the severe constraints imposed by the deficit, reoriented economic policy in a direction Democrats favored. The most significant deviation from the initial proposal and the biggest compromise necessary for passage was substituting a modest gas tax hike for the more ambitious Btu tax.

Democrats accomplished this legislative success by working together across the institutional divide. Throughout the process, Clinton maintained an enormous amount of personal contact with congressional Democrats. The president gave congressional Democrats opportunities to influence the substance of his package and immersed himself in the process of getting it enacted. In early February he invited every member of the House to the White House to consult with him in small groups on the components of the economic plan; he made numerous appearances at Democratic Caucus meetings on the Hill to buck up Democrats; he conducted innumerable one-on-one conversations. A willing participant in the whipping effort, the president learned over time how to nail down a commitment. Early on, congressional participants report, Clinton was too willing to accept excuses from members. The administration also quickly learned to deploy the cabinet and other high-ranking officials to good effect; the ties many of them had to members of Congress served them well in persuasion efforts. "White House budget director Leon E. Panetta, a former House member, and Treasury Secretary Lloyd Bentsen, a former senator, spent so much time on Capitol Hill the week of July 26 that it was easy to forget they ever left the Congress," Congressional Quarterly reported (Hook 1993, 2024). Throughout the process, the Democratic congressional leadership worked closely and loyally with the administration.

As important as cooperation between the president and the congressional majority was to success, the president's program would never have passed were it not for the special procedures the leadership had available and used to maximum effect. In both chambers the leaders worked out postcommittee adjustments to the legislation in order to build majority coalitions. In the House restrictive special rules were crucial to keeping the supportive coalition together. Most important, of course, was the budget process and the packaging it makes possible. Despite voters' professed desire for deficit reduction in the abstract, a real deficit-cutting package will unavoidably contain some unpalatable provisions, and it is unlikely to be popular. Had it been procedurally necessary to bring up those elements as separate bills, few of the provisions would have survived. Packaging allows popular and less popular elements to be combined and reduces the number of fights that need to be won. It also raises the stakes so high that members are faced with repudiating and severely weakening their leaders if they desert them; that makes it high risk for leaders but also gives them leverage. Budget rules give the budget resolution and the reconciliation bill protection against a filibuster and amendments in the Senate that is enormously advantageous.

The budget process makes comprehensive policy change possible; it makes it a bit less difficult for the Congress to make hard choices and unpopular decisions. However, as shown by the saga of Clinton's economic program in 1993 and even more by the Republicans' attempt in 1995 to enact nonincremental policy change, it certainly does not make either comprehensive policy change or hard choices easy.

Success also requires favorable political circumstances. Without a Democratic Congress, President Clinton's economic program would have had no chance at all. With stronger public support, the compromises necessary to pass it would have been less extensive.

The Republican Revolution and the Budget Process

DURING THE 1994 ELECTIONS Republicans promised that, were the voters to make them the congressional majority, they would balance the budget in seven years and enact a host of major policy changes. House Republicans had formalized a number of their promises in their Contract with America, which they pledged to bring to a vote within the first 100 days of the 104th Congress.

In early January 1995 the new Republican majorities in the House and Senate confronted a monumental task in delivering on their promises. Balancing the budget (without touching social security or reducing defense spending, as they had promised) would require restructuring and vastly reducing large, complex federal programs such as Medicare, Medicaid, and farm programs. House Republicans had included a big tax cut in the Contract; fulfilling that promise would, of course, make balancing the budget that much harder. The Contract committed House Republicans to revamping federal welfare programs, especially Aid to Families with Dependent Children (AFDC), and Senate Republicans too were dedicated to that task. To deliver on their campaign promises, Republicans had to make a myriad of highly significant and extraordinarily complex policy decisions, many of which would inflict pain on constituents and thus be extremely controversial, and they had to do so quickly. House Republicans believed they had to bring all the Contract items to the floor within the promised 100 days, but even the full two years of a Congress is not much time to thoroughly overhaul large numbers of programs that have developed over decades.

Furthermore, Republicans faced enacting such far-reaching policy change with narrow margins of control in both chambers and a hostile president in the White House.[1] The radical character of the Republicans' agenda ensured that the battle over its enactment would be hard fought and that opponents would attempt to stop them using all available weapons. Certainly, opponents would appeal to the court of public opinion and attempt to make voting for the components of the program prohibitively expensive in reelection terms for many Republicans. Given the ideological gulf between President Bill Clinton and congressional Republicans, the president with his veto and his bully pulpit would be one of those opponents.

The budget process provided the primary procedural tool through which Republicans would attempt to enact their agenda. Without it, the "Republican revolution" of a balanced budget in seven years would have had no chance whatsoever; the Republican congressional leaders knew that getting a large number of major and often painful changes through both chambers and past the president as separate bills was a hopeless task. The budget process allowed packaging, it provided protection against the Senate filibuster, and, combined with an adept strategy, it might make it possible to force Clinton to sign the legislation.

Fulfilling the Contract: Welfare Reform and Tax Cuts

Tax cuts and welfare reform, which were both in the Contract, would eventually become part of the reconciliation bill. To meet the 100-day deadline, however, House Republicans had to bring them up before the budget resolution was ready. Welfare reform legislation was referred to the committees on Ways and Means, Economic and Educational Opportunities, and Agriculture, which reported their provisions by early March. Under strict instructions from the party leadership, Republican committee leaders had pushed the measures through their committees with limited debate and on largely party-line votes. The leadership then combined the provisions from the three committees, making alterations where that

---

1. At the beginning of the 104th Congress, House membership stood at 230 Republicans, 204 Democrats, and 1 Independent; over the course of the Congress, five Democrats (all conservative southerners) switched to the Republican Party. Senate membership stood at 53 Republicans (including Richard Shelby of Alabama who switched from Democrat to Republican on November 9, 1994) and 47 Democrats. Ben Nighthorse Campbell of Colorado switched from Democrat to Republican in 1995.

seemed advisable. The welfare reform bill ended welfare as an entitlement and turned the responsibility over to the states. The federal government would give the states block grants to fund welfare, but the federal contribution would be less than it would have been under AFDC, so the legislation saved money.

The bill was brought to the floor under a tight rule that barred votes on several amendments that would have split Republicans. For example, "pro-life" Republicans, who feared that cutting off benefits to teenaged unwed mothers would encourage abortion, were denied a chance to offer amendments deleting such provisions. The rule was narrowly approved, but then the bill passed on a 234–199 party-line vote (Katz 1995b, 872–875).

Welfare reform passed on March 24; the tax bill followed on April 5. Passing the last and, in the words of Speaker Newt Gingrich, R-Ga., the "crowning jewel" of the Contract proved to be a tough test for House Republicans, one that required party leaders to make use of a number of their procedural tools (Rubin 1995a, 1010–1014). Although Ways and Means reported the bill cutting taxes by $189 billion over five years ($353 billion over seven years) on a party-line vote, many Republicans were concerned about the size of the tax cut and about the eligibility for the $500-per-child tax credit of families with incomes of up to $200,000. Democrats, claiming the tax cuts would benefit mostly the rich, were scoring points in the media. Over a hundred House Republicans signed a letter to the leadership asking for a vote on lowering the income ceiling for eligibility.

Few Republicans wanted to vote for tax cuts that could be painted as ballooning the deficit, so the leadership planned to package tax provisions with spending cuts. Some of these proved to be highly controversial on their own. The Government Reform and Oversight Committee refused to report a bill substantially increasing federal workers' contributions to their retirement plans and lowering their benefits; Washington-area Republicans on the committee, aware the provisions would cost their constituents substantial amounts of money, joined Democrats in blocking the bill. The Republican party leadership nevertheless inserted it into the legislation that went to the floor.

To appease deficit hawk members, the leadership added a provision to the bill requiring that, before the tax cuts could be enacted, a reconciliation bill putting the deficit on a path to zero had to be passed. The special rule made this language as well as the federal pension provisions and other postcommittee adjustments a part of the base bill that went to the floor. Members who opposed the high ceiling on the per-child credit were cajoled and pressured by their colleagues, the leaders, and interest groups, especially the Christian Coalition; but no

TABLE 11.1   1995 Budget Process: A Chronology

House Action	Senate Action	Appropriations and Debt Limit Legislation
	Budget Resolution and Reconciliation	
3/21, 3/22, 3/30, 4/4 Budget Committee holds hearings.	1/26, 2/1 Budget Committee holds hearings.	
5/10, 5/11 Budget Committee considers, marks up, and approves budget resolution.	5/8, 5/9, 5/10 Budget Committee considers and marks up budget resolution.	
5/16 Rules Committee grants modified closed rule allowing votes on four substitutes and suspending the automatic adoption of an increase in the debt limit.	5/11 Budget Committee completes markup and approves budget resolution.	
5/17 House adopts rule.	5/18, 5/19, 5/22, 5/23, 5/24 Senate considers budget resolution.	
5/18 House considers and adopts budget resolution, H.Con. Res. 67, by a 238–193 vote.	5/25 Senate completes consideration and approves budget resolution, S.Con. Res. 13, by a 57–42 vote.	
6/8 House conferees named.	6/7 Senate conferees named.	
6/8 Conference begins.		
Gingrich and Dole negotiate an agreement on taxes.		
6/22 Conferees reach agreement.		
6/29 House and Senate approve conference report by votes of 239 to 194 and 54 to 46.		
Budget resolution having been approved by both chambers is now in effect.		

7/19–10/11 House committees, under instructions by the budget resolution, hold hearings. They then consider and mark up their recommendations.

8/1 Budget reconciliation recommendations are ordered reported by the National Security Committee.

9/12 Budget reconciliation recommendations are ordered reported by the Judiciary Committee.

9/19 Budget reconciliation recommendations are ordered reported by the Banking and Financial Services Committee and the Resources Committee.

9/21 Budget reconciliation recommendations are ordered reported by the Ways and Means Committee.

9/22 Budget reconciliation recommendations are ordered reported by the Commerce Committee.

9/27 Budget reconciliation recommendations are ordered reported by the International Relations Committee.

9/28 Budget reconciliation recommendations are ordered reported by the Economic and Educational Opportunities, Transportation and Infrastructure, and Veterans' Affairs committees.

7/11–10/19 Senate committees, under instructions by the budget resolution, hold hearings. They then consider and mark up their recommendations.

9/18 Budget reconciliation recommendations are ordered reported by the Armed Services Committee.

9/19 Budget reconciliation recommendations are ordered reported by the Environment and Public Works Committee.

9/20 Budget reconciliation recommendations are ordered reported by the Banking, Housing and Urban Affairs Committee and Veterans' Affairs committees.

9/21 Budget reconciliation recommendations are ordered reported by the Energy and Natural Resources Committee and the Judiciary Committee.

9/22 Budget reconciliation recommendations are ordered reported by the Labor and Human Resources Committee.

TABLE 11.1 *(Continued)*

House Action	Senate Action	Appropriations and Debt Limit Legislation
	Budget Resolution and Reconciliation	
	9/28 Budget reconciliation recommendations are ordered reported by the Agriculture Committee and the Commerce, Science and Transportation Committee.	10/1 1997 fiscal year begins; FY 1996 appropriations run out; continuing resolution (CR) extending funding through November 13 in effect.
	10/19 Budget reconciliation recommendations are ordered reported by the Finance Committee.	
10/12 Budget Committee marks up and orders reported the reconciliation bill, HR2491.	*Dole negotiates with moderates.*	
Republican party leaders engage in intense bargaining and agree on postcommittee adjustments.	10/20 Budget Committee marks up reconciliation bill.	
10/20 Budget chair Kasich unveils the omnibus reconciliation bill, HR2517. (It includes Medicare, welfare, and tax cut bills passed separately earlier and cuts in agricultural subsidies and in federal pensions that the committees of jurisdiction refused to report.)	*Dole and moderates and other holdouts agree on postcommittee adjustments to be offered as amendments on the floor.*	
Republican party leaders continue their negotiations and agree on more postcommittee adjustments.	10/23 Budget Committee completes markup and orders reconciliation bill reported.	
10/25 Rules Committee grants rule allowing a vote on one substitute and including a self-executing provision incorporating last-minute deals into the bill.	10/25, 10/26, 10/27 Senate considers reconciliation bill.	

10/26 House approves rule and debates and approves the reconciliation bill, HR2491, which incorporated HR2517. The vote was 227–202.

10/30 House conferees named.

10/27 Senate passes reconciliation bill, S1357, by a 52–47 vote.

11/13 Senate conferees named.

11/15 Conferees agree to file conference report.

11/17 House agrees to conference report, 237–189. Portions of bill stricken in Senate as violations of the Byrd rule. Senate agrees, 52–47, to conference report without stricken provision. (Amendments between the chambers used.)

11/18 House agrees to conference report as altered in the Senate, 235–192.

11/30 Bill presented to the president.

12/6 President Clinton vetoes reconciliation bill, HR2491.

11/1 Clinton and Republican congressional leaders meet to discuss budget issues.

11/9, 11/10 House and Senate pass and clear for president a short-term debt limit increase with "strings."

11/8, 11/13 House and Senate pass and clear for president a CR with extraneous matter that Clinton opposes.

11/13 Clinton vetoes CR and debt limit increase; old CR runs out.

11/14 Federal government shuts down.

11/19 Clinton and Republican congressional leaders reach agreement to open the government and to hold high-level talks; group of sixteen chosen to negotiate deal.

11/19, 11/20 Senate and House pass and clear for president a CR funding government until December 15.

11/28 Negotiations begin.

Negotiations continue in fits and starts.

12/6 Clinton vetoes reconciliation bill.

TABLE 11.1 *(Continued)*

Budget Resolution and Reconciliation	Appropriations and Debt Limit Legislation
	12/15 CR runs out and federal government shuts down again.
	12/19 Clinton and Republican congressional leaders agree to peak-level summit with Clinton participating.
	12/22 Clinton, Dole, and Gingrich meet at White House.
	Talks continue intermittently.
	1/2/96 Senate passes "clean" CR.
	1/5/96 House passes CR, ending the longest government shutdown ever.
	More talks, maneuvering, and negotiations; short-term CRs keep government open. Republican leaders and Clinton administration negotiate deal on debt limit increase.
	3/28/96 Long-term debt limit extension passes.
	Congressional party leaders and appropriators and administration negotiate deal on remaining appropriations.
	4/24/96, 4/25/96 House and Senate pass and clear for president omnibus appropriations bill funding government for the rest of FY 97.
	4/26/96 Clinton signs omnibus appropriations bill, HR3019.

NOTE: Official actions are in roman type; behind-the-scenes, unofficial actions are in italics.

change in the bill was made, nor did the rule give them a vote on an amendment.

The leadership brought the bill to the floor under a rule allowing only one substitute to be offered by the minority leader. When the rule passed on a narrow 228–204 vote, Republicans who objected to specific provisions were faced with a choice: vote against the last item of the Contract and thereby possibly contribute to the Republican Party ending the 100 days with an ignominious defeat or swallow hard and vote with their party colleagues. All but eleven Republicans, mostly those with many federal workers in their districts, supported the bill and it passed 246–188.

Committing to a Balanced Budget: The Budget Resolution

Fulfilling the promise of bringing to the floor all of the Contract items in the first 100 days left the new Republican majority in the House with little time for anything else, so the budget process began late. The budget resolution is supposed to be passed by April 15, a deadline seldom met, though it was in 1993; in 1995 the House Budget Committee did not report its resolution until May 11.

John R. Kasich of Ohio, the new chair of the Budget Committee and a part of the Republican leadership's inner circle, had not been idle. Knowing that making cuts of the magnitude necessary to balance the budget would require restructuring and in some cases abolishing programs, not just marginally trimming spending, he had set up in January a number of working groups to develop proposals. By including top Republicans from the authorizing and appropriations committees with Budget Committee members, he hoped to reach consensus on specific policy changes to reduce spending. Policy at this level, however, is not in the Budget Committee's jurisdiction; the committee is supposed to propose broad guidelines that are then filled in by other committees. A number of Republican committee leaders objected to Kasich's overstepping, and to keep peace within the Republican Party Speaker Gingrich had to tell him to back off (Jacoby 1995).

Drafting the Budget Resolution

The chairman of the Senate Budget Committee, Pete V. Domenici, R-N.M., beat his House counterpart to the mark. In early April the outlines of Domenici's budget plan began to emerge. Initially unwilling to commit himself to offering a budget plan that would lead to a balanced budget in seven years because he feared his colleagues lacked the political will to pass such a plan, Domenici changed his mind and made clear he would submit such a plan. He had at first intended to propose a plan that made a down payment toward balance but decided such a plan would bring much of the pain but none of the gain that a balanced budget plan would (Rubin 1995a, 1012–1013). That a balanced budget plan, particularly under the ground rules the Republicans had established during the elections, would entail real pain was evident; although Domenici's plan included no tax cuts, getting to a balanced budget without raising taxes, touching social security, or reducing defense required huge cuts in Medicare, Medicaid, and other entitlement programs, as well as in appropriations for discretionary domestic programs.

Domenici had intended to formally unveil the plan and start markup on May 1, but the difficulty of amassing sufficient support delayed action. Majority Leader Bob Dole of Kansas and Budget Committee member Phil Gramm of Texas, both running for the Republican presidential nomination, were unhappy with the lack of a big tax cut in the Domenici proposal. Gramm and some like-minded colleagues threatened to withhold their support from any budget resolution that lacked substantial tax cuts. The cuts in Medicare immediately became controversial, making a lot of Republicans nervous. A public opinion poll released in late April showed that 62 percent of those questioned did not want Congress to cut Medicare to reduce the deficit. Democrats had been charging that the Republicans' proposed cuts would gut Medicare, and their criticism had begun to take hold. "There's a lot of queasiness here," Domenici said. "I'm queasy myself" (Hager 1995b, 1166).

Senate and House Republicans jointly planned a public relations counteroffensive on Medicare.[2] A report by the Medicare trustees released in early April gave them ammunition; the report predicted that the Medicare hospital insurance trust fund would go bankrupt by 2002 unless changes were made. Republicans trumpeted the report and altered their rhetoric. No longer were they cutting Medicare to balance the budget; they were reforming it to save it from going broke. Congressional Republicans also tried to lure the president into giving them cover on Medicare cuts, demanding that he, as the country's highest leader, present his own

---

2. Throughout the controversy, Republicans argued that because the dollar amount they proposed to spend on Medicare would go up over the next seven years, it was inaccurate and unfair to say that their plan cut Medicare. Democrats argued that because the amount Republicans proposed to spend would not go up as much as health care costs, the amount of health care the dollar amount would buy would, in fact, decrease and thus the Republicans' plan did represent a cut.

plan to save Medicare. Clinton refused to take the bait. Instead he criticized Republicans for being so tardy with their budget resolution and excoriated them for cutting programs for the elderly to pay for tax cuts for the wealthy. "I will not support proposals to slash these programs, to undermine their integrity, to pay for tax cuts for people who are well-off," Clinton said at a White House conference on the problems of aging (Hager and Rubin 1995a, 1227).

The Senate Budget Committee began marking up the budget resolution on May 8 and on May 11, after four days of highly charged partisan debate, approved the resolution on a 12–10 party-line vote. Democrats failed in all their attempts to amend the resolution significantly. Domenici had presented to the committee a compromise on tax cuts: the "economic bonus" (up to $170 billion that the Congressional Budget Office figured a balanced budget would yield) could be used for tax cuts but only after a balanced budget plan was enacted and certified to actually achieve balance by the CBO. Domenici's compromise was sufficient to hold all the Republicans, though Gramm vowed to offer a tax-cutting plan similar to the House's on the floor.

The same day the House Budget Committee ended a fifteen-hour session by approving a budget resolution on a near party-line vote of 24 to 17; the only committee member to cross party lines was Mississippi Democrat Mike Parker, who later switched his partisan affiliation. The resolution proposed balancing the budget in seven years. Because it also included the previously passed tax cut that would cost $353 billion over seven years, it proposed even deeper spending cuts than had the Senate Budget Committee's resolution; entitlements such as Medicare and Medicaid and domestic discretionary programs were slated to be severely slashed, with spending for programs to aid the poor being especially hard hit (Hager 1995c, 1302).

Passing the Budget Resolution

The Republican party leadership brought the budget resolution to the House floor under a highly restrictive rule; only four comprehensive substitutes were allowed. For a number of years budget resolutions had been considered under restrictive rules that made in order votes on a limited number of entire substitutes but barred votes on narrow amendments targeting some unpopular feature of the measure. This rule went even further, however, in demanding that any substitute meet the Republicans' goal of balancing the budget in seven years.

The rule allowed Democrats to offer two substitutes, a Black Caucus plan and a proposal put together by a group of conservative Democrats known as the Coalition. Republican deficit hawks were permitted to offer an alternative that balanced the budget in five years. To twit the president for his failure to offer a balanced budget plan, the Republican leadership included in the rule a provision allowing the minority leader to offer a substitute "consisting of a revised budget submitted by the president to the Congress that achieves a balanced budget by the fiscal year 2002" (*Congressional Record,* May 16, 1995, D616).

Anticipating difficulty in getting Clinton to accept legislation enacting the policy changes the budget resolution required, the Republican leadership inserted a special provision in the rule: it suspended a House budget process rule that automatically raised the debt limit by providing for the automatic adoption of a debt limit identical to the level contained in the conference report on the budget resolution. Republican House leaders wanted to keep the need to increase the debt limit as a weapon in the confrontation with the president that they knew would eventually come.

None of the three substitutes that were offered commanded much support; the Coalition's did best, receiving 100 votes, 90 of them from Democrats. Democrats had not been able to agree on a more broadly supported alternative to the Republican plan. Many believed that their minority status relieved them of the necessity of offering an alternative and that their best political strategy was simply to attack the Republican plan; that, after all, is what Republicans had done in 1993 and 1994, and doing so had paid off handsomely for them at the polls. On May 18 the House approved the budget resolution its Budget Committee had reported by a vote of 238 to 193; only one Republican opposed it, and only eight Democrats supported it.[3]

Senate floor consideration began on May 18. Because of the importance of the measure in both policy and political terms, it attracted a multitude of amendments. Senator Gramm's amendment to include a big tax cut similar to that in the House resolution lost on a 31–69 vote, with twenty-three Republicans voting against it. Although they knew their chances of prevailing were slim, minority Democrats forced votes on almost fifty amendments and thereby made Republicans go on the record on the most painful cuts—in education, Medicaid, Medicare, and other popular programs.

---

3. The one Republican who voted against the budget resolution on passage (and on the conference report) was Michael Patrick Flanagan, an Illinois freshman who defeated Dan Rostenkowski, then under indictment, in a heavily Democratic district in Chicago. Flanagan lost his seat in 1996.

Although they had to beat back a barrage of amendments, not all of them offered by opposition party members, Senate Republicans were aided in passing their resolution by budget process rules. Those rules restrict total debate time and so prohibit a filibuster by opponents. They also require that an amendment increasing spending in one area must be paid for with cuts in another, which tends to work against major changes. Only two significant amendments were passed, both by sizable bipartisan margins; one restored some of the cuts in the student loan program, and the other restored cuts in the budget of the National Institutes of Health. On May 25 the Senate passed the budget resolution by a vote of 57 to 42 with every Republican and three Democrats supporting it.

The President Enters the Budget Arena

On June 13 President Clinton on national television unveiled a new budget that reached balance in ten years. The budget that Clinton had submitted to Congress in early 1995 had included no deficit reduction beyond that approved in the 1993 budget deal. Clinton knew that the Republicans' big electoral victory in 1994 and the fact that the budget resolution does not require the president's signature severely reduced his influence during the early parts of the budget process. Having gotten no credit for the deficit reduction that he and congressional Democrats enacted in 1993, Clinton also had no intention of providing political cover to Republicans for the big and painful cuts that balancing the budget would entail. When the budget committees reported out their budget plans, the administration had strongly criticized the priorities they incorporated and had warned that, were they incorporated into law, the president would exercise his veto.

Given the ambitiousness and painfulness of the task, it was by no means certain in early 1995 that Republicans would be able to come up with a budget resolution that met their targets. When both chambers passed such a resolution, the strategic situation for the president changed. If Republicans did, in fact, send him a reconciliation bill that led to a balanced budget in seven years—still not a certainty but considerably more likely—Clinton would be in a weak position if he had no credible budget of his own. To prepare for that eventuality, Clinton proposed his plan.

When different parties control the presidency and Congress, the strategy that most effectively furthers the president's political goals may conflict with that best for the congressional members of his party. Congressional Democrats who believed they were making large political gains by criticizing the Republicans' budget plan were furious with Clinton for proposing a budget plan that cut spending on popular programs; Clinton had pulled the rug out from under them, they believed, by blurring the differences between the parties and taking the spotlight off the Republicans' heartless spending cuts and big tax breaks for the wealthy.

Resolving House-Senate Differences

The conference between the House and the Senate had begun June 8. Although there were many differences to resolve, the biggest issue and the most difficult problem was the tax cut. Not only did the two chambers have substantially different provisions, but this was an issue on which many Republicans held passionate beliefs. Even before the budget resolution came to the Senate floor, eight Senate Republicans had written Majority Leader Dole expressing their opposition to a tax cut of the size the House supported. In the House seventy-nine Republicans signed a letter threatening to withhold their support from the conference report if it "significantly" diminished the House-approved tax cuts (Hager 1995d, 1619). Senator Gramm warned that he, too, would oppose a budget plan without big tax cuts.

After two weeks of tough bargaining among congressional Republicans (Democrats having been relegated to the sidelines), Speaker Gingrich and Majority Leader Dole reached an agreement on taxes. With the Fourth of July recess approaching and most other differences already resolved, the two top leaders agreed to a $245 billion tax cut. To a very considerable extent, the House won. Three factors worked to the advantage of the House. The House Republicans' iron commitment to a big tax cut made senators realize that only a long and bloody war of attrition was likely to budge the House conferees. Because Senate rules prevent movement on appropriations bills until a budget resolution has been approved, the Senate was more eager than the House to complete action. Bob Dole's presidential ambitions made him especially eager to get quick agreement on a resolution that included a big tax cut. Conservative Republicans who make up the bulk of the primary electorate strongly favored big tax cuts. If the process dragged on, Dole would look like an ineffective leader.

On June 29 both chambers approved the conference report. The big tax cut the compromise plan included led the three Democrats who had voted for the Senate plan to vote against the conference report, but all the Republicans, even those who had been most adamantly opposed to a large tax cut, supported the measure, and it passed the Senate 54–46. House approval came on a 239–194 vote, with again one Republican and eight Democrats defecting from their party's position.

Republicans were ecstatic about what they had accomplished. "We are changing directions," said Domenici, the elated Senate Budget Committee chairman. "It is the framework to change the fiscal policy of America and to change the way the federal government operates" (Hook 1995a, A28). They were determined to finish the job, Republicans said, no matter how recalcitrant Clinton was. "This is a revolution," declared moderate Republican representative Christopher Shays of Connecticut, vowing to refuse to raise the debt ceiling if Clinton did not agree to a balanced budget. "We are prepared to shut the government down in order to solve this problem," proclaimed House Budget Committee chairman Kasich (Hager and Rubin 1995b, 1905).

Shooting with Real Bullets: Reconciliation

As difficult as enacting the budget resolution had been, a bigger and more politically difficult task lay ahead. The budget resolution is a blueprint; by its passage the Congress had promised to make the changes in law necessary to reach balance in the federal budget by 2002. Now Republicans had to deliver; as Bob Dole had said at the same stage in the budget process in 1993, "From now on we're shooting with real bullets."

The budget resolution committed Congress to making savings of $894 billion over seven years. It instructed twelve House and eleven Senate committees to change law under their jurisdictions so as to meet spending targets. Much of the savings were slated to come from entitlement programs: $270 billion from Medicare, $182 billion from Medicaid, and $175 billion from other mandatory spending programs such as food stamps, farm subsidies, welfare, and federal pensions. The committees of jurisdiction were free to decide just how to reach these targets, but the magnitude of the required savings dictated a major restructuring of the programs.

The budget resolution also prescribed $190 billion in savings in nondefense discretionary spending, which funds all those government activities—from the federal courts to Head Start to national park maintenance—that are not entitlements. The budget resolution contained a multitude of suggestions for how these cuts could be made. The budget committees had proposed closing down whole departments, agencies, and programs. Such specifics just provide guidance; they are not binding. The appropriations committees would be responsible for deciding how to make the cuts.[4] Given the magnitude of the cuts—about 10 percent in the first year—drastic changes would be required.

---

4. The authorizing committees with jurisdiction would be in charge of making major changes in the programs, or abolishing them; however, Appropriations, by cutting funding drastically, can have the same effect.

About the only pleasant task mandated by the reconciliation instructions was for the taxing committees to cut taxes by $245 billion; however, given the disagreements within the Republican Party about whether a sizable tax cut made political and policy sense, even that task promised to be difficult. And finally, all this had to be done in a very short period of time. The thirteen appropriations bills are supposed to be enacted by October 1, the beginning of the federal government's fiscal year. The budget resolution instructed the committees to report their provisions for the reconciliation bill by September 22.

Congress returned to work in early September after an August recess of heated rhetoric in members' districts and on the airwaves. Democrats accused Republicans of sacrificing the elderly's health care in order to pay for huge tax cuts for the wealthy; Republicans claimed they were restructuring Medicare in order to save it from bankruptcy and that Democrats were acting irresponsibly. Returning members from both parties reported that their constituents supported their positions. Republicans thus were fortified to proceed with the difficult task ahead.

Although committees had begun their work on complying with their reconciliation instructions well before the recess, the most contentious issues, which were often the most complex, had not been resolved. If the September 22 deadline were to be met or even approached, an enormous amount would have to be done quickly.

Welfare Reform in the Senate

On September 19 the Senate finally managed to pass a welfare reform bill. The House had passed its welfare reform legislation in March, but the Senate Finance Committee did not report a bill until May 26. Problems within the majority party immediately became apparent. Republicans from the South and Southwest who represent fast-growing states with relatively low welfare benefits objected to the funding formulas that based the amount of federal funds a state received on past welfare expenditures; the most conservative senators decried the dropping of House provisions aimed at reducing out-of-wedlock births such as one barring unwed teenaged mothers from receiving welfare; Republican moderates believed the legislation did not provide enough money for child care and would allow states to cut their own welfare spending too much.

Because of the saliency and political popularity of the issue, no one (including most Democrats) really wanted to vote against a welfare reform bill. Had the Republican leadership been able to force an up or down vote, the committee bill might well have passed. But because he had no way of protecting the legislation from a barrage of amendments on the floor or from a filibuster, Senate Majority Leader Dole had to deal. He and Sen. Bob Packwood, R-Ore., the chairman of the Finance Committee, took on the task of rewriting the bill. In early August, after several months of negotiations, Dole unveiled a revised bill aimed at satisfying the various factions; it consisted of a modified version of the Finance Committee bill but also incorporated in revised form three other pieces of legislation—a bill from the Agriculture Committee that overhauled the food stamp program and child care and job training bills approved by the Labor and Human Resources Committee. Adding these provisions provided a greater scope for compromise.

Floor debate began August 7, and it soon became evident that problems still existed, and the bill would not pass before the scheduled recess. Republicans blamed the Democrats, charging that they intended to offer fifty amendments, but, in fact, the GOP itself was split. On September 6, after the recess, Dole brought the bill back to the floor, but he still lacked a secure winning coalition and continued to make changes to placate various groups of Republicans. He also began talking with Democrats, and on September 15 a major compromise was reached; among other provisions, it added substantial funds for child care. Four days later Dole and Minority Leader Tom Daschle, D-S.D., offered an amendment that incorporated the compromise. It passed on an 87–12 vote, with mostly hard-line conservative Republicans voting in opposition. Acceptance of the amendment significantly moderated the Senate's welfare overhaul bill, which was already more moderate than the House bill. The Senate passed the bill as amended 87–12, with only one Republican voting in opposition. Welfare reform was expected to be included in the reconciliation bill, and the differences between the two chambers' provisions presaged difficult negotiations.

The House Agriculture Committee Revolts

On September 20 the reconciliation process hit a major snag when the House Agriculture Committee refused to approve a bill making the required $13.4 billion in cuts. Despite strong pressure from the Republican leadership, four southern Republicans refused to support the "Freedom to Farm" proposal for overhauling farm programs offered by the committee's chairman, Pat Roberts, R-Kan. The four joined with all the Democrats to defeat it. On September 14 the Speaker, majority leader, and whip had sent a letter to the committee warning, "If the committee fails to report such reforms . . . we would consider bringing a farm bill to the floor within the next two weeks under an open rule. Alternatively, the leadership would have the ability to replace the committee's legislation with true reforms before reconciliation is considered on the floor."

Chairman Roberts reiterated the warning during the markup: "It is a decision of whether we do this [in committee] or . . . others will do it for us, or to us," he said (Hosansky 1995b, 2875).

In this case appeals to party loyalty and threats of dire consequences for members' House careers swayed members less than did the opinions of their constituents. The defecting Republicans saw the legislation as a direct and substantial threat to their constituents' interests. Like their Washington area colleagues when asked to increase significantly what their constituents had to pay for their federal pensions, these southern Republicans voted to protect their constituents' farm programs. The Senate Agriculture Committee was also badly split, and Chairman Richard G. Lugar, R-Ind., avoided the likelihood of a similar embarrassment by postponing a scheduled markup.

Medicaid and Formula Politics

On September 20 the House Commerce Committee began to mark up legislation revising and cutting the Medicaid program, which provides health care for the poor. House Republicans had unveiled their plan only the day before, timing that outraged committee Democrats. The product of months of consultation with Republican governors, it transformed the program from an entitlement to a block grant. The states would be given extremely wide latitude to decide who would be covered, for what, and how.

Committee Republicans were almost completely successful in maintaining unity during three days of markup as Democrats offered amendments to reinstate guarantees of coverage, to maintain federal nursing home standards, and to protect spouses of nursing home residents from financial disaster. On only one issue did Republicans split. The Republican governors had come to a consensus on everything except the formula for how federal money would be divided among the states. The formula issue divided committee members as well. However, Democrats as well as Republicans split, and an amendment to alter the formula was defeated. The committee approved the legislation on a 27–18 vote with only one conservative Democrat crossing party lines.

Medicare Politics in the House

Committee hearings on Medicare, begun in early February, had been held sporadically throughout 1995, mostly by Ways and Means and Commerce, the primary committees with jurisdiction. The real action, however, was taking place elsewhere. Because successful Medicare reform was essential to attainment of the Republican Party's policy and electoral goals, Speaker Gingrich decided to direct the effort himself. He designated a "design team" of eight from the party leadership and the Ways and Means and Commerce committees to put together the legislation; the group, which he chaired, met over the course of four months, sometimes daily. Gingrich took on the primary job of promoting the politically perilous endeavor with House Republicans and in the media (Koszczuk 1995a, 3049; Hook 1995b, A20).

By mid-September House Republicans had still not made public a concrete proposal. Delay was in part the result of the complexity of the issues involved and of the time required to negotiate with the myriad interest groups influential on health care. Republicans had decided early in the process to adjust the contents of their proposal to gain the support of influential groups where possible and their neutrality where not; much of the bargaining was conducted by the top party leadership. "The speaker has done a superb job of figuring out what was important to all the health care groups and what it would take for them to support it given some of the less attractive parts of the plan," the lobbyist for a group of large health care companies said (Rubin 1995b, 2895). The delay, however, also was part of a deliberate strategy by Republicans to deprive their opponents of a clearly defined target. Republicans had learned from President Clinton's health care reform experience that exposing a proposal to lengthy scrutiny by potential critics reduces its chances of enactment. Democrats were outraged by the stealth strategy but could do little but fume.

Consequently, on September 22, when the Ways and Means Committee held its only day of hearings on the Republicans' proposal, only an outline of the legislation was available. On the same day the Senate Finance Committee Republicans outlined a plan for revamping Medicare and Medicaid that was similar to the House Republicans' plan. On September 29 Republicans finally produced details when their plan was introduced by Ways and Means Committee chairman Bill Archer, R-Texas, as HR2425 and referred to the committees on Commerce, Judiciary, Rules, and Ways and Means.

On October 10 the influential American Medical Association (AMA) announced its support for the GOP plan. Negotiations with Speaker Gingrich had won the AMA concessions on doctors' fees. The American Association of Retired Persons (AARP), important because of its huge membership, came out strongly against the plan and launched a major publicity campaign to spread its views.

On October 11, after three days of often bitterly partisan markup, the Ways and Means Committee approved the legislation on a party-line vote of 22 to 14. Democrats offered three substitutes and numerous other amendments, but the committee accepted no changes of great significance. Only hours later the Commerce Committee reported a slightly different version of the bill by a 27–22 vote. That markup had featured a walkout by Democrats to protest the lack of committee hearings on the legislation, the arrest of senior citizen demonstrators, and much heated rhetoric. The theatrics had little effect on the outcome; with one relatively minor exception, all of the Democrats' amendments were rejected.

To undercut the Democrats' argument that changes in Medicare were being made to pay for tax cuts, the House Republican leadership made a move to decouple those two issues. It decided to pass Medicare reform as free-standing legislation rather than just roll it into the giant reconciliation bill. Their success with the AMA and the party unity on the two reporting committees encouraged the leaders to believe that this was doable. Putting together the majority to pass the bill on the floor nevertheless required further substantive adjustments to the legislation. The Speaker and other high-ranking party leaders had begun that fine tuning even before the committees reported; now their efforts shifted into high gear. A group of rural Republicans, believing their constituencies would be unfairly hurt, threatened to oppose the bill if alterations were not made. After several attempts Gingrich came up with a revision in the payment formula for rural providers that brought the rural Republicans on board. To placate other Republicans, adjustments were made in provisions on the funding of medical education, on fraud and abuse, and on other more minor issues.

The leadership changes were incorporated in a substitute that combined the slightly different versions of the legislation reported by the two committees, and on October 18 this new bill was sent to the Rules Committee.[5] The deal Gingrich had struck with the AMA was also included in the leadership's alterations. The revised bill deleted a number of provisions adopted during the committees' markups, including the Democrats' only successes.

After hearing from more than thirty members who wanted to offer floor amendments, the Rules Committee approved a highly restrictive rule; only one substitute was allowed, general debate was limited to three hours, and debate on the substitute was limited to one hour. The substitute made in order was the one offered by the ranking Democrats on the

---

5. On the 16th the House had by unanimous consent discharged the Judiciary and Rules committees, which had also received referral of the legislation but had not considered it.

two reporting committees, Sam M. Gibbons of Florida and John D. Dingell of Michigan, and was the Democratic-leadership-approved Democratic substitute. The Rules Committee refused to allow the Coalition, the group of conservative Democrats, to offer their compromise alternative. This more moderate plan to revamp Medicare might have confronted some Republicans with a much tougher vote than the more liberal Democratic version. (Democratic leader Richard A. Gephardt of Missouri also refused to incorporate the Coalition's alternative into his motion to recommit the bill with instructions, the minority party's other opportunity to amend the bill. That alternative presented a number of Democrats with a difficult vote as well.)

The special rule also waived the provisions of a House rule that requires a three-fifths vote on any amendment or measure containing an increase in the federal income tax rate. The Republicans had proudly passed that new House rule at the beginning of 1995. Ever since, Democrats had used it to harass them, and they had often had to waive it in special rules. (In every case Republicans claimed the rule did not really apply, but the rule's language left that a matter of interpretation.)

Debate was passionate; both sides agreed that truly fundamental changes in Medicare were at stake. Republicans argued that they were rescuing Medicare and making it better and that, as evidenced by the free-standing bill up for consideration, the enterprise had nothing to do with tax cuts. "There are no tax cuts today. There is no budget today," Gingrich emphasized in his closing remarks. "This is about Medicare" (Fraley 1995, 3209). Democrats responded that how the policies are packaged is irrelevant, that the bill made far greater cuts in Medicare than necessary to save the program. Republicans charged that Democrats were unjustifiably scaring senior citizens. Democrats responded that the legislation gave seniors good reason to be frightened. "With this vote, we turn back 30 years of progress, 30 years of trust and 30 years of hope that our parents and our grandparents will always have the health care they need," Democratic whip David E. Bonior of Michigan declared (Fraley 1995, 3210).

The outcome was never really in doubt; the Republican leadership would not have brought the bill to the floor if it did not have the votes. On October 19 the House passed the bill by a vote of 231 to 201; four conservative Democrats voted for the legislation; six Republicans opposed it, each because he believed it treated his district unfairly.

Medicaid Politics in the Senate

Although the Senate did not intend to vote on a free-standing Medicare bill, the Finance Committee was nevertheless under pressure to move on its huge reconciliation workload. On September 26 the committee began marking up Medicare, Medicaid, and earned-income tax credit provisions, even though it still lacked formal legislative language. Moderate Republican John H. Chafee of Rhode Island joined Democrats in a number of efforts to temper the bill but with little success. His vote, and that of all the Democrats on the Senate Finance Committee, produced a 10–10 tie, and an amendment must get a majority to pass.

Republicans did need Chafee's vote to approve the package; in return for his support, committee Republicans agreed to two amendments to the Medicaid provisions, the most important of which would retain some limited entitlement status for poor pregnant women, children twelve years old and younger, and the disabled. On September 30 the Finance Committee approved the package.

After Finance approved its Medicaid provisions, twenty-four Republican governors wrote Majority Leader Dole to complain about restrictions in the bill and especially about the Chafee amendment's requirement that the disabled be covered. Dole, after a meeting with Finance Committee Republicans, seemed inclined to accede to the governors' wishes, and Finance Committee staff claimed that, since the final language was still being written, changes were possible. Although Democrats were outraged and Chafee was miffed, the language that Finance sent to the Budget Committee for inclusion in the reconciliation bill allowed the states to define "disabled," which in effect negated the entitlement. Democrats could only fume, but if he wanted to, Chafee together with his like-minded party colleagues could make real trouble. The bill could not pass without them.

Packaging Reconciliation in the House

Although this imbroglio was only one of a number of problems that developed as the reconciliation process moved toward its belated climax (the deadline set by the resolution having long since passed), by the end of September the pieces were coming together. Ten House committees had reported their provisions. In the Senate all except Finance had reported. On September 28 the Senate Agriculture Committee managed to approve a revision of farm policy that cut subsidies but was considerably less radical than the proposal the House Agriculture Committee had turned down.

The House Budget Committee on October 12 approved on a single 24–16 vote the approximately $562 billion in spending cuts made by the authorizing committees. In addition, the bill that went to the floor would include the Medicare cuts, the welfare bill, tax cuts, and cuts in agriculture subsidies and federal pensions. The Agriculture Committee and the Government Reform Committee, which have jurisdiction over farm subsidies and federal pension legislation respectively, had not been able to report those provisions; too many committee members believed they hurt their constituents. Nevertheless, at the instructions of the party leadership and under authority provided by the budget resolution, they were to be included in the bill. The leadership's plan to dismantle the Commerce Department would also be incorporated in the package. Budget Committee chairman Kasich announced that he would assemble these pieces himself and ask the Rules Committee for a self-executing rule that would roll all the elements into one big bill (Hager 1995e, 3119).

The House Republican leadership devoted the week preceding floor consideration to last-minute bargaining and intense persuasion. The enormous scope of the bill and its importance to the Republican Party made it hard for Republicans to oppose it. The same features also ensured that many members would strongly dislike some provisions and that all but the most committed would be tempted to extract a price for their vote. The party leaders had been centrally involved in the budget process from its beginning; now they became the preeminent players.

To assuage the concerns of some moderates and members from high-growth states, Gingrich agreed to restore $12 billion in Medicaid spending and to distribute the money to states particularly hard-hit by the committee's plan. Although the agricultural provisions were not altered, disgruntled farm-state members were brought back on board with implied promises that changes would be made in conference. They were reminded that since the Senate provisions were less radical than those of the House, the conference compromise would almost certainly be more to their liking.

Moderates upset by environmental provisions were not given any concessions; the provision to open the Alaskan Arctic National Wildlife Refuge to oil drilling, which they especially opposed, was left in the bill. In a move aimed at moderates, the leadership did agree to drop the repeal of the Davis-Bacon Act, which requires federal contractors to pay the prevailing wage (Hook 1995b, A20). As a sweetener for representatives from the Washington suburbs, a provision increasing parking fees for federal employees was dropped. Rep. Fred Upton, R-Mich., won a provision important to a major business in his district that allowed drug companies to sell their products abroad without approval from the Food and Drug Administration.

Many of these changes were included in the revised bill, HR2517, that Chairman Kasich put together and unveiled on October 20. The numerous last-minute deals the leadership made after October 20 were incorporated into the bill by the rule. The rule granted by the Rules Committee on October 25 contained a self-executing provision specifying that when the House approved the rule it thereby approved HR2517 as modified by the last-minute leadership amendments as a substitute for the bill the Budget Committee had reported. This procedure allowed the leadership to avoid having to offer their changes and additions to the bill reported by the Budget Committee as amendments on the floor. The rule allowed only one amendment, a minority party substitute, to be offered, and it waived the House rule requiring a three-fifths vote on measures containing a federal income tax rate increase.

Passing Reconciliation in the House

Because the feverish bargaining continued until floor consideration was scheduled to begin, general debate actually started before the rule was approved. The majority and the minority agreed to go ahead with three hours of general debate under a unanimous consent agreement. When the rule was brought to the floor on October 26, Democrats protested the rule, the process by which the bill had been crafted, and the bill's substance. Rules Committee Democrat Anthony C. Beilenson of California argued:

> [W]e strongly oppose the rule, and the legislation it makes in order—the budget reconciliation bill drafted by the Republican leadership.
>
> The importance of the legislation before us cannot be overstated. It is a measure that makes drastic changes in a huge number of Federal programs and services; a measure that will directly affect virtually every American. Yet the rule for its consideration allows the House to consider only one substitute, and one motion to recommit. And, the rule limits the remaining time for general debate to just 3 hours, plus 1 hour for debate on the substitute.
>
> It is true, as our friends on the other side of the aisle have pointed out, that this is a typical rule for a budget reconciliation bill. But this is not a typical reconciliation bill; it is not a bill that has been developed through the normal reconciliation process but, rather, one that has been brought to the House floor through actions of the Republican leadership that constitute an extremely serious abuse of the legislative process. . . . The bill before us now . . . contains critical changes in agriculture programs, in the civil service retirement system, in tax policy, in the structure of a Federal department, and other important provisions that were not considered by the committees of jurisdiction, nor reviewed by the Budget Committee. Some of the provisions were not even finalized until last night. These portions of the bill were drafted behind the closed doors of the Speaker's office, where decisions were also made to drop certain provisions from the committee reported version of the bill. Even as the Rules Committee was conducting its hearing yesterday—

and even as general debate on the bill had begun on the floor—decisions were still being made by the Republican leadership about the contents of the plan we would be asked to vote on today.

We find the disregard for the normal legislative process that has been demonstrated by this process profoundly disturbing. We believe it is a huge injustice to the Members of the House and, far more important, to the people we represent. . . .

Mr. Speaker, this is a bad rule for a terrible bill. I urge Members to vote "no" on the previous question, "no" on the rule, and "no" on the bill (*Congressional Record,* October 26, 1995, H10859).

Republicans argued that the House faced a historic moment. Budget Committee chairman Kasich extolled the budget resolution as a momentous accomplishment and praised his party colleagues for their courage:

Mr. Speaker, they said it could not be done. Here we have before us today the Seven Year Balanced Budget Resolution certified by the Congressional Budget Office. . . . [I]n seven years we will, in fact, balance the Federal budget and save this country and save the next generation. . . . [I]t took courage. Some of my colleagues know what it is like to go home and have to take the heat when people do not understand all the programs and what we are doing.

Mr. Speaker, I am proud of these people. I am proud to serve with them. Why? It is courage. It is the courage to be willing to put an election on the line; do the right thing (*Congressional Record,* October 26, 1995, H11364).

The Democratic leadership did not draft its own alternative; the leaders knew a Democratic substitute would have no chance, and they feared it would only distract media attention from the Republican plan just when public opinion seemed to be turning against it. Instead Minority Leader Gephardt allowed the Coalition to offer its alternative. This group of conservative and moderate Democrats had drafted a budget plan that, like the Republican plan, reached balance in seven years but, because it did not include a tax cut, made much less Draconian cuts in spending for programs such as Medicare and Medicaid. The plan received seventy-two votes, sixty-eight from Democrats.

The Republican leaders' combination of fervent, high-minded exhortation and nitty-gritty deal making paid off. The biggest and most ambitious reconciliation bill ever considered by the House passed on a 227–203 vote, with only ten Republicans defecting.

Packaging and Passing Reconciliation in the Senate

In the Senate, Finance Committee Republicans finally managed to come to an agreement on the tax provisions of the reconciliation bill; on

October 19 they reported that section by a party-line vote. Five of the committee's eleven Republicans had serious reservations about a big tax cut, but after a series of closed door meetings, they agreed to go along with $245 billion in cuts. An agreement to limit the $500-per-child tax credit to families with income below $110,000 made acquiescence easier for moderates like Chafee. Furthermore, most of the reluctant senators did not want to weaken Bob Dole in his contest for the presidential nomination with ardent tax-cut proponent Phil Gramm (Rubin 1995c, 3058; 1995d 3189). As majority leader and a member of the Finance Committee, Dole would be considered responsible if the committee failed.

Finance Committee action cleared the way for the Budget Committee to put the reconciliation package together and report it. Starting well before the Budget Committee reported the bill on October 23 and continuing even as the bill was being debated on the floor, Majority Leader Dole held a series of meetings with Republican moderates who had deep concerns about a number of the bill's provisions. Because of the narrow Republican margin in the Senate, these senators had considerable bargaining power, and several threatened to vote against the legislation if changes were not made. Dole agreed to restore about $13 billion in Medicaid spending, reduce cuts in education funding, and reinstate some federal nursing home standards. These restorations were to be offered as floor amendments. In addition, Dole promised that Senate conferees would move substantially toward the House's lower cuts in the earned-income tax credit for the working poor.

Although the Budget Act protects reconciliation bills from a filibuster, Senate floor procedure on such legislation is still much more open—and potentially chaotic—than is House procedure. The Senate spent three days on the bill, during which it took fifty-eight roll call votes. Scores of amendments, large and small, were offered and a considerable number were adopted. Especially during the last frenzied day of floor consideration, the Senate took on the guise of a "legislative bazaar." "In a dizzying blizzard of detailed changes that many senators themselves had trouble keeping track of, dozens of amendments—some worth hundreds of millions of dollars—won approval" (Rubin 1995f, 3359). Although budget rules require that any increases in spending be offset by cuts, when the vote on passage came, no one really knew if the bill as a whole was still in balance.

The restoration amendments incorporating Dole's deal with the moderates were offered and approved. An amendment by Chafee defining "disability" for Medicaid coverage won on a 60–39 vote, with a large majority of Republicans opposing it. Many moderates and liberals were concerned about a provision allowing companies to use excess corporate pension funds for other purposes. When Sen. Nancy Landon Kassebaum, R-Kan., and Sen. Edward M. Kennedy, D-Mass., offered an amendment to strike the provision, it passed on a 94–5 vote. Most of the amendments approved were narrower in scope than the Chafee or Kassebaum-Kennedy amendments; many were agreed to by the leadership in order to keep various Republican members happy. Democrats' amendments to delete or fundamentally alter the most politically sensitive components of the package lost, but Democrats did force Republicans to go on the record in support. Democrats nevertheless had an impact on the legislation when they used the Byrd rule barring extraneous matter in reconciliation bills to knock out big chunks of the welfare bill as well as a number of other provisions.

The bill passed on a 52–47 vote; no Democrat voted for it, but every Republican except moderate William S. Cohen of Maine supported it. Dole's concessions as well as a few additional victories on the floor brought all the other Republican moderates on board. Ironically, Clinton's vow to veto the bill made it easier for moderate Republicans to provide the votes to pass it. "We know this isn't the last station," Chafee said (Rubin 1995e, 3290).

Reconciling House-Senate Differences

Resolving the differences between the House and Senate bills was a task of formidable scope. The bills, after all, dealt with hundreds of issues and programs. Agriculture, Medicare, Medicaid, and welfare were expected to present the trickiest problems. The two chambers' provisions on agricultural programs were very far apart. Medicare is a politically sensitive program, and the two bills made cuts in different ways. At issue on Medicaid was the formula for distributing funds to the states, always a potentially divisive matter. Both Medicaid and welfare involved highly charged ideological issues—guaranteed coverage for certain groups and cutting off funds to teenaged mothers, for example.

Tax provisions were also a potential source of conflict. After the budget resolution specified a tax cut of $245 billion, the House did not rewrite its original $353 billion bill but sent it to conference with instructions that the size of the tax cut be reduced there; among the many differences in the two chambers' bills was the income ceiling for the $500-per-child tax credit.

In addition to being faced with many tough issues, the negotiators were constrained by the numerous promises that had been made during the effort to pass the bill. In both chambers the leaders had over and over again promised members concerned with some provision that "we'll fix it in conference."

Countering this formidable set of problems was the momentum passing the legislation in both chambers had created. Members had made a host of difficult decisions; they had put their careers on the line; if no agreement were reached it would all be for naught. And, given that important deadlines had already been missed, more long delay was likely to hurt the Republican Party's image. The leaders were determined to get a bill to the president before Thanksgiving.

The conference committee consisted of forty-three senators divided into twelve subgroups and seventy-one House members divided into fourteen subgroups. Had Gingrich not assertively exercised the Speaker's discretion in the appointment of conferees, the House delegation could easily have been much larger. Fearing that sheer numbers would delay resolution, Gingrich chose whenever possible members who could do double duty because they served on the Budget Committee and another concerned committee; in this and other ways he kept the number of conferees down.

A subgroup of eight House members had authority over the entire bill and included, in addition to high-ranking Budget Committee members, a number of party leaders—Majority Leader Dick Armey of Texas, Whip Tom DeLay of Texas, and Conference chairman John A. Boehner of Ohio on the Republican side and Whip David Bonior on the Democratic side. In the Senate, the group of three that had authority over the entire bill was confined to the Budget Committee leaders. The other subgroups consisted of members from the committees with provisions in the bill and had authority over those provisions only. The Republican members of these subgroups made most of the many detailed decisions that a bill of such broad scope required. On the big, tough issues, however, the party leaders were centrally involved. Gingrich and Dole working with shifting groups of committee leaders, depending on the issue, hammered out agreements on the most sensitive issues such as agriculture and Medicaid.

On agriculture the agreement provides an example of the power of conferees; much of the fairly radical House language was adopted even though the House Agriculture Committee had turned it down, and the Senate version entailed less drastic change. The chair of the House Agriculture Committee, who was the author of the "Freedom to Farm" version, headed the House conferees and the top House party leaders supported him; the chair of the Senate Agriculture Committee also liked much of the House version even though his committee had reported a more moderate bill.

Bound by the many promises they had made to gain votes, Dole and Gingrich cut Medicaid savings by almost $20 billion below the figure specified in the budget resolution. To settle the formula dispute with its party-splitting potential, they agreed to let each state choose whichever of the two chambers' formulas gave it the most money. They retained some federal nursing home standards and a requirement that states provide some care for pregnant women and children under thirteen but dropped the requirement that the disabled be covered.

The House accepted the Senate's $110,000 family income ceiling for the $500-per-child tax credit; the agreement also specified that a part of the tax cuts be retroactive so that voters would receive some of it before the 1996 elections.

The conferees approved the conference report on November 15, and on November 17 both houses approved it on largely party-line votes. Democrats in the Senate again used the Byrd rule to force deletion of a number of extraneous provisions; as during initial floor consideration, Republicans could not muster the sixty votes needed to waive the rule. Since the House had already approved the conference report with the offending provisions, the legislation had to go back to the House for approval in altered form. When on November 20 the House concurred in the Senate amendment, both chambers had passed the bill in identical form.

Why Nonincremental Change?

"This is what they said we could never do," crowed House Budget Committee chairman John Kasich after the House approved the reconciliation bill (Hager 1995f, 3287). Congressional Republicans had passed a bill of enormous scope and consequence, one that significantly shrank the size and responsibilities of the federal government and restructured some of the biggest and most complex federal programs including Medicare, which because of its popularity with the middle class had long been considered untouchable.

In our system of government, political scientists agree, nonincremental policy change is difficult to effect; when that policy change entails pain for major constituency groups, elected representatives are even less inclined to make the necessary decisions. So why were Republicans able to pass a reconciliation bill that did represent nonincremental change?

A part of the answer lies in the fact that there were powerful organized interests that did, in fact, benefit mightily from the bill. Business interests in particular gained, especially but not only from the tax provisions. Conversely, the biggest losers, the poor, are neither powerful nor organized. The political circumstances that the 1994 elections created were, however, crucial. Republicans in 1995 were able to stay united and pass legislation radically redirecting policy because their leaders skillfully exploited the sense of mandate the election results produced and because they had the congressional budget process available as a tool.

The 1994 elections brought into the House, and to a lesser extent into the Senate, a group of new members who were strongly committed to effecting policy change; the seventy-three-member strong House freshman Republican class joined a sizable group of sophomore Republicans that shared its fervent ideological belief in budget balancing, tax cutting, and government downsizing. They and many more senior House Republicans as well believed that the 1994 elections had mandated them to make major changes in government; their signing of the Contract with America, of course, heightened and focused that belief. Furthermore, the voter cynicism about Congress, which they had so effectively exploited, meant they had to deliver, Republicans realized; if they failed to keep their promises, voters were likely to punish them. The Republican leadership, especially in the House, brilliantly capitalized on such fears to keep its members unified. Over and over the leaders emphasized that, if they hoped to retain their congressional majorities, Republicans had to keep their promises, had to show they could govern, and doing so meant passing a balanced budget plan (Koszczuk and Cloud 1995, 2769).

As the process moved forward and members went on the record with more and more difficult decisions, the prospect of receiving no political or policy payoff became increasingly unthinkable; any member responsible for failure had to know his party colleagues would make him pay dearly. The fear of voter retribution for coming up empty influenced moderate Republicans who had qualms about specific policy changes and hard-liners who abhorred all compromise. "The last time I checked, every single Republican enjoyed being in the majority," remarked moderate Sherwood Boehlert, R-N.Y. "So I think that's going to weigh heavily on the minds of some people who might be cantankerous and find the plan unacceptable for one or two or three reasons" (Koszczuk and Cloud 1995, 2770). But even with these favorable political circumstances, it is unlikely that Republicans could have accomplished what they did without the congressional budget process. The packaging the process allows and the protection it provides in the Senate were essential.

Summitry: Struggling to Reconcile Irreconcilable Differences

Politics and procedure had relegated President Clinton to the sidelines during much of the budget process. Convinced that the 1994 elections had given them a mandate that superseded any Clinton may have had and finding nothing of value in either of the budget plans Clinton had proposed, Republicans had proceeded on their own. Since the budget resolution does not require the president's signature, Republicans were not forced to take Clinton's preferences into account. The president, however, can veto the reconciliation bill, and Republicans knew they could not muster the votes to override.

As Republicans were crafting their bill, President Clinton made clear that he strongly opposed many of its provisions. The bill, Clinton argued, cut much too deeply in Medicaid, Medicare, welfare, education, and the environment; ending poor people's entitlement to health care under Medicaid and slashing the earned-income tax credit for the working poor while providing huge tax cuts to the well off were unacceptable.

Bargaining Chips and Strategy

If, as he had repeatedly threatened, Clinton vetoed the reconciliation bill, Republicans would have to bargain with him; otherwise the legislation on which they had spent so much of their first year in power would die. Yet the differences between their position and Clinton's were enormous and reflected basic philosophical disagreement about the appropriate role of government. Reconciliation legislation is not in the strict sense "must-pass" legislation, and this put the Republicans at a disadvantage. To be sure, when the Congress passes a budget resolution with reconciliation instructions, it promises to pass a reconciliation bill, and if it does not the Congress looks ineffective. Furthermore, most Republicans were convinced that public judgment of their performance would rest on their enacting legislation that balanced the budget in seven years as they had promised. Thus, congressional Republicans considered the bill to be must-pass legislation. Failure of a reconciliation bill does not, however, entail direct and concrete negative consequences of the sort that pressure an opposition party president to sign it.

Republicans controlled the fate of true must-pass legislation that they could use to shore up their bargaining position. To provide the funds necessary to keep the government functioning, appropriations legislation has to be passed every year; otherwise large chunks of the government must shut down. Perhaps even more of a weapon, Congress must periodically pass legislation raising the debt ceiling so that the federal government can borrow the funds necessary to pay its debts; if borrowing authority runs out, the federal government would have to default on its obligations, a course potentially disastrous for the economy and the credibility of the United States. From very early in the year, Republicans had been contemplating using these measures as bargaining tools. They hoped that public opinion, which they were convinced strongly supported a balanced budget, would provide the main pressure on Clinton to agree to a deal to their liking. If that failed, they had a backup plan: the threat of shutting down the federal government or bringing it to the brink of default.

All thirteen appropriations bills are supposed to be enacted by October 1, the beginning of the new fiscal year. In 1995 the process was far behind schedule, slowed by the time the House had spent on the Contract, the big cuts that the appropriations committees were required to make, and legislative "riders." With the party leadership orchestrating the effort, House Republicans, eager to make changes in law quickly, attached controversial legislative provisions—known as "riders"—to appropriations bills. Intended to protect the provisions from a presidential veto, the strategy in many cases made House-Senate agreement on the bills excruciatingly difficult. Compared with hard-line House Republicans, moderate Senate Republicans were much less enthusiastic about hamstringing the Environmental Protection Agency, imposing new restrictions on abortion, or effectively barring liberal interest groups from lobbying.

By late September only two of thirteen appropriations bills had been cleared for the president. Not wanting to call attention to their inability to meet deadlines, congressional Republicans agreed with the president on a continuing (appropriations) resolution (CR) to fund government programs for forty-four days. This was a "clean" continuing resolution because it contained no extraneous provisions and was noncontroversial.

The continuing resolution would expire November 13, about when Republicans hoped to have completed work on their reconciliation bill. By then, Robert Rubin, the secretary of the Treasury, estimated, the federal government would reach the debt ceiling.

The Early Rounds and the First Government Shutdown

Both sides knew that the time when they would have to talk to each other was fast approaching. Leon Panetta, then White House chief of staff, and Pete Domenici, the chairman of the Senate Budget Committee, had been meeting informally for months trying to find common ground in preparation for serious talks. On November 1 President Clinton and the Republican leadership met for two hours at the White House to discuss budget issues including the debt limit. Republicans reiterated that any agreement must balance the budget in seven years according to conservative CBO estimates; House Republicans would not vote for anything less, Speaker Gingrich declared.[6] Clinton made it clear he would not cave

---

6. For more on such estimates, see Chapter 5.

in as many Republicans seem to have hoped. "If you're determined to undermine the government's role in things I believe in, you'll have to put someone else in that chair," the president said, pointing to his big leather chair (Nelson 1995, A33). Although both sides called the meeting useful, no agreements were reached.

Implementing their strategy of using must-pass legislation to pressure the president into an agreement, congressional Republicans passed a continuing resolution and a debt ceiling increase, including in both pieces of legislation provisions the president strongly opposed. The debt limit bill prohibited the administration from using a financial strategy that the secretary of the Treasury was considering to avoid default, and it would have plunged the U.S. government into default as soon as the temporary increase ran out on December 12, thus forcing Clinton to agree with Republicans on a plan by then. The House version had also included a provision abolishing the Commerce Department, but that was stripped out of the bill at the insistence of Senate Republican moderates. The continuing resolution contained deep cuts, especially for Clinton's priorities, and prevented a decrease as current law dictated in Medicare premiums. On November 13 Clinton vetoed both bills as he had said he would.

In a final attempt to avert a government shutdown, Clinton sent Panetta to the Hill to confer with Gingrich and Dole; however, when Panetta insisted that congressional Democrats be included in the talks, the Republican leaders refused, and no negotiations took place. On November 14 the federal government shut down. Only two of the regular appropriations bills had been signed into law by the president, though Congress had completed several others; more than half, including such large and contentious bills as the one funding the departments of Labor, Education, and Health and Human Services were unfinished, many hung up by House-Senate disagreements. A number of appropriations bills were under veto threat.

Under law, "essential" government services (law enforcement, for example) continue even if appropriations bills are not passed; but all other services and programs not yet funded have to close down. About 800,000 federal employees were sent home all across the country; national parks were shut; the Small Business Administration stopped processing loan requests; new applicants for social security were out of luck, though the checks (an entitlement and not funded by appropriations) continued to go out.

On November 15, with no debt limit bill having passed, Treasury secretary Rubin made use of an extraordinary procedure to prevent default. Two days later both chambers passed their reconciliation bills.

Agreements, Disagreements, and the
Second Government Shutdown Begins

On November 19 President Clinton and Republican leaders announced an agreement to end the six-day shutdown. To their surprise, Republicans found the public blaming them rather than the president by a 2-to-1 margin. Threats of defection by significant numbers of congressional Democrats put Clinton under pressure as well. After Clinton's vetoes, Republicans had brought to the floor a continuing resolution without the extraneous provisions in the previous one but with a provision committing the president and Congress to a budget balanced in seven years using CBO numbers; in both chambers a substantial number of Democrats had joined Republicans in support. With both sides concerned about prolonging the shutdown, the talks that had proceeded by fits and starts bore fruit.

The deal struck on November 19 and incorporated in a continuing resolution passed the next day funded the government until December 15 and bound the president and Congress to enacting a budget that the CBO certified as balanced by 2002 and that, at the same time, protected future generations, ensured Medicare solvency, reformed welfare, and provided adequate funding for Medicaid, education, agriculture, national defense, veterans, and the environment (Rubin 1995g, 3598).

Disagreement about what the agreement meant surfaced almost immediately. Republicans contended that it bound Clinton to putting on the table a plan that met the criteria, and on November 22 Republican leaders sent the president a letter calling on him to submit a detailed budget plan. Democrats argued that they had promised to reach a balanced budget at the end of the negotiations, not to start from that point.

To carry out the face-to-face negotiations, a group of sixteen was chosen, eight from each side. The Republican group consisted of a combination of party and Budget Committee leaders from each chamber. House Republicans were represented by Majority Leader Armey, Whip DeLay, Budget Committee chairman Kasich, and Robert S. Walker of Pennsylvania, a high-ranking member of the Budget Committee and a close confidant of the Speaker; Whip Trent Lott of Mississippi, Budget Committee chairman Domenici, and Charles E. Grassley of Iowa and Don Nickles of Oklahoma, the two next most senior members of the Budget Committee, made up the Senate Republican contingent. The administration was represented by Chief of Staff Panetta, Secretary Rubin, and Alice Rivlin, the director of the Office of Management and Budget.

Republicans had wanted to limit participants to representatives of the administration and congressional Republicans; the White House, however, had insisted that congressional Democrats be included. The difficult political environment for Democrats since the 1994 elections had strained relations between the White House and congressional Democrats; excluding them from the talks was a prescription for disaster. Therefore, Rep. Martin Olav Sabo of Minnesota and Nebraska senator Jim Exon, ranking members of the House and Senate budget committees respectively, House Democratic whip David Bonior, Charles W. Stenholm, a senior member of the House Budget Committee and a leader of the Coalition, and North Dakota senator Byron L. Dorgan, representing the Senate Democratic leadership, were included (*Congressional Quarterly Weekly Report,* December 2, 1995, 3640). In the background would be Speaker Gingrich, Senate Majority Leader Dole, and the president, all of whom would have to sign off on any deal.

The negotiators met for the first time on November 28 in the Capitol. After three bargaining sessions of a few hours each, the talks stalled on November 30. Each side accused the other of bad faith. Republicans charged that Clinton had still not proposed a detailed alternative plan; the White House responded that Republicans refused to follow a previously agreed upon agenda for the meetings.

On December 6 the president vetoed the reconciliation bill, using the pen with which President Lyndon Baines Johnson had signed the Medicaid/Medicare bill into law thirty years before. At the same time Clinton announced that he would unveil a seven-year alternative budget. On December 7 he sent Leon Panetta to meet with Republicans to explain it. Clinton's new budget did not rely on the more pessimistic CBO numbers (which required deeper cuts) as the Republicans had demanded, and they dismissed it out of hand. Gingrich and Dole again demanded that Clinton submit another budget plan.

With the talks seemingly stuck and the continuing resolution running out, Panetta on December 13 signaled that the White House intended to bring still another White House proposal to the table, one that he hoped would narrow the differences with the Republicans' plan. Both sides expressed optimism that a breakthrough was at hand. After discussing it with congressional Democrats on December 14, Panetta presented the new plan to the negotiating group the next day. Republicans turned it down flat, claiming it did not represent a good faith effort; it relied substantially on different economic assumptions rather than on real cuts, they claimed. "It's almost an insult," Senate Republican Whip Trent Lott said of the proposal. Clinton charged that Republicans were demanding "unconscionable" cuts in Medicaid and Medicare as preconditions to negotiations. "Every time we move, every time we add additional savings, they say, 'That's not good enough,'" Panetta added (Hager and Rubin 1995c, 3789).

With the talks again stalled, Republicans refused to approve another short-term continuing resolution, and the government shut down again. Many were convinced that the president did not really want a balanced budget deal and that they would have to play hardball to force him to agree. Treasury secretary Rubin's extraordinary but legal financial maneuvering had, at least temporarily, removed the debt limit as a lever. Thus appropriations remained the Republicans' best weapon. Vowing that the House would not pass another continuing resolution, Gingrich-confidant Bob Walker said, "We will politically endure as much pain as it takes to get a [balanced-budget] deal" (Hager 1995g, 3876).

Peak-Level Negotiations and the Longest Shutdown

On December 19 President Clinton called Gingrich and Dole and invited them to the White House; that afternoon, after a two-hour meeting with the president, the Republican leaders announced a breakthrough—Clinton had agreed to negotiate by the end of the year a seven-year budget deal starting from CBO numbers. Furthermore, Clinton had promised to participate personally in the negotiations.

Republican leaders had promised that once good faith talks were under way Congress would pass a continuing resolution. House Republicans, however, absolutely refused. A statement by Vice President Al Gore seeming to dispute that Clinton had agreed to CBO numbers, though quickly contradicted by the White House, fed already suspicious Republicans' distrust and hardened their inclination to hold fast. By a near unanimous vote, the House Republican Conference voted to hold out until Clinton agreed to a balanced budget deal. The freshmen, many of whom lacked political experience and disdained compromise, were especially adamant. "This government is going to remain shut down until he [President Clinton] realizes that we are not going to compromise on a balanced budget," warned Wisconsin representative Mark W. Neumann. "If that makes us radical freshmen, then so be it" (Fiore 1995, A1). Gingrich's fellow leaders even agreed that in future meetings with the president, Majority Leader Dick Armey should accompany him to prevent Gingrich from being sweet-talked by Clinton.

President Clinton condemned a "radical fringe" of House Republicans for blowing up the agreement. They are "determined to keep the government closed unless they get their way," he charged (Peterson and Richter 1995, A24).

Despite this inauspicious start, the talks proceeded. On December 21 aides and members of the original negotiation team met to prepare the ground for a meeting of the principals. The meeting the next day at the

White House of Clinton, Dole, and Gingrich was, the participants reported, a good one, though a great deal of work remained to be done. They agreed to meet again December 29, but in the meantime aides would continue to talk.

The House and Senate passed a "rifle shot" appropriations bill to fund veterans' benefits, welfare payments, and the District of Columbia and then recessed on December 22 for a belated Christmas vacation.

When Congress returned in early January, the government shutdown had lasted far longer than any before. Although several more appropriations bills had become law before the second shutdown started, six were still outstanding. The press was full of articles about the harm the shutdown might cause—preparation of next year's flu vaccine was being hindered, for example—and of the suffering of federal employees. The public was blaming Republicans far more than the president for the impasse. Never enthusiastic about the strategy of closing the government down and concerned that the focus had shifted from budget balancing to the shutdown, Majority Leader Dole on January 2 pushed through the Senate a condition-free continuing resolution to fund the government until January 12 while budget talks proceeded. To move the legislation so quickly, Dole took up a most-favored-nation bill for Bulgaria and offered the CR as a substitute amendment to it, a maneuver that the Senate's loose rules on germaneness made possible. When the Senate adopted the "amendment," the CR was substituted for the original bill.

Dole's move put the responsibility for the shutdown squarely on House Republicans. Many of them had become even more convinced that Clinton did not want a balanced budget, and they were deeply frustrated that they had not been able to force him to capitulate. The House turned down Dole's continuing resolution on a procedural vote, with only two Republicans defecting. But behind the scenes, cracks in the united front were beginning to appear; in a closed-door meeting of the Republican Conference on January 3, more than fifty members voted in favor of a compromise CR.

Budget talks had resumed in late December. After a January 4 meeting with Panetta and Domenici, Kasich said he saw "no visible signs of progress" (Hook and Richter 1996, A16). Dole, however, contradicted him. In obvious disarray, Republican leaders canceled their scheduled meeting with Clinton to allow for "internal communications" (Taylor 1996, 56).

The House Republican leadership decided that House Republicans were in a politically untenable position; a change in strategy was needed. The leaders proposed a CR that would run through March 15, but at a contentious Republican Conference the membership refused to go along.

"I am vehemently and steadfastly opposed to this . . . defeatist strategy, which is going to blur the differences between the parties," protested Frank Riggs of California, reflecting the views of many of his fellow freshmen (Hook and Richter 1996, A16). Republican leaders regrouped, came up with another plan, and at a Conference meeting the next morning pressured their members to support it. House Republicans had been so successful in 1995 because they had acted as a team, Gingrich told them. If they wanted to stay a part of the team, they would vote for the CR, he added pointedly. Later in the day the leadership-supported measures were approved by the House; fifteen determined Republicans refused to vote for reopening the government.

Legislative Legerdemain and Its Limits

The January 5 passage of a new continuing resolution by no means ended the crisis. The CR funded through September 30, the end of the fiscal year, a number of politically sensitive government functions (Meals on Wheels, passport services, veterans' programs, national park visitor services, for example), and it funded some others until March 30. Although the CR authorized all government workers to return to work until January 26, it did not, in most cases, fund the programs they administered. Another measure provided operating funds as well, but, in an unusual procedure, it would be sent to the president only if Clinton proposed a budget balanced in seven years as scored by the CBO (Taylor 1996, 56).

Showing just how flexible a tool special rules are, the rule for H.J. Res. 134, the continuing resolution with operating funds, included a self-executing provision by which adoption of the rule automatically meant adoption of H.Con. Res. 131, which established "procedures making the transmission of the continuing resolution (H.J. Res. 134) to the President contingent upon the submission by the President of a 7-year balanced budget using updated economic and technical assumptions of the Congressional Budget Office." Specifically, the concurrent resolution read, "The Committee on House Oversight . . . shall not present to the President the joint resolution (H.J. Res. 134) . . . until the Speaker of the House notifies that committee that the requirements of this concurrent resolution have been met." To make sure the Senate did not block the concurrent resolution and thus the condition on providing operating funds, the rule further stated "that the clerk shall not transmit the joint resolution to the Senate until it has agreed to H.Con. Res. 131 as adopted in the House" (*Congressional Record,* January 5, 1996, D12).

Dole and Gingrich had met with the president shortly before floor action on the continuing resolutions and had emerged optimistic that he would soon submit a plan that met the requirements. The next day Clinton did so, and Congress sent him the second CR.

Clinton's putting forth his own plan to balance the budget in seven years according to CBO numbers initially seemed like a breakthrough; he had finally met what Republicans claimed was their one "non-negotiable" demand. But the talks soon stalled again. Increasingly, it was becoming clear that the policy differences between the president and congressional Republicans were too great to bridge. Even as negotiations narrowed the dollar amount differences between the sides, Republicans found the ways in which the administration proposed balancing the budget unacceptable because they did not include the sort of basic restructuring of entitlement programs to which Republicans were committed; the president and congressional Democrats, although they had conceded on balancing the budget, deemed the Republicans' means of doing so unacceptable because they weakened or destroyed government programs they considered essential. "It's not a debate about numbers; it's a debate about policies," Majority Leader Bob Dole said succinctly (Rubin and Hager 1996, 89).

With the prospects of an agreement dimming but with neither side wanting to throw in the towel and reap the blame for failure, negotiations spluttered along, more frequently in suspension than in full throttle. In late January congressional Republicans and the White House worked out a mutually agreeable continuing resolution that extended funding until mid-March.

Raising the Debt Limit

Not long into the new year the debt limit reemerged as a front-burner issue; Treasury secretary Rubin was running out of stopgap measures to ward off default. The Republican House leadership no longer talked blithely about preferring default to compromise; the government shutdown had cost the Republican Party dearly with the public; Republicans could not afford another such debacle. Yet the leaders desperately wanted to be able to claim if not a victory at least not a total defeat; and they, of course, had to amass a majority vote for the debt limit increase. Both considerations dictated adding provisions favored by Republicans to the debt limit bill.

The debate within the Republican Party over what to include as sweeteners in the bill was intense and prolonged. Some—especially junior House Republicans—wanted to include welfare, Medicaid, and perhaps even Medicare reform; others argued for coming up with a bill that Clinton would sign even if that meant modest additions; still others had favorite pieces of the Contract with America that they wanted to force

Clinton to accept by including them in the package. After buying time by passing two short-term extensions, Republican leaders decided on the low-risk strategy. They negotiated a deal with the Clinton administration to include in the bill providing for a long-term increase in the debt ceiling some regulatory relief for small business, an increase in the earnings limit for social security recipients, and the line-item veto.

This strategically designed package accomplished a number of purposes. It would avoid a confrontation between the administration and Congress and a possible default. The big item in it—the line-item veto—was one Clinton had long supported. Including the line-item veto in must-pass legislation gave it some protection from a filibuster by adamant opponents such as Sen. Robert Byrd, D-W.Va. The sweeteners, especially the line-item veto, were sufficient to enable most Republicans, even the hardline House freshmen, to vote for the debt limit increase and to give the Republican Party something to brag about. Essentially, Republican leaders made the best of a weak hand.

House leaders' control over special rules made that possible. Under leadership instructions, the Rules Committee packaged the items together into HR3136 and specified that the bill be considered under a closed rule. Since the line-item veto had already passed, it was the conference report that was included. Since the rule allowed no amendments, members could justify their vote for the debt ceiling increase as required in order to enact the line-item veto. In an even more unusual procedure, the rule provided that if the Senate approved the line-item veto conference report before March 30 and the House passed HR3136, the House "will be deemed to have adopted the conference report on S4, the line-item veto conference report," and the line item veto would be struck from HR3136 and be sent to the president as a free-standing bill (*Congressional Record*, March 28, 1996, H2974). The House thereby kept pressure on the Senate to approve the line-item veto, but it also specified a return to more normal procedures if the Senate moved expeditiously.

Both chambers passed HR3136 on March 28 and Clinton signed it the next day, thereby ending the threat of default but also depriving Republicans of the lever they had hoped to use to force the president to accept their policy proposals.

With a Whimper: The Budget Battle Ends

The curtain finally came down on the 1995 budget battle in late April when Congress passed and Clinton signed an omnibus appropriations bill to fund the nine departments and dozens of agencies covered by the five regular appropriations bills never enacted. After fourteen continuing resolutions and two government shutdowns, the government was finally funded for the fiscal year ending October 1, 1996.

Both chambers passed their own versions of the omnibus appropriations bill in March, but reaching a final agreement required weeks of negotiations between House and Senate Republicans and with the White House. Funding levels and policy riders were at issue. Hard-line House Republicans were resistant to increasing funding—especially for the programs such as AmeriCorps (the national service program) and Goals 2000 (an education program) dearest to Clinton's heart—and to dropping controversial policy riders on issues such as abortion and the environment. Clinton, buoyed by his increasing popularity, also hung tough. Senate Republicans often found themselves in between. There was much less support for the policy riders in the Senate than in the House, and the Senate bill included more money than did the House bill, though not as much as Clinton wanted.

House and Senate appropriators meeting in small groups hammered out a multitude of compromises. The more difficult issues were pushed up to the core negotiating group of White House chief of staff Leon Panetta and the chairs and ranking minority members of the House and Senate Appropriations Committees. After a series of talks, the core group reached agreement on Wednesday, April 24. House Republicans were forced to make major concessions on both funding levels and policy riders; considerable money for Clinton's priorities in the areas of education and the environment was restored, and most of the riders were dropped or the president was given the authority to waive them. "We got rolled," House freshman Mark E. Souder, R-Ind., complained (Hook 1996, A15). Despite much grumbling by House Republicans, the House as well as the Senate overwhelmingly approved the conference report that contained the agreement. As senior House Republican and appropriator Bill Young, R-Fla., said succinctly, "At this stage, we've got to get it settled" (Hook 1996, A15).

The Budget Process and "Revolutionary" Policy Change: Possibilities and Limits

Using the budget process, the new Republican majorities managed to cut domestic appropriations by 9 percent over the previous year, a very considerable achievement from their perspective (Hager 1996, 1156). They failed in their much more ambitious attempt to cut spending for, and fundamentally restructure, the big entitlement programs, especially Medicare and Medicaid.

The procedures and practices of unorthodox lawmaking were essential tools in the Republicans' strategy to accomplish their ambitious goal; without the packaging the budget process allowed and the protection from filibusters it afforded the legislation in the Senate, such nonincremental policy change could not have been passed. Other tools of unorthodox lawmaking were instrumental at a number of stages in the process as well. As employed by an activist party leadership, special rules were especially important to Republican strategy; such rules were used to hold the package together at crucial stages. They also allowed the House to accomplish objectives not otherwise easily attained; for example, the leaders used a complex rule to make the sending of legislation to the Senate and to the president contingent on actions these actors took.

The procedures and practices of unorthodox lawmaking are, however, just tools. They are by no means sufficient to produce fundamental change in policy direction. Summits are, in fact, a procedure of last resort. The president and Congress agree to try to settle their differences through a summit when more orthodox procedures have failed. The American governmental system of separate institutions sharing power has a status quo bias; making major policy changes is difficult and usually requires compromise. Sometimes the philosophical differences between the president and the congressional majority are so great that what one considers a reasonable compromise the other regards as selling out. When this happens, significant policy change is unlikely unless the actor advocating change can marshal strong public support and thereby make holding out too costly in electoral terms for the other actor. In fact, in the summer of 1996, Republicans scored an impressive victory when President Clinton signed a welfare overhaul bill. Although Clinton had extracted significant compromises, the legislation ended welfare as an entitlement and, in other provisions as well, bore a clear Republican stamp. This was a case in which the Republicans were backed by a strong public desire for policy change; Clinton and many other Democrats feared the electoral consequences of killing the legislation. On the budget, Republicans had hoped that public support for a balanced budget in the abstract would translate into strong public pressure on Clinton to make a deal on their terms. Instead, the Democrats' warnings that the Republicans' plan would cut Medicare, education, and environmental protection proved more persuasive. When Clinton won the battle for public opinion, Republicans lost their chance of winning the policy war.

The Consequences of Unorthodox Lawmaking

Unorthodox LAWMAKING HAS BECOME standard operating procedure in the U.S. Congress. Not only does the textbook model no longer describe how most major legislation becomes—or fails to become—law, no single model has replaced it. Variety, not uniformity, characterizes the contemporary legislative process.

After briefly reviewing the contours of unorthodox lawmaking, this chapter examines its consequences. Do the procedures and practices that constitute unorthodox lawmaking as here defined enhance or hinder a bill's chances of becoming law? Are there other less measurable costs and benefits of unorthodox lawmaking? Overall, how should observers of Congress assess unorthodox lawmaking?

Lawmaking in the Contemporary Congress

Once, most major legislation followed a single, well-defined process; the question at each stage was simply whether the bill would survive (and in what form) to go on to the next. Now bills and other important measures confront a series of decision points where more complex choices are at issue. Will the bill be referred to more than one committee? In the House rules of committee jurisdiction are the most important determinant of the answer, but the Speaker does have some discretion. Usually the Speaker designates one lead committee, but he may bring in other committees through additional initial referrals, and he likely will impose on those committees time limits for action, which may be generous or tight. When a number of committees work on a bill, many perspectives and interests are represented in the bill-drafting process. If the committees come to an agreement among themselves, the supportive coalition for the bill becomes formidable. But the more committees involved, the longer the process is likely to take and the more difficult working out disagreements among the committees is likely to be.

In the Senate, committee leaders usually work out problems of conflicting jurisdiction among themselves, sometimes by agreeing to multiple referral, more often informally; the majority leader lacks the procedural powers the Speaker has and is less likely to take a hand. Fairly frequently, several Senate committees work on different bills that deal with the same subject; this was the case with regulatory reform in 1995 (see Chapter 8). Such instances can raise many of the same questions and problems as multiple referral does in the House.

Although in both chambers most legislation is referred to committee, the option of bypassing the committee stage altogether does exist; it is one that, most of the time, only the party leaders can exercise. Bypassing committee can speed up the process significantly. For that reason, committee leaders sometimes agree wholeheartedly to the strategy, particularly if the committee reported the bill or a very similar one in the previous Congress. Party leaders occasionally bypass committee and draft the legislation themselves or delegate the drafting to a special task force because they believe the committee will not do a satisfactory job. They fear that, because of its membership or the political delicacy of the issue, the committee will not be able to come to an agreement in a reasonable period of time or that it will produce a bill that cannot pass the chamber or that is unsatisfactory to significant numbers of majority party members. When legislation is drafted in a task force, the party leadership controls the composition of the drafting group and, in the House, can and often does exclude all minority party members. Speaker Newt Gingrich, R-Ga., for example, headed a task force that drafted the Medicare overhaul plan in 1995; the Republican leaders of the committees of jurisdiction were included on the task force, but no Democratic members of the committee were (see Chapter 11). Frequent bypassing of committees is, however, likely to engender considerable hostility from the membership, majority as well as minority, and leaders who need their party members' votes for reelection to their positions are unlikely to do so except under extraordinary circumstances.

Once a bill has been reported from committee, the majority party leadership must decide if the bill as reported is ready for floor consideration. That decision depends on the answers to a series of questions. If the bill has been reported from several committees, are there major outstanding differences between the committees' versions? Does the bill as reported command enough support to pass the chamber? Is it satisfactory to most majority party members? If the answer to any of these questions is no, postcommittee changes to the legislation will have to be negotiated. Once leaders decide postcommittee adjustments are necessary, they are faced with a host of choices about the form such changes should take.

In the House the next decision centers on the type of special rule under which to bring the legislation to the floor. Are there special problems that confront the legislation as a result of multiple referral? Do special provisions have to be made for incorporating a postcommittee compromise into the bill? Are there amendments that members very much do or do not want to vote on? The majority party leadership in consultation with the Rules Committee majority designs a rule intended to give the legislation its best chance on the floor. Whereas in the past most rules were simple open rules, and the rest were simple closed rules, now only leaders' creativity and the need for House approval limit the form of rules. A majority of the House membership can defeat a rule, but because leaders are sensitive to their party members' preferences, this seldom happens.

In the Senate the majority leader has no such powerful tool at his command. He will often try to work out a unanimous consent agreement for expeditious and orderly consideration of the legislation on the floor; but, for success, he is dependent on the acquiescence of all senators.

The prerogatives individual senators possess give them choices to make at this stage. If they dislike the legislation, should they try to block it from being brought to the floor by putting a "hold" on it? Should they explicitly threaten to filibuster it? Should they make known to the bill's supporters that they are willing to negotiate? Whatever their sentiments about the bill, if it does come to the floor, what amendments will they offer to the legislation? Should they offer measures that are not related to the bill's subject matter as nongermane amendments—either to load down the legislation and hurt its chances of enactment or to piggy-back their own pet ideas on a popular bill? If a bill they strongly dislike passes the chamber, should they try to prevent it from going to conference or filibuster the conference report?

These are the sorts of choices confronting actors in the legislative process on more-or-less ordinary major bills—the kind of legislation discussed in Chapters 7 and 8. Legislative actors can also choose or be faced with new forms of legislation and entirely new processes. For example, leaders can decide to package a broad array of provisions into an omnibus bill—in order to raise the visibility of individually modest measures on a popular issue or to make passing unpalatable but necessary provisions possible by bundling them with more popular ones. The budget process makes omnibus measures a regular part of the legislative process and forces majority party leaders regularly to deal with the problems passing such broad measures create. Central leaders—the majority party leaders but also the president—can use the budget process as a mechanism for attempting to make comprehensive policy change, something that the legislative process as it functioned before the 1974 Congressional Budget and Impoundment Control Act made extremely difficult.

When the president and the congressional majority cannot come to an agreement on major legislation through normal processes, they may decide to try a summit—formal negotiations between congressional leaders and high-level representatives of the president or even the president himself.

Congressional actors—especially congressional majority party leaders but also individual senators—now have more choices, and the alternatives they choose lead to different legislative processes. Party leaders make most of their choices with the aim of facilitating the passage of legislation; individual senators may have quite different aims in mind. When, as they often do, congressional actors make choices that produce a legislative process that is unorthodox by the standards of the old textbook model, what is the effect on whether the bill becomes a law?

Unorthodox Lawmaking and Legislative Outcomes

I have argued that changes in the legislative process can be seen as the responses of members to the problems and opportunities that the institutional structure and the political environment present as members pursue, as individuals or collectively, their goals of reelection, influence in the chamber, and good public policy. Specifically, I contended that a number of the innovations and modifications were driven by the difficulties in legislating that internal reforms and a hostile political climate created for majority Democrats. If the aim was to facilitate successful lawmaking, does unorthodox lawmaking, in fact, do so?

Most bills do not become law. The House has been passing considerably less than 20 percent of the bills introduced by its members in recent Congresses and the Senate less than 30 percent, and, of course, passage in one chamber does not ensure enactment (Ornstein, Mann, and Malbin 1994, 153–155). Thousands of bills are introduced in each chamber during each Congress; neither chamber could possibly consider each one, so most are referred to committee and die there without any further action. Members introduce legislation for a variety of reasons ranging from placating a pesky interest group in their home state or district to publicizing a little recognized problem or an innovative approach to an acknowl-

TABLE 12.1   The Fate of All Major Legislation, 1987–90, 1993–94

	Percentage of major measures	Number of major measures
Total measures	100	158
Reached House floor	92	146
Reached Senate floor	89	140
Passed House	88	139
Passed Senate	80	127
Passed House and Senate	78	123
Became law[a]	71	112

SOURCE: Computed by the author.

[a] Or otherwise successfully completed the legislative process. This means approval of the conference report in both chambers in the case of budget resolutions and approval by two-thirds vote in each chamber in the case of constitutional amendments.

edged problem. Members may not expect certain of their bills to pass and, sometimes, may not even want them to.

Major legislation is different; by definition, it is significant legislation that has made it onto the congressional agenda where it is being seriously considered. As Table 12.1 shows, its prospects are considerably brighter than that of all legislation. Most major measures get to the floor of at least one chamber, and those that do usually pass—though the likelihood is greater in the House than in the Senate. A little more than three out of four major measures pass both chambers, and seven out of ten become law or otherwise successfully finish the process.[1] Thus, measures that have attained the status of being considered major legislation on the congressional agenda do tend to become law, but it is no sure thing; about three out of ten do not succeed.

How do the special procedures and practices that often characterize the legislative process on these major measures affect the measures' probability of successful enactment? An examination of the relationship between the number of special procedures and practices used and legislative success provides at least a partial answer. The cumulative indexes introduced in Chapter 5 are used. For each of the major measures in three recent Congresses (the 100th, 101st, and 103rd), the House measure counts the number of the following special procedures and practices

---

1. Legislative success is defined as enactment in the case of bills, as approval of the conference report in both chambers in the case of budget resolutions, and as approval by two-thirds vote in each chamber in the case of constitutional amendments.

TABLE 12.2   The Effect of Unorthodox Lawmaking on Legislative Success, by Chamber, 1987–90, 1993–94

Chamber	Number of special practices and procedures[a]	All major measures	
		Percentage that passed chamber	Percentage enacted
House	0	80	57
	1	80	64
	2	96	77
	3 or more	97	87
Senate	0	77	68
	1	78	65
	2 or more	96	92

SOURCE: Computed by the author.

[a] The number of the following special procedures and practices that the legislation encountered as it worked its way through the chamber: for the House, multiple referral, omnibus legislation, legislation was the result of a legislative-executive branch summit, the bypassing of committees, postcommittee adjustments, and consideration under a complex or closed rule; for the Senate, all of the above except consideration under a complex or closed rule.

that the legislation encountered as it worked its way through that chamber: multiple referral, omnibus, the result of a summit, committee bypassed, postcommittee adjustments, and consideration under a complex or closed rule. The Senate measure is identical except that it does not include consideration under a complex or closed rule.

When the legislative process on a bill in the House includes two or more special procedures or practices, that legislation is considerably more likely to pass the House than if it includes one or none (see Table 12.2). The same relationship holds in the Senate. The likelihood of a bill becoming law increases with the number of special procedures and practices employed in the House. Again the relationship is similar for the Senate. Because becoming law requires that both chambers pass the legislation, the combination of special procedures and practices in the two chambers should make a difference. As Table 12.3 shows, it does. Of measures subject to two or more special procedures and practices in both chambers, 91 percent were successful; at the other extreme, if subject to none in either chamber, only 63 percent were successful. In sum, legislation is more likely to complete the legislative process successfully if that process includes these special procedures and practices.

When the circumstances that stimulate the employment of unorthodox lawmaking are considered, these findings are all the more impressive.

TABLE 12.3   The Cumulative Effect of Unorthodox Lawmaking on Legislative
Success, 1987–90, 1993–94

Number of special procedures and practices[a]	Percentage of all major measures enacted
None in either chamber	63
None in one chamber, one in the other chamber, or one in each chamber	59
All other combinations except two or more in both chambers	77
Two or more in both chambers	91

SOURCE: Computed by the author.

[a] The number of the following special procedures and practices that the legislation encountered as it worked its way through the chamber: for the House, multiple referral, omnibus legislation, legislation was the result of a legislative-executive branch summit, the bypassing of committees, postcommittee adjustments, and consideration under a complex or closed rule; for the Senate, all of the above except consideration under a complex or closed rule.

Leaders are unlikely to employ the special procedures and practices under their control unless they expect passing the bill in satisfactory form to be problematical. Negotiating postcommittee adjustments and crafting and passing restrictive rules, not to mention bypassing committee, take time and resources; if the legislation is going to pass without trouble, why expend either? Therefore, when the legislative process displays several of the special procedures and practices, the chances are the bill was in some trouble and that, without intervention, its chances of legislative success were lower than those of other legislation. Since the data show a higher frequency of legislative success, these special procedures and practices do appear to accomplish their purpose.

The special practices stemming from the Senate's unique rules are under the control of individual senators and may well be employed for different purposes and have different consequences than those that are primarily leadership tools. What impact do amending marathons and filibusters have on legislative outcomes?

Amending marathons are associated with legislative success. Bills subject to ten or more Senate amendments decided by roll call votes are more likely to pass the Senate and more likely to become law than are other measures (see Table 12.4). The adoption of floor amendments may enhance a bill's chances of ultimate legislative success; amendments may make a bill more broadly attractive or at least give the sponsors of successful amendments a greater stake in the legislation's enactment. However, the substantial differences in success rates between bills subject to high

TABLE 12.4   Amending Marathons, Filibusters, and Legislative Outcomes for
Major Measures, 1987–90, 1993–94 (in percentages)

	Amending marathon[a]		Filibuster problem	
Outcome	Yes	No	Yes	No
Passed Senate	97	89	75	87
Enacted	92	78	65	77

SOURCE: Computed by the author.

[a] An amending marathon is defined as ten or more amendments offered and pushed to a roll call vote. Only measures that reached the Senate floor are included.

amending activity and those subject to low amending activity (regardless of whether the amendments that were offered passed) strongly suggest that senators engage in amending marathons on bills highly likely to become law; senators use such bills as vehicles for lawmaking. Senators sometimes use the Senate's permissive amending rules to try to kill legislation, but that is not their primary use.

The uses senators make of extended debate are much less benign in purpose and in effect. Legislation subject to a filibuster problem (a hold, a threatened filibuster, or a filibuster) is less likely to pass the Senate and less likely to become law than is other legislation (see Table 12.4). In recent Congresses 87 percent of legislation that did not encounter any extended debate–related problem passed the Senate and 77 percent became law; in contrast, only 75 percent of measures that ran into a filibuster-related problem passed the Senate and 65 percent became law. Half of the major measures that failed to pass the Senate encountered a filibuster problem. Of all measures that failed to complete the entire process, 39 percent encountered a filibuster problem.

Extended debate–related problems have had quite different effects on legislative success in different Congresses. In the 101st Congress whether a measure ran into a filibuster problem had little impact on its chances of enactment, and the same is true for the 97th Congress for which data are also available; in the 100th and 103rd Congresses the impact was major. In the 100th, a Congress in which Senate Republicans (newly in the minority) openly waged a partisan filibuster strategy, all of the major measures not subject to a filibuster-related problem passed the Senate, and 91 percent were enacted; of those subject to such a problem, 75 percent passed the Senate, and 67 percent were enacted. In the 103rd, during which minority party Republicans again pursued a strategy heavily based on the filibuster, 85 percent of major measures not subject to an extended debate–related problem passed the Senate, and 82 percent were enacted; 71 percent of those that encountered a filibuster problem passed the Senate, and 58 percent were enacted. Since almost half the major legislation in the 103rd Congress was subject to a filibuster problem, the impact on enactment was substantial. About two-thirds of measures that failed encountered a filibuster problem. Extended debate has its most severe impact on legislative outputs when it is employed as a partisan tool.

Of course, filibusters, actual and threatened, can influence outcomes without killing the legislation at issue. The perpetrators' aim, in fact, may be to extort substantive concessions from the bill's supporters rather than to kill the bill altogether. Those measures that became law despite a filibuster problem show a very high incidence of postcommittee adjustments (48 percent), suggesting that substantive alterations were required to overcome the filibuster problem.

Other Costs and Benefits

What effect does unorthodox lawmaking have beyond its impact on legislative outcomes? Scholars long ago learned that even planned changes in complex organizations and processes are likely to have unintended consequences; many of the changes examined here were not planned but evolved out of ad hoc responses to pressing problems.

Congress has long done its serious substantive work on legislation in committees. A number of the procedures and practices that constitute unorthodox lawmaking were a response to the decline in the committees' autonomy and power; however, procedures and practices such as multiple referral, postcommittee adjustments, and the bypassing of committees have further eroded the committees' influence, at least to some extent. Has the result been less expertly crafted legislation and less deliberation at the pre-floor stage of the process? If so, this would be a serious negative byproduct of unorthodox lawmaking since this is when real deliberation takes place, if it takes place at all.

At least before the 104th Congress, pre-floor deliberation had not, by and large, been sacrificed. It is when committees are bypassed that the possibility that deliberation will be truncated is greatest. Yet, in many cases when a committee is bypassed in a particular Congress, the committee had, in fact, reported the legislation in a previous Congress. In those instances when Democratic House leaders used task forces rather than committees to draft legislation, they chose as task force leaders members who brought great substantive as well as political expertise to bear on the issue (Sinclair 1995, 188–192).

During the 104th Congress, House Republican leaders put extraordinary pressure on committees to report legislation quickly. Hearings, if they were held at all, were perfunctory; markups were often so hurried, and held before most members had had an opportunity to study the legislative language at issue, that they were, in effect, pro forma. Party leaders directly, and task forces on which inexperienced freshmen predominated, exercised considerable influence on the substance of legislation in committee or through postcommittee adjustments; and committees were frequently bypassed both to move legislation more quickly and for substantive reasons. Deliberation and the quality of legislation did suffer. Many Republicans, members and staff alike, concede privately that the legislation brought to the floor was sloppy at best; the careful substantive work had not been done.

The power of the Congress, especially that of the House, in the political system depends on its specialized, expert committees. The issues and problems with which the federal government deals are too numerous, diverse, and complex for any one person to master. For a relatively small body such as Congress to hold its own vis-à-vis the executive branch and outside interests, it must divide labor and rely on its members' expertise in their area of specialization. Has unorthodox lawmaking decreased the incentives for members to specialize and gain expertise?

Were the modes of decision making prevalent in the 104th House to become standard operating procedure, incentives would decline substantially; substantive expertise and hard work on one's committee had relatively little payoff in influence during that Congress, especially during 1995. Those modes of decision making arose, however, out of highly unusual circumstances—a new House majority after forty years and the attendant sense of mandate—and were a temporary response to them. To be sure, some greater centralization is likely to be the 104th Congress's legacy for some time to come. Yet committees had begun to regain influence during 1996, the second year of the 104th Congress, and in the foreseeable future are unlikely to be again relegated to the subordinate role they played in 1995.

The incentives for members of the House to develop committee expertise, although weaker than in the committee government days before the mid-1970s, are still strong. Becoming a committee specialist is not the only route to influence, but it remains a major one. Senators do specialize less than they used to, but notable specialists still exist. The effective senator must develop some expertise; a senator must know what she or he is talking about to be taken seriously. To some extent, senators can substitute staff expertise for personal expertise, and in both chambers the increase in staff has made it possible for members to involve themselves effectively in more issues than once was possible.

In sum, unorthodox lawmaking has not reduced the influence of committees so much that members no longer find it worthwhile to develop committee-related expertise; expertise still pays off in influence. Nevertheless, central leaders do need to be aware that their strategies affect members' incentives and that, for the good of the institution, they should avoid seriously undermining their members' incentives to develop expertise.

As important as expertise to an effective legislative process is ensuring that the broadest possible range of interests is heard and considered. What effect has unorthodox lawmaking had on the likelihood that the full range of views and interests will find a hearing? From that perspective, unorthodox lawmaking as practiced in the 104th House was problematical. When, as was common during the Contract with America period in early 1995, committees do not hold meaningful hearings, an important forum for the expression of a diversity of views is unavailable. To an unprecedented extent, the minority party was excluded from decision making at the pre-floor stage; committee procedures made meaningful participation impossible, and often the real decisions were made elsewhere, within Republican-only task forces or by the Republican leadership itself. Interest groups that the Republican Party considered hostile—environmental groups, for example—were not given access to make their case, while the party's business allies participated in drafting legislation in which they had a direct interest.

Understandably, the first Republican House majority in forty years had a lot it wanted to accomplish; these extraordinary circumstances led to such a truncated process. Furthermore, Republicans paid a price for their exclusionary procedures. Because neither the committees nor the leadership did the hard and often ideologically painful work of building a coalition broad enough to survive the entire process, much of the legislation passed by the House did not become law; excluded interests blocked it elsewhere. Because the costs of exclusion were high, the 104th is not likely to set a precedent.

Although the minority exclusion practiced by House Republicans in the 104th was extraordinary, Democrats, when they were the majority party, employed some of the practices and procedures of unorthodox lawmaking in a way that excluded the minority from effective decision making in the pre-floor legislative process in the House. In the 1980s and early 1990s, most though not all Democratic task forces consisted of Democrats only. When Democratic leaders negotiated postcommittee adjustments to bills, they were most likely to do so among Democrats. As a more diverse party and one accustomed to governing, Democrats did not exclude major interests from receiving a hearing, nor did they truncate the committee process in the way Republicans did. However, the ideological gulf between the parties that grew ever wider during the 1980s and 1990s made bipartisan decision making increasingly difficult and continues to do so today.

Although unorthodox lawmaking in the House can be employed to cut legitimate actors out of certain stages of the process, it also can have just the opposite effect. Multiple referral involves more members, and thus more and different perspectives and interests, in policy making and gives more members opportunities to participate in the legislative process on issues that interest them. The way postcommittee adjustments are made often does the same, though the members brought into the process are usually only majority party members.

Finally, in evaluating the effects of unorthodox lawmaking on the inclusiveness of the pre-floor legislative process in the House, one must remember that the orthodox process could often be highly exclusionary. One committee had a monopoly on legislative action in a given area and was not necessarily responsive to the wishes of the chamber or of the majority party. Decisions were made behind closed doors. And the membership of many committees was biased in a way that favored some interests and excluded others. Diffuse interests—consumer and environmental interests in particular, which are seldom represented by wealthy and well-connected organizations—had little access.

Have specially tailored and usually restrictive special rules for House floor consideration of legislation degraded floor deliberation as both Republican and Democratic minorities have claimed? That contention is based on a false premise; it is unrealistic, I would argue, to expect deliberation, as a great many people use the term, to take place on the floor of either chamber and certainly not in the House. If deliberation is defined as the process by which a group of people get together and talk through a complex problem, mapping the problem's contours, defining the alternatives, and figuring out where they stand, it is unrealistic to expect all of that to occur on the chamber floors. Deliberation is a nonlinear, free-form process that depends on the size of the group being strictly limited; subcommittees, other small groups, and possibly committees are the forums where it might be fostered. Deliberation so defined certainly did not occur on the House floor before restrictive rules became prevalent.

What we can and should expect on the chamber floors is informed and informative debate and sound decision making. Restrictive rules can, in fact, contribute toward those goals. Rules can provide order and predictability to the floor consideration of complex and controversial legislation; they can be used to ensure that floor time is apportioned in a reasonably sensible way, both within a given bill and across legislation, and that debate focuses on the major alternatives, not on minor or side issues. In addition, through the use of restrictive rules, committee compromises can be protected from being picked apart on the floor.

One's conclusions about the appropriate form of special rules depend on what sorts of decisions one believes can and cannot be made well on the House floor. The membership as a whole can and should make the big decisions; it can and should choose among the major alternatives that have been proposed. A body of 435 should not, I believe, get involved in a detailed rewriting of legislation on the floor via multitudes of individual amendments; the institution is too large and unwieldy, the necessary expertise often is lacking, and the time almost always is too short for a full consideration of the impact of proposed changes. Restrictive rules, in and of themselves, have not damaged the quality of House floor consideration. To be sure, both Democrats and Republicans, when in the majority, have sometimes used rules that were unnecessarily restrictive. Nevertheless, despite the rhetoric implying otherwise, the House seldom considers legislation under closed rules barring all amendments. Most rules, by making in order one or more major substitutes, do allow the membership as a whole to make at least the biggest decisions.

Informed floor decision making requires that members not directly involved in the crafting of legislation nevertheless have available sufficient information to make a considered choice. When Congress legislates through large omnibus measures, the likelihood that members will not know about or understand all the measures' provisions increases. When high-level summits make legislative decisions, members are also likely to face information problems. This is not a problem unique to such unorthodox processes of lawmaking; it also occurs with much other complex legislation. In all these cases the problem can be ameliorated by strictly abiding by layover rules that require that language be available for a given period of time before a vote can be taken.

Summits as decision-making mechanisms raise another problem. Their frequent use would undermine the committee system, but the costs to party leaders of summit decision making are sufficiently high that that is unlikely. Because summits are an exclusionary rather than an inclusionary mode of decision making, they leave most members feeling cut out of the action and thus disgruntled.

The procedures and practices of unorthodox lawmaking discussed to this point entail limited costs and have the benefit of facilitating lawmaking. Senators' increasingly frequent exploitation of extended debate, however, hinders lawmaking. Does this trend in the Senate have consequences beyond the blocking of specific legislation? Are there benefits not otherwise attainable that outweigh the costs?

The habitual exploitation of extended debate by senators has a pervasive impact on the legislative process that extends far beyond its effect on specific legislation. By requiring a super majority to pass legislation that is at all controversial, it makes the coalition building process much more difficult and increases a status quo–oriented system's tendency toward gridlock. The costs of prolonged gridlock can be severe; a government that cannot act, that cannot respond satisfactorily to its citizens' demands, loses its legitimacy.

Supporters of the filibuster argue that it promotes deliberation; by slowing the legislative process, it provides an opportunity for second thoughts and perhaps for cooler heads to prevail. Furthermore, many argue, it gives extra weight to intensity in the process, allowing an intense minority to protect itself from a tyrannical majority.

In reply one can argue that, quite apart from extended debate in the Senate, the legislative process advantages intensity. For example, the committee assignment process (in which members' preferences are given substantial weight) and members' considerable freedom in both chambers to choose the issues to which they will devote their time result in those with the more intense preferences on an issue generally exercising greater influence (Shepsle 1978; Hall 1987). Deliberation is promoted by ensuring that a minority has time to attempt to raise public opposition to a proposal it believes unwise, but guaranteeing the minority an opportunity to publicize its views does not require such a difficult cloture procedure. If Rule 22 were altered so that the longer a measure is debated on the floor, the smaller the super majority needed for cloture, the minority would have the floor time to make its case but would not be able to block action on majority-supported legislation forever.

Proposed Senate rules changes can be filibustered and imposing cloture requires a two-thirds vote—a higher threshold than for cloture on legislation. Therefore, major rules changes are extraordinarily difficult to enact in the Senate. Either the new rules must benefit almost all senators or the public demand for change must be overwhelming.

Assessing Unorthodox Lawmaking

Overall, then, how do we rate unorthodox lawmaking? A broader assessment of unorthodox lawmaking requires some discussion of the appropriate criteria for judging Congress. Unless we are clear about what it is we want Congress to do, how are we to evaluate the impact of unorthodox lawmaking?

Certainly, we expect Congress to represent; we expect members to bring into the legislative process the views, needs, and desires of their constituents, and we expect Congress as an institution to provide a forum where the interests and demands of all segments of society are expressed. But, while we want Congress to be a forum for debate where the full range of views is expressed, we also want Congress to make decisions—to pass laws.

This second criterion has sometimes been labeled lawmaking, but obviously not just any laws will do. In characterizing what sort of laws Congress is expected to pass, two criteria are frequently mentioned and often conflated. Congress should pass laws that reflect the will of the people; that is, Congress should be responsive to popular majorities. Congress should pass laws that deal promptly and effectively with pressing national problems. These two criteria, which can be labeled responsiveness and responsibility, are distinct. Only in a perfect world would what the majority wants always accord with what policy experts deem most likely to be effective—especially in the long run. Both responsiveness and responsibility are values we would like Congress to further in its lawmaking, yet at times they may come into conflict.

In popular and journalistic discourse, members of Congress are admonished to "do what's right, not what's popular." But do we really want Congress to regularly thwart popular majorities? Furthermore and critically, uncertainty about the link between a specific policy choice and the societal outcome means that, in most major policy areas, legitimate differences of opinion as to what constitutes good public policy can and do exist. Members of Congress are also told to pay attention to the people, not to the special interests or the out-of-touch experts; yet how should Congress respond when what the people want is based on faulty logic or incorrect information, a not infrequent occurrence given citizens' inattention to public policy problems? And what if the majority in question is a slim or relatively indifferent one and the minority passionately dissents?

Some tension among the values of representation, responsiveness, and responsibility is unavoidable. The institutional structures and processes most conducive to each are not necessarily the same. A decentralized, open, permeable body in which individual members have considerable resources and autonomy of action has great potential for representation— for articulating the broad variety of opinions and interests in our society. A more centralized, hierarchical body is more capable of expeditious decision making. Decision-making processes highly exposed to public scrutiny further responsiveness; those that are less visible may promote responsibility. Representation takes time, especially when there are a great variety of viewpoints; by definition, lawmaking requires closure, an end to debate, and, implicitly or explicitly, a choice among competing alternatives. Thus, it is logically impossible to maximize all three values simultaneously. It would require an institution and a legislative process that makes decisions quickly and slowly at the same time, one that both exposes its members to the full force of public opinion and one that provides some insulation.

If we expect a Congress that gives all interests a full and fair hearing on each issue and then, in every case, expeditiously passes legislation that both satisfies a majority, preferably a large one, and effectively addresses the problem in question, we are doomed to disappointment. Congress has never been able to come up to that standard and the environment in which the contemporary Congress functions makes that even less feasible than in the past. The problems facing the country are highly complex. On many, there is little consensus among the experts about the appropriate governmental response; on others, the experts' prescriptions are unpalatable. Citizens are divided, unclear, and often ambivalent in their views as to what they want government to do. Political elites including the representatives citizens elect are sharply divided in their views as to what constitutes good public policy.

If, as I have argued, it is logically impossible for Congress to be perfectly representative, responsive, and responsible at the same time, and if the climate in which it currently functions is an especially difficult one, how should we evaluate unorthodox lawmaking? I would argue that so long as unorthodox lawmaking facilitates Congress's ability to make decisions without sacrificing deliberation or restricting significantly the range of interests with access to the process, it performs an extremely important function.

Unorthodox lawmaking has made it possible for Congress to carry out its essential function of lawmaking during an exceedingly tough time. And that in a very important sense is the bottom line; "representation" by a body powerless to make decisions is just meaningless talk. Institutions, like other complex organisms, are faced with the challenge of adapting to their changing environment or succumbing. In the case of the Congress, the threat is not that the institution will cease to exist but that it will become irrelevant. If it does not and cannot carry out its legislative functions satisfactorily, those tasks are likely to be taken over, in fact if not in form, by other entities—the executive branch most likely.

The development of what I have called unorthodox lawmaking is the latest chapter in an ongoing story of congressional adaption and change. Confronted by a political and institutional environment that made lawmaking difficult, congressional leaders modified and sometimes transformed existing procedures and practices as they attempted to do their job of facilitating lawmaking. The result, unorthodox lawmaking, is often not neat and not pretty, especially on those highly salient and contentious issues that are most likely to lead the news. It is, however, highly flexible and so can be tailored to the problems—political, substantive, and proce-dural—that a particular major measure raises. To be sure, one compo-nent of unorthodox lawmaking—the frequent use of extended debate in the Senate—has contributed to gridlock. The difficulty of changing Sen-ate rules threatens the adaptability of the chamber.

Even so, unorthodox lawmaking on balance represents successful adaption to a tough environment. During much of the past two decades, all of the ingredients for gridlock have been present: divided control of the presidency and Congress, large and deeply felt differences in policy preferences between the parties, and big deficits that make the policy choices facing politicians unpalatable ones. The political system has failed to solve the big problems facing the country, though on some, such as the deficit, progress has been made. The conflicting political and policy goals of the president and the congressional majority during much of this period, the hard choices confronting decision makers, and the public's ambivalence about what it wants have produced gridlock in this sense. Yet throughout this difficult time, Congress has with few exceptions produced essential legislation and kept the government functioning; the failure to do so in 1995–96 resulted in such negative public opinion that Congress is unlikely to shut down the federal government again. The Congress has also managed to pass some significant measures that were not simple "must-pass" bills (Mayhew 1990). Unorthodox lawmaking has given Con-gress the capacity to produce such legislation within an environment more conducive to gridlock.

Furthermore, unorthodox lawmaking has made it possible for Con-gress to make decisions without, most of the time, sacrificing deliberation or restricting significantly the range of interests with access to the process. The development of expertise is still rewarded and deliberation is still fos-tered by the committee system. Overall, the Congress as an institution and its legislative process are much more open to the full range of societal views and interests than in the prereform era, and while the procedures and practices of unorthodox lawmaking can narrow participation, they more frequently broaden it.

Unorthodox lawmaking has not made it possible for Congress consis-tently to make laws that both reflect the will of the people and deal promptly and effectively with pressing national problems. No process can ensure that. It has made it possible for our most representative branch to continue to perform its essential function of lawmaking in a time of popu-lar division and ambiguity; it has thereby given us all the opportunity to work toward a political system in which the branch closest to the people better performs the tough tasks we assign to it.

References

Bach, Stanley. 1994. "Legislating: Floor and Conference Procedures in Congress." In *Encyclopedia of the American Legislative System*, vol. 2, ed. Joel Silbey. New York: Scribner's.

Bach, Stanley, and Steven S. Smith. 1988. *Managing Uncertainty in the House of Representatives.* Washington, D.C.: The Brookings Institution.

Benenson, Bob. 1995a. "House Panels Take Quick Action on Risk Assessment Provisions." *Congressional Quarterly Weekly Report,* February 11, 450–453.

———. 1995b. "Complaints Don't Delay Action on Regulatory Overhaul Bills." *Congressional Quarterly Weekly Report,* February 18, 520–521.

———. 1995c. "Bipartisan Regulatory Rewrite Breezes Through Committee." *Congressional Quarterly Weekly Report,* March 25, 867.

———. 1995d. "Panel, Mired in Squabbling, Throws Bill to Full Senate." *Congressional Quarterly Weekly Report,* April 29, 1174.

———. 1995e. "Bill to Scale Back Process Gets Bipartisan Nod." *Congressional Quarterly Weekly Report,* June 24, 1836.

———. 1995f. "Opponents Whittle Away at Dole's Overhaul Bill." *Congressional Quarterly Weekly Report,* July 15, 2051.

Beth, Richard. 1994. "Control of the House Floor Agenda: Implications from the Use of the Discharge Rule, 1931–1994." Paper delivered at the annual meeting of the American Political Science Association, New York, September 1–4.

———. 1995. "What We Don't Know About Filibusters." Paper delivered at the meeting of the Western Political Science Association, Portland, Oregon, March 15–18.

Binder, Sarah. 1996. "The Partisan Basis of Procedural Choice: Parliamentary Rights in the House, 1798–1990." *American Political Science Review,* March 8–20.

———. forthcoming. *Minority Rights, Majority Rule: Partisanship and the Development of Congress.* New York: Cambridge University Press.

Burger, Timothy J. 1995. "After Defeat House Leaders Must Regroup." *Roll Call,* July 17, 1, 22.

Canon, David. 1992. "Unconventional Lawmaking in the United States Congress." Paper presented at the annual meeting of the American Political Science Association, September 3–6, Chicago.

Cheney, Richard B. 1989. "An Unruly House." *Public Opinion* 11: 41–44.

Cloud, David S. 1995. "Industry, Politics Intertwined in Dole's Regulatory Bill." *Congressional Quarterly Weekly Report,* May 6, 1219–1224.

Cloud, David S., and George Hager. 1993. "With New Budget Deal in Hand, Clinton Faces Longest Yard." *Congressional Quarterly Weekly Report,* July 31, 2023–2028.

Cloud, David S., George Hager, and Alissa Rubin. 1993. "Deal on Deficit Sets Stage for Senate Floor Fight." *Congressional Quarterly Weekly Report,* June 19, 1542–1545.

Cohen, Richard E. 1992. *Washington at Work: Back Rooms and Clean Air.* New York: Macmillan.

———. 1996. "Appropriators Losing Clout." *National Journal,* January 20, 130–131.

Congress and the Nation. 1993. Washington, D.C.: Congressional Quarterly.

Congressional Quarterly Almanac. Various years. Washington, D.C.: Congressional Quarterly.

Connelly, William, and John Pitney. 1994. *Congress' Permanent Minority? Republicans in the U.S. House.* Lanham, Md.: Rowman & Littlefield.

Cooper, Joseph. 1981. "Organization and Innovation in the House of Representatives." In *The House at Work,* ed. Joseph Cooper and G. Calvin Mackenzie. Austin: University of Texas Press.

Cooper, Joseph, and Cheryl D. Young. 1989. "Bill Introduction in the Nineteenth Century: A Study of Institutional Change." *Legislative Studies Quarterly* (February): 67–106.

Cox, Gary, and Mathew McCubbins. 1992. *Legislative Leviathan: Party Government in the House.* Berkeley: University of California Press.

Cranford, John. 1987. "Highlights of HR 3, the House-Passed Trade Bill." *Congressional Quarterly Weekly Report,* May 2, 813.

Davidson, Roger H. 1981. "Two Avenues of Change: House and Senate Committee Reorganization." In *Congress Reconsidered,* ed. Lawrence C. Dodd and Bruce I. Oppenheimer, 2d ed. Washington, D.C.: CQ Press.

———. 1989. "Multiple Referral of Legislation in the U.S. Senate." *Legislative Studies Quarterly* 14: 375–392.

Davidson, Roger H., and Walter Oleszek. 1977. *Congress against Itself.* Bloomington: Indiana University Press.

Davidson, Roger H., and Walter Oleszek. 1992. "From Monopoly to Management: Changing Patterns of Committee Deliberation." In *The Postreform Congress,* ed. Roger H. Davidson. New York: St. Martin's.

Dodd, Lawrence C., and Bruce I. Oppenheimer. 1977. *Congress Reconsidered.* New York: Praeger.

Drew, Elizabeth. 1996. *Showdown: The Struggle between the Gingrich Congress and the Clinton White House.* New York: Simon and Schuster.

DSG (Democratic Study Group). 1994. "A Look at the Senate Filibuster." DSG Special Report, June 13, 103–128, Appendix B (compiled by Congressional Research Service).

Eilperin, Juliet. 1996. "House Bills Bypass Committee Process." *Roll Call,* March 18, 1, 27.

Ellwood, John W., and James A. Thurber. 1981. "The Politics of the Congressional Budget Process Re-examined." In *Congress Reconsidered,* ed. Lawrence C. Dodd and Bruce I. Oppenheimer, 2d ed. Washington, D.C.: CQ Press.

Evans, C. Lawrence, and Walter J. Oleszek. 1995. "Congressional Tsunami? Institutional Change in the 104th Congress." Paper delivered at the annual meeting of the American Political Science Association, Chicago, August 31–September 3.

Fenno, Richard. 1973. *Congressmen in Committees.* Boston: Little, Brown.

Fessler, Pamela. 1993. "If People Get Behind President, Congress Is Likely to Follow." *Congressional Quarterly Weekly Report,* February 20, 380–381.

Fiore, Faye. 1995. "Unyielding GOP Freshmen Lead Balanced-Budget Siege." *Los Angeles Times,* December 21, A1.

Fraley, Colette. 1995. "Historic House Medicare Vote Affirms GOP Determination." *Congressional Quarterly Weekly Report,* October 21, 3206–3210.

Freedman, Allan. 1995. "Property Rights Bill Advances But Faces Uncertainty." *Congressional Quarterly Weekly Report,* December 23, 3884–3885.

Gamm, Gerald, and Kenneth Shepsle. 1989. "Emergence of Legislative Institutions: Standing Committees in the House and Senate, 1810–1825." *Legislative Studies Quarterly* (February): 39–66.

Gilmour, John B. 1990. *Reconcilable Differences?* Berkeley: University of California Press.

Gold, Martin, Michael Hugo, Hyde Murray, Peter Robinson, and A. L. "Pete" Singleton. 1992. *The Book on Congress: Process, Procedure and*

Structure. Washington, D.C.: Big Eagle Publishing Co. Supplements published biannually.

Granat, Diane. 1984. "The Big Conference: Getting to Be Old Hat." *Congressional Quarterly Weekly Report,* June 2, 1298.

Hager, George. 1993. "President Throws Down Gauntlet." *Congressional Quarterly Weekly Report,* February 20, 355–359.

———. 1995a. "House GOP Pushes Budget Cuts as Political Stakes Mount." *Congressional Quarterly Weekly Report,* March 18, 794–798.

———. 1995b. "Senate Drafting Session Delayed to Build Support for Cuts." *Congressional Quarterly Weekly Report,* April 29, 1166.

———. 1995c. "Caustic Four-Day Scrap Portends a Long Haul in the Senate." *Congressional Quarterly Weekly Report,* May 13, 1302.

———. 1995d. "Tax Cuts Dominate Agenda as Conference Begins." *Congressional Quarterly Weekly Report,* June 10, 1619.

———. 1995e. "Pivotal Floor Votes Are Up Next as GOP Budget Lurches Ahead." *Congressional Quarterly Weekly Report,* October 14, 3119.

———. 1995f. "In the House, GOP Leadership Scores Comfortable Win." *Congressional Quarterly Weekly Report,* October 28, 3287.

———. 1995g. "Budget Battles Set to Continue After Christmas Cease-Fire." *Congressional Quarterly Weekly Report,* December 23, 3874–3878.

———. 1996. "Congress, Clinton Yield Enough to Close the Book on Fiscal '96." *Congressional Quarterly Weekly Report,* April 27, 1155–1157.

Hager, George, and Alissa J. Rubin. 1995a. "With Cuts Ahead, GOP Works to Build a Sense of Urgency." *Congressional Quarterly Weekly Report,* May 6, 1227–1230.

———. 1995b. "Congress Gives Resounding Yes to Balanced-Budget Plan." *Congressional Quarterly Weekly Report,* July 1, 1899–1905.

———. 1995c. "As Budget Talks Break Down, Finger-Pointing Escalates." *Congressional Quarterly Weekly Report,* December 16, 3789–3792.

———. 1996. "Chances of a Budget Deal Now Anyone's Guess." *Congressional Quarterly Weekly Report,* January 13, 89–91.

Hager, George, and David S. Cloud. 1993a. "Leaders Scramble to Win Votes for Deficit-Reduction Bill." *Congressional Quarterly Weekly Report,* May 22, 1277–1279.

———. 1993b. "Democrats Pull Off Squeaker in Approving Clinton Plan." *Congressional Quarterly Weekly Report,* May 29, 1340–1345.

———. 1993c. "Democrats Tie Their Fate to Clinton's Budget Bill." *Congressional Quarterly Weekly Report,* August 7, 2122–2129.

Hall, Richard L. 1987. "Participation and Purpose in Committee Decision Making." *American Political Science Review* 81 (March): 105–127.

Hibbing, John, and Elizabeth Theiss-Morse. 1995. *Congress as Public Enemy.* New York: Cambridge University Press.

Hook, Janet. 1993. "In Fight for Votes, White House . . . Here, There and Everywhere." *Congressional Quarterly Weekly Report,* July 31, 2023–2028.

———. 1995a. "Congress Passes Landmark GOP Plan to Balance Budget." *Los Angeles Times,* June 30, A28.

———. 1995b. "Budget Battle Forces Gingrich into the Trenches." *Los Angeles Times,* October 21, A20.

———. 1996. "White House, Congress Reach Deal on Budget." *Los Angeles Times,* April 25, A1, A15.

Hook, Janet, and Paul Richter. 1996. "House GOP Leaders, in Shift, Act on Shutdown." *Los Angeles Times,* January 5, A1, A16.

Hosansky, David. 1995a. "Chipping Away at Opposition, Senate Passes Mandates Bill." *Congressional Quarterly Weekly Report,* January 28, 276–279, 307–309.

———. 1995b. "Panel Rejects Farm Overhaul in a Rebuke to Leadership." *Congressional Quarterly Weekly Report,* September 23, 2875–2879.

Idelson, Holly. 1994. "Clinton, Democrats Scramble to Save Anti-Crime Bill." *Congressional Quarterly Weekly Report,* August 13, 2340–2343.

Idelson, Holly, and Richard Sammon. 1994. "Marathon Talks Produce New Anti-Crime Bill." *Congressional Quarterly Weekly Report,* August 20, 2449–2454.

Jacoby, Mary. 1995. "GOP Battles over Budget's Role." *Roll Call,* January 30, 1.

Katz, Jeffrey L. 1995a. "Provisions of House Welfare Bill." *Congressional Quarterly Weekly Report,* March 18, 815–818.

———. 1995b. "House Passes Welfare Bill; Senate Likely to Alter It." *Congressional Quarterly Weekly Report,* March 25, 872–875.

King, David. 1994. "The Nature of Congressional Committee Jurisdictions." *American Political Science Review* (March): 48–62.

Koszczuk, Jackie. 1995a. "Gingrich Puts More Power into Speaker's Hands." *Congressional Quarterly Weekly Report,* October 7, 3049–3053.

———. 1995b. "Gingrich's Abortion Strategies." *Congressional Quarterly Weekly Report,* November 4, 3376.

Koszczuk, Jackie, and David S. Cloud. 1995. "GOP Leaders Tell the Troops, It's Time to Lock Hands." *Congressional Quarterly Weekly Report,* September 16, 2769–2770.

Kriz, Margaret. 1995. "Risky Business." *National Journal,* February 18, 417–421.

Kuntz, Phil. 1992. "Drawn-Out Denouement Mirrors Character of 102nd Congress." *Congressional Quarterly Weekly Report,* October 10, 3127–3128.

———. 1994. "Hard-Fought Crime Bill Battle Spoils Field for Health Care." *Congressional Quarterly Weekly Report,* August 27, 2485.

Lawrence, Christine C. 1988a. "Senate Breaks Deadlock, Passes Anti-Drug Bill." *Congressional Quarterly Weekly Report,* October 15, 2978.

———. 1988b. "Drug Bill Delays Conclusion of 100th Congress." *Congressional Quarterly Weekly Report,* October 22, 3032–3036.

———. 1988c. "In Its Last Act, Congress Clears Anti-Drug Bill." *Congressional Quarterly Weekly Report,* October 29, 3145, 3170.

Longley, Lawrence, and Walter Oleszek. 1989. *Bicameral Politics.* New Haven: Yale University Press.

Matthews, Donald E. 1960. *U.S. Senators and Their World.* New York: Vintage Books.

Mayhew, David R. 1991. *Divided We Govern: Party Control, Lawmaking, and Investigating, 1946–1990.* New Haven: Yale University Press.

Nelson, Jack. 1995. "Clinton Draws Line in the Sand on Budget, Aides Say." *Los Angeles Times,* November 10, A33.

Oleszek, Walter J. 1996. *Congressional Procedures and the Policy Process.* 4th ed. Washington, D.C.: CQ Press.

Oppenheimer, Bruce. 1994. "The Rules Committee: The House Traffic Cop." In *Encyclopedia of the American Legislative System,* vol. 2, ed. Joel Silbey. New York: Scribner's.

Ornstein, Norman J., Thomas E. Mann, and Michael J. Malbin. 1990. *Vital Statistics on Congress 1989–1990.* Washington, D.C.: American Enterprise Institute.

———. 1994. *Vital Statistics on Congress 1993–1994.* Washington, D.C.: Congressional Quarterly.

Owens, John E. 1996. "The Return of Party Government in the U.S. House of Representatives: Central Leadership-Committee Relations in the 104th Congress." Paper presented at the annual meeting of the Political Studies Association of the United Kingdom, University of Bristol, January 4–6.

Peterson, Jonathan, and Paul Richter. 1995. "Budget Talks Accepted after Pointed Accusations." *Los Angeles Times,* December 21, A24.

Risjord, Norman K. 1994. "Congress in the Federalist-Republican Era." In *Encyclopedia of the American Legislative System,* vol. 1, ed. Joel Silbey. New York: Scribner's.

Rohde, David. 1991. *Parties and Leaders in the Postreform House.* Chicago: University of Chicago Press.

Rubin, Alissa J. 1995a. "Finishing the 'Contract' in Style, House Passes Tax-Cut Bill." *Congressional Quarterly Weekly Report,* April 8, 1010–1014.

———. 1995b. "Spadework on Medicare Pays Off for GOP." *Congressional Quarterly Weekly Report,* September 23, 2895.

———. 1995c. "Finance Committee Republicans Divided over Tax Cut." *Congressional Quarterly Weekly Report,* October 7, 3058.

_____. 1995d. "Unified GOP on Senate Finance Approves $245 Billion Tax Cut." *Congressional Quarterly Weekly Report,* October 21, 3189–3192.

_____. 1995e. "Senate GOP Appeases Moderates, Gets Majority Behind Bill." *Congressional Quarterly Weekly Report,* October 28, 3290.

_____. 1995f. "A Flurry of Amendments." *Congressional Quarterly Weekly Report,* November 4, 3359.

_____. 1995g. "Reality of Tough Job Ahead Dampens Joy over Deal." *Congressional Quarterly Weekly Report,* November 25, 3397–3399.

Rubin, Alissa J., and George Hager. 1996. "Chances of a Budget Deal Now Anyone's Guess." *Congressional Quarterly Weekly Report,* January 13, 89–91.

Salant, Jonathan D. 1995. "Term Limits: Procedure OK'd on Floor Vote." *Congressional Quarterly Weekly Report,* March 18, 787.

Schick, Allen. 1980. *Congress and Money.* Washington, D.C.: The Urban Institute.

Shepsle, Kenneth. 1978. *The Giant Jigsaw Puzzle: Democratic Committee Assignments in the Modern House.* Chicago: University of Chicago Press.

Sinclair, Barbara. 1983. *Majority Leadership in the U.S. House.* Baltimore: Johns Hopkins University Press.

_____. 1989. *The Transformation of the U.S. Senate.* Baltimore: Johns Hopkins University Press.

_____. 1991. "Governing Unheroically (and Sometimes Unappetizingly): Bush and the 101st Congress." In *The Bush Presidency: First Appraisals,* ed. Colin Campbell and Bert Rockman. Chatham, N.J.: Chatham House.

_____. 1995. *Legislators, Leaders and Lawmaking.* Baltimore: Johns Hopkins University Press.

_____. 1996. "Trying to Govern Positively in a Negative Era: Clinton and the 103rd Congress." In *The Clinton Presidency: First Appraisals,* ed. Colin Campbell and Bert Rockman. Chatham, N.J.: Chatham House.

Smith, Steven S. 1989. *Call to Order: Floor Politics in the House and Senate.* Washington, D.C.: The Brookings Institution.

_____. 1995. *The American Congress.* Boston: Houghton Mifflin.

Smith, Steven S., and Marcus Flathman. 1989. "Managing the Senate Floor: Complex Unanimous Consent Agreements since the 1950s." *Legislative Studies Quarterly* (August): 349–374.

Stockman, David Alan. 1986. *The Triumph of Politics.* London: Bodley Head.

Strom, Gerald, and Barry Rundquist. 1977. "A Revised Theory of Winning in House-Senate Conferences." *American Political Science Review* 71 (June): 448–453.

Taylor, Andrew. 1995. "Line-Item Veto Compromise Easily Passes Senate." *Congressional Quarterly Weekly Report,* March 25, 854–856.

———. 1996. "A Piecemeal Solution." *Congressional Quarterly Weekly Report,* January 6, 56.

Thurber, James, and Samantha Durst. 1993. "The 1990 Budget Enforcement Act: The Decline of Congressional Accountability." In *Congress Reconsidered,* 5th ed., ed. Lawrence C. Dodd and Bruce I. Oppenheimer. Washington, D.C.: CQ Press.

Tiefer, Charles. 1989. *Congressional Practice and Procedure.* Westport, Conn.: Greenwood Press.

Waldman, Steven. 1995. *The Bill.* New York: Viking.

Young, Gary, and Joseph Cooper. 1993. "Multiple Referral and the Transformation of House Decision Making." In *Congress Reconsidered,* 5th ed., ed. Lawrence C. Dodd and Bruce I. Oppenheimer. Washington, D.C.: CQ Press.

Zuckman, Jill. 1993. "Echoes of Slavery." *Congressional Quarterly Weekly Report,* July 24, 1960.

Index